EMIL AND KATHLEEN SICK SERIES IN WESTERN HISTORY AND BIOGRAPHY

With support from the Center for the Study of the Pacific Northwest at the University of Washington, the Sick Series in Western History and Biography features scholarly books on the peoples and issues that have defined and shaped the American West. Through intellectually challenging and engaging books of general interest, the series seeks to deepen and expand our understanding of the American West as a region and its role in the making of the United States and the modern world.

Seattle
FROM THE
Margins

EXCLUSION, ERASURE, AND THE MAKING OF A PACIFIC COAST CITY

MEGAN ASAKA

University of Washington Press

Seattle

Seattle from the Margins was made possible in part by a grant from the Emil and Kathleen Sick Fund of the University of Washington's Department of History.

4
CULTURE

This publication was also supported by a grant from the 4Culture Heritage Special Projects Program.

Additional support was provided by the University of California President's Faculty Research Fellowship in the Humanities, MRP-19-600791.

Copyright © 2022 by the University of Washington Press

Maps by Ben Pease.

26   25   24   23   22   5   4   3   2   1

Printed and bound in the United States of America

CENTER FOR THE STUDY
OF THE PACIFIC NORTHWEST
sites.uw.edu/cspn/

UNIVERSITY OF WASHINGTON PRESS
uwapress.uw.edu

LIBRARY OF CONGRESS CATALOGING-IN-PUBLICATION DATA

Names: Asaka, Megan, author.

Title: Seattle from the margins : exclusion, erasure, and the making of a Pacific Coast city / Megan Asaka.

Description: Seattle : University of Washington Press, [2022] | Series: Emil and Kathleen Sick book series in Western history and biography | Includes bibliographical references and index.

Identifiers: LCCN 2021057703 (print) | LCCN 2021057704 (ebook) | ISBN 9780295750675 (hardcover) | ISBN 9780295750682 (ebook)

Subjects: LCSH: Minorities—Washington (State)—Seattle—History. | Migrant labor—Washington (State)—Seattle Region—History. | Indians of North America—Washington (State)—Seattle Region—Economic conditions. | Indians of North America—Washington (State)—Seattle Region—Social conditions—History. | Asian Americans—Washington (State)—Seattle Region—Economic conditions. | Asian Americans—Washington (State)—Seattle Region—Social conditions—History. | Immigrants—Washington (State)—Seattle—History. | Seattle (Wash.)—Emigration and immigration—History. | Seattle (Wash.)—Social conditions—History. | Seattle (Wash.)—Race relations—History.

Classification: LCC F899.S49 A24 2022 (print) | LCC F899.S49 (ebook) | DDC 305.8009797/772—dc23/eng/20211220

LC record available at https://lccn.loc.gov/2021057703

LC ebook record available at https://lccn.loc.gov/2021057704

♾ This paper meets the requirements of ANSI/NISO Z39.48-1992 (Permanenceof Paper).

CONTENTS

ACKNOWLEDGMENTS

THE QUESTIONS THAT ANIMATE THIS BOOK HAVE BEEN WITH ME for a very long time. Growing up in Seattle, I became aware of a disconnect between history as lived and experienced by my family and history as presented in scholarship. The expulsion of Japanese Americans from the city in 1942 and their incarceration during the war was often treated as a footnote, an aberration tied to the specific context of the war and hysteria of Pearl Harbor. But it seemed to me that this act of racialized exclusion held the key to understanding something else, a very different narrative of Seattle history that had gone unacknowledged in scholarly literature and public memory.

This desire to understand what I recognized as a troubling absence in the historical narrative brought me to Brown University, where I spent my undergraduate years. It was at Brown as an ethnic studies major where I first began to connect my family's experience with other histories of displacement and exclusion. I learned that such omissions were not accidental, but reflected a bias in historical practice that elevated certain voices and forms of knowledge over others. During this time, I was lucky to have met Jesús Hernández, Neetu Khanna, Briana Masterson, and Hentyle Yapp, friends who have become like family over the years. I first discovered my love of archival research in classes with James Campbell. My advisor, Bob Lee, introduced me to the field of Asian American studies and was a continual source of support at Brown, for me and many other students.

In college, I found an internship back home in Seattle with Densho, an organization that sought to preserve the stories of the World War II incarceration of Japanese Americans through a digital archive. Densho's mission of preservation coupled with popular education and social justice resonated with me, and after graduation I began working there full-time as an oral historian and archivist. I will be forever grateful to Tom Ikeda, who took a chance on me and gave me the freedom at Densho to pursue my interests and make the work my own. Dana Hoshide, Virginia Yamada, and Naoko Tanabe inspired me with their commitment to Densho's mission and their deep knowledge of Japanese American history.

In some ways, though, my time at Densho didn't provide the answers I was looking for, but instead raised more questions. As an oral historian, I saw firsthand what people decided to leave out—what made it into the historical record and what did not. I realized that no archive is ever complete and began looking into graduate programs to explore these questions around silence, erasure, and the production of historical knowledge. At Yale, I benefited tremendously from the guidance and mentorship of Mary Lui and Dolores Hayden, two scholars who understood right away the value of my work and gave me the confidence to find my own scholarly voice. They also introduced me to geography and the built environment as a way of illuminating marginalized histories, an influence that shaped the development of this book. I also thank Ned Blackhawk, who affirmed my commitment to telling a new kind of Seattle history and always pushed me to be ambitious in my scholarship. At Yale, I was surrounded by many brilliant people whose support and humor helped to sustain me throughout graduate school. I would especially like to acknowledge Khalil Johnson, Talya Zemach-Bersin, Melanie Yazzie, Carolee Klimchock, Claudia Calhoun, Michelle Morgan, Alex Beasley, Sigma Colon, Assef Ashraf, Nazanin Yvonne Sullivan, David Minto, Lisa Furchtgott, Simeon Man, Monica Muñoz Martinez, Quan Tran, and LiLi Johnson.

I was hired in 2014 as an assistant professor of public history at the University of California, Riverside, in many ways a dream job for someone like me who straddles both worlds. At UCR, Cathy Gudis has been my biggest source of support—a brilliant, community-engaged scholar who offers many of us a sense of what's possible beyond the narrow scope of the academy. Molly McGarry, Dana Simmons, Cliff Trafzer, and Devra Weber have also helped me immeasurably as I've tried to navigate the pressures of academic life. Special thank-you to my assistant professor cohort at UCR: Crystal Baik, Ademide Adelusi-Adeluyi, Jody Benjamin, Maile Arvin, Natasha McPherson, Philipp Lehmann, and Jorge Leal. I don't think I would have managed during these last few years without the organizational expertise of Michael Austin and Allison Palmer in the history office.

I am fortunate to have received financial support from several fellowship programs, which gave me much-needed time to develop and write this book. The Hellman Foundation Fellowship and UC Regents Fellowship provided a course release and research funds to complete two research trips. A semester-long residency at Dumbarton Oaks as a Mellon Fellow in Urban Landscape Studies offered an intellectual space to explore the interdisciplinary aspects of my book and to connect with scholars and practitioners from many different fields within and outside the academy. I especially valued my conversations with Burak Erdim and Adam Goldwyn. The UC President's Faculty Research Fellowship in the Humanities came at a crucial moment in my career and offered time off from teaching to finalize the book.

Research for this project would not have been possible without the guidance of archivists and librarians. Anne Frantilla at the Seattle Municipal Archives was the first to recommend the records of the fire department when I hit a wall in my research on Japanese hotel operators. Conor Casey at the University of Washington, Special Collections, recommended a few critical records that helped me fill out the picture of labor during the early twentieth century. Maggie Weatherby at the Washington State Historical Society identified key images in the final days of the project.

I am grateful to many people who helped me along the way. I learned so much from the conversations I had with Harumi Guiberson, Bea Kumasaka, and Page Tanagi. Naoko Tanabe and my great-aunt Hisa Tamura translated key documents from Japanese into English. My great-uncle, Toshio Tamura, spoke with me about my great-grandfather's life and helped to fill out the picture of his early life in the Pacific Northwest. Densho provided office space during my research trips back to Seattle. Matt Klingle has been the most generous mentor, always taking the time to offer feedback and advice.

The wonderful folks at UW Press have been nothing but supportive. They embraced my project from the beginning and helped me hone the book's arguments. Mike Baccam went above and beyond as an editor. He became a valued interlocutor who knew exactly what I wanted to say and helped me find the words to say it. Josh Reid read the entire manuscript and gave crucial feedback that improved the book immensely. Chad Attenborough answered my (many) questions about images and permissions. Thank you as well to the anonymous reviewers who took the time to read and comment on an earlier draft.

The biggest thank-you goes to my family. My parents, Jan Asaka-Burgett and Gary Asaka, have supported me in everything I've done. I wouldn't be here writing this book without their hard work and sacrifices. A special shout-out to my dad who dropped everything to help me during the last frantic days of finishing this book. I have much gratitude for my extended family: Barbara Asaka; Scott Burgett; Jason Lombard and my nieces Kaiya and Emiko; Shannon, Brian, Ellie, and Grace Laskey; and the Lentacker family.

My partner, Antoine Lentacker, has believed in me and encouraged me every step of the way. He's the smartest and most generous person I know, who read pretty much every version of every chapter of this book. My little Alex burst into our lives four years ago and forever changed them for the better. Her school, Altadena Children's Center, provided the best, most loving care during my stressful and time-consuming years on the tenure clock. I will never forget how they reopened at the height of the pandemic so the children could return and have a sense of normalcy.

This project started many years ago when I began to question the rosy view of Seattle and broader US history that was being taught in school. My sister, Jamie Asaka, was the first to open my eyes to alternative histories and community formations that forever changed how I saw the world. She has kept me grounded over the years and reminds me to never lose sight of where we came from and to whom we are most accountable. I dedicate this book to her.

Portions of this manuscript originally appeared as "Incendiary City: Fire and Race in Seattle's Progressive Era," *Pacific Northwest Quarterly* 111, no. 2–3 (2020): 95–104; and "40-Acre Smudge": Race and Erasure in Prewar Seattle," *Pacific Historical Review* 87, no. 2 (Spring 2018): 231–63.

Seattle Unsettled

ON JUNE 6, 1927, SIXTEEN-YEAR-OLD FRANK KUBO STEPPED OFF the *Arabia-Maru*, a transpacific steamship, and onto the docks in Seattle. The three-week journey from Yokohama had seemed endless to Frank, who spent the bulk of the trip seasick, unable to eat or sleep. Frank had taken this journey once before, in reverse, as a child. His mother and father were among the first Japanese migrants to arrive in Auburn, a rural town on the outskirts of Seattle. They worked as tenant farmers for several years before going bankrupt and losing the farm, their only source of income. With their dreams of wealth and prosperity in the United States no longer possible, they returned to Japan with Frank, then six years old, and his younger brother and sister. A US citizen by birth, Frank grew up in Japan, spoke no English, and held only the faintest memories of his birthplace. As he approached adulthood, however, Frank wanted to return to the United States to pursue his studies. Against his father's wishes, he purchased a ticket on the *Arabia-Maru*, which left Yokohama and arrived in Seattle on a clear spring day.[1]

Frank's uncle came to greet him at the docks and led him to a place called the New Home Hotel, located several blocks away. There, Frank dropped off his belongings and wondered what to do next. "Since it was already summer all the schools were closed," he recalled. "My uncle therefore took me to Nishimura Employment Office to apply for an Alaskan salmon cannery job." The next week, he hopped on another steamship, this one filled with Japanese men of all ages who were headed to work in Petersburg, Alaska.

After two months, the salmon runs died down and the cannery slowed its operation, and Frank returned to Seattle with $120 cash. After paying his uncle and sending money back to Japan, Frank was left with very little. School would have to wait. Frank set out to find more work to support himself and his family. He was quickly hired by a Japanese import company and traveled around the region peddling food and supplies to Japanese labor camps. Weeks turned into months, which turned into years: summers in Alaska, fall and spring on the road, and winters in the Seattle hotels and lodging houses.[2]

Frank's life of continual movement was not uncommon for the era's working-class urban residents across the American West. As environmental historian William Cronon has argued, in the late nineteenth and early twentieth centuries cities developed as economic centers that controlled vast regional hinterlands devoted to resource extraction and agriculture. Cronon traces the resulting flow of raw materials in and out of Chicago, which became a gateway city connecting western resources with eastern markets.[3] Though Cronon focuses mainly on commodities, the same system applied to workers. As cities extended their economic reach outward, they created linkages for the regional circulation of people. Just as commodities moved in and out, so too did individuals. This phenomenon was especially pronounced along the Pacific Coast, where ports allowed access to wider networks of labor. Migrants moved through cities constantly, in search of jobs or else on their way to mining sites and agricultural camps ringing the urban centers.

Workers like Frank played a key role in building cities, but their historical presence has gone largely unacknowledged in urban scholarship. As a field, urban history has devoted considerable attention to workers' lives and the emergence of an industrial working class in the period after the Civil War and before World War II.[4] These discussions have focused overwhelmingly on Chicago, New York, and a handful of other industrial centers, although recent scholarship has diversified considerably in terms of geography as well as race and region.[5] Still, the typical urban experience during this period is presented as a process of permanent settlement: a one-way migration to the cities in search of jobs, and the formation of neighborhoods, communities, and institutions. This gives the impression of a working-class population as stable, rooted in place, and skewed mostly toward the white male factory worker. A large literature does exist on loggers, miners, agricultural workers, and others who labored in the extractive and seasonal industries across the American West; however, they are almost exclusively discussed in terms of rurality and associated with nonurban environments.[6]

This absence is particularly glaring in the case of Seattle, a city quite literally built around the movement of workers.[7] From the mid-nineteenth century through the 1930s, Seattle's urban economy became tightly intertwined with the broader regional economy of the Pacific Northwest, which revolved around industries such as logging and lumber processing, fishing, salmon canning, coal mining, and agriculture.[8] The regional economy's demand for highly mobile labor brought successive waves of workers through Seattle, which served as an ever-expanding hub of local, regional, and transnational migrations. In the 1920s, an academic study estimated that Seattle had one of the highest transient populations in the entire country.[9] When he arrived in 1927, Frank joined a migratory labor stream as old as Seattle itself; in camps, forests, and hotels in and around the city, Indigenous, Asian, European, and US-born white workers came into contact and conflict with one another.

Reorienting our study of the urban past around workers like Frank, who passed through or resided in the city temporarily, reveals an entire class of laborers often ignored in urban scholarship—and also highlights the structural forces that made them itinerant in the first place. Seattle's urban growth and development required the constant disruption and uprooting of people, beginning with the dispossession of the Duwamish, the first people of Seattle, and their displacement to the southern edge of the city for the purposes of labor. This book traces how the city was structured—spatially, socially, economically, and politically—around this demand for mobile labor, a pool of available workers able to move from place to place. Urban life during this period was one of profound dislocation for the poor and itinerant laborers of the Pacific Northwest. Centering their experiences exposes the exclusionary roots of the city's rise as a modern metropolis, dramatically shifting our understanding of Seattle history.

EMPIRE AND MIGRATION IN THE PACIFIC NORTHWEST

Seattle is best understood as a Pacific city, situated at the heart of a maritime network that revolves around the Pacific Ocean.[10] This link to the sea is palpable from anywhere in the city, the smell of saltwater or call of seagulls offering a constant reminder of Seattle's maritime roots. While the city itself doesn't directly touch the Pacific Ocean—it's not a coastal city in that sense—it is connected to the Pacific through the Salish Sea, which links the Strait of Georgia in British Columbia, the Puget Sound in Washington State, the Strait of Juan de Fuca, and many smaller inlets, forming a vast marine space that flows into the ocean. Seattle occupies a central location within the Salish Sea, easily accessible by water.[11] It sits along the eastern shore of the Puget Sound and serves as a connection point for the many river systems of the Cascade mountain range. In Lushootseed, the language of the region's Indigenous peoples, Seattle was known as dᶻidᶻəlalič, or the place where one crosses over.[12]

Too often, we understand the history of the American West as a linear process that follows the movement of settlers from east to west. The railroad figures centrally within this national mythology, presenting white settlement as a foregone conclusion and associating the "real" origins of Western cities with the introduction of railway technology. In the Pacific Northwest, however, water played a far more crucial role in the development of urban societies and capitalist economies. Seattle's maritime geography integrated the city into a Pacific-oriented economy, bringing it closer to Asia and the Pacific world than to the rest of the continental United States. The unique maritime environment of the Pacific Northwest, and Seattle's location within it, allowed for the movement of people and goods before the arrival of the railroad. During the mid-nineteenth century, for example, the largest markets for Pacific Northwest lumber, the region's most lucrative export, were all accessible by water and included California and Hawaii.[13]

Highlighting these "Pacific connections" reveals more than just a new geography. It also brings the question of empire to the forefront. Moving beyond the borders of the nation and situating Seattle's history within a Pacific framework helps clarify the imperial context of the city's growth and its enmeshment with the broader dynamics of US empire-building. As historian Kornel Chang has pointed out, the Pacific Northwest's capitalist development was shaped by imbricated processes of empire. While historians have tended to study US empire in two district phases—continental expansion on one hand and overseas expansion on the other—Chang argues that the two were mutually reinforcing, with "the development of one being utterly dependent on the development of the other."[14] The capitalist economy required both land and labor, as well as markets to absorb lumber, coal, and other Pacific Northwest commodities. The invasion of sovereign Indigenous nations and military incursions into Asia formed the basis of what scholar Manu Karuka calls the imperial economy, which we see very clearly taking root in Seattle during this period.[15]

Bringing empire to the forefront reveals the intersecting histories of Indigenous and Asian peoples in the region and their role in building the city. For Indigenous peoples, the economy's orientation around maritime networks opened up a space of autonomy within the growing constraints of colonial society. While the formation of the economy in the Pacific Northwest relied upon the colonization of Indigenous lands, Indigenous people didn't simply disappear. As maritime peoples, they remained present in the seasonal workforce, often living and working alongside settlers and other migrant laborers. Grouped under the designation "Coast Salish," which has been used to identify commonalities of language and culture among peoples of the coastal Northwest (running from Washington through British Columbia), Puget Sound Indigenous inhabitants also formed their own distinctive and autonomous tribal societies.[16] This included the Duwamish, the first people of Seattle, who moved along the waters of the Puget Sound during spring, summer, and fall, fishing, socializing, and resource gathering, while residing in permanent villages during the winter months. Their maritime mobility persisted well after the arrival of the first white settlers and helps to explain the high participation of Duwamish and other Coast Salish peoples in the wage economy. As historian Paige Raibmon argues, the seasonal nature of the industries, including fishing, canning, and agriculture, and the location of the various worksites along rivers and coastal areas allowed Indigenous peoples to weave "political and cultural imperatives into their travel itineraries," while also earning wages.[17]

As the Duwamish and other Coast Salish peoples became more integrated into the wage economy, they encountered Asian workers whose migration and arrival to the Pacific Northwest also took place within a maritime world.[18] The expansion of Western imperialism and military aggression across Asia beginning in the mid-nineteenth century created the conditions for mass emigration, disrupting traditional economies, destabilizing political systems, and impoverishing and uprooting millions of people.[19] At the same time, the US pursuit of Asian markets created financial linkages and migration routes that pulled successive waves of Chinese,

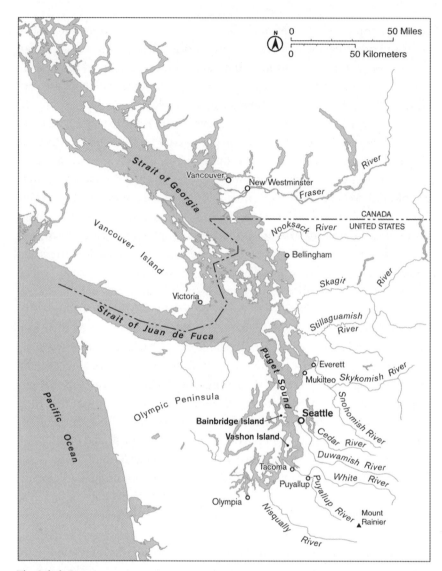

The Salish Sea

Japanese, and Filipino laborers to the Pacific Northwest, where they were funneled into the low-wage, seasonal workforce.[20] As the region secured greater connections with Asia and the Pacific world, Seattle emerged as a crucial hub of Asian migration and labor: from the 1860s to 1880s with Chinese migration, the 1890s to 1910s with Japanese migration, and, finally, the 1920s to 1930s with Filipino migration. During this period, Asian laborers worked in the same industries and traversed the same maritime networks as their Indigenous counterparts. They labored alongside one another, competed over jobs, and forged unexpected alliances within the marine and coastal spaces of the Puget Sound.

The maritime orientation of the economy and the movement of Indigenous and Asian laborers through it laid the groundwork for a larger system of labor migration and recruitment that also drew in Europeans and US-born whites, who came in growing numbers beginning around the turn of the twentieth century. Scholarship on Seattle history has not really examined the presence of European and white laborers within these regional circuits of migration. Some work has been done on so-called "hobos," single men who traveled widely around the American West in search of jobs, but these studies don't connect to the bigger picture of migratory labor that also included Indigenous and Asian workers.[21] Most white and European laborers who arrived in Seattle during this time were also migrants, moving around from place to place and working in the same kinds of seasonal or temporary jobs. They did not fit the image of the stable factory worker so dominant in the scholarship on the urban white working class. In fact, their very uprootedness and nonconformity to settled family life cast them as suspicious and potentially disruptive to the social order.[22]

These Indigenous, Asian, European, and white workers often converged in Seattle, which anchored a much larger regional network of migration and labor. Within the city, they made their way to the district south of Yesler Way, along the waterfront, where they found temporary accommodations, entertainment venues, cafés, bathhouses, employment agencies, and other businesses that popped up to serve the mobile workforce. The name of this area changed many times over the years, from the Sawdust to the Tenderloin to simply "below the line" (meaning "below Yesler Way"), reflecting its constantly changing population.[23] Though the district played a central role in the broader economy by concentrating the workforce into one bounded area, it also was a heterogeneous, highly fluid urban environment. Laborers and migrants of all kinds mixed and mingled with Indigenous and Asian residents, single men and women, interracial families, sex workers, and the poor and unemployed. The district defied easy categorization, forged through the shifting and unstable demands of a Pacific-oriented economy and the maritime routes that sustained it.

COLONIAL ROOTS OF SEGREGATION

Seattle's urban landscape developed around the segregation and containment of this south-end district. Segregation dominates the literature on race in US cities, often through discussions of redlining. As the Great Depression created massive financial instability and caused many Americans to lose their homes, the federal government became more involved in the housing sector via the New Deal, creating various programs to assist first-time homebuyers and those who could no longer pay their mortgages. These programs, however, produced racial segregation by denying home loans and other financial support to those who lived in "redlined" districts, neighborhoods deemed risky financial investments and thus undesirable for federal loans. As scholars have found, the real estate agents and mortgage brokers who contracted with the federal government to produce these assessments almost always measured Black and other nonwhite and immigrant neighborhoods as "risks," making it almost impossible for these groups to obtain home loans. Coupled with other mechanisms of racial exclusion, redlining trapped nonwhite people in poorly resourced districts, a process that greatly accelerated after World War II.[24]

In Seattle, though, redlining tells only part of the story. Though Seattle has its own ugly history of redlining, which deserves far more attention than it currently receives, the process of segregation started much earlier, with the founding of the city itself in the mid-nineteenth century, and did not involve the federal government. At that time, white settlers removed the Duwamish people and segregated them in the southern fringes of the city, eager to take their lands but also to make them available as workers.[25] Settlers even blocked efforts by the federal government to create a reservation for the Duwamish on their ancestral homelands because it would interfere with the city's access to a steady labor supply.[26] Seattle did not have reliable land-based transportation until the late nineteenth century, and even then water remained a primary mode of transportation, making the Duwamish and other Coast Salish peoples a valuable source of labor. Marked as a disorderly slum, the south end became a container for all of the city's racialized and marginalized populations, which, in turn, served to further mark them as undesirable and unworthy for inclusion into urban society. This included Asian migrants, who were also restricted south of Yesler Way, and single male laborers, whose deviation from normative family life also made them racially suspect in the eyes of the settler elites. Seattle's urban landscape developed around this north-south orientation, with the north as a "residence district" for white families and the south as a stigmatized slum district for the city's heterogeneous workforce.

This example reveals the colonial roots of racial segregation, as well as the function of racial segregation in forming the urban and regional economy. The south end was not a stable district with a racially defined population, but one that constantly changed according to the needs of the broader economy and the kinds of workers available at that particular moment. In this way, Seattle shares historical commonalities with Vancouver, Melbourne, and other cities across the Anglophone Pacific world that developed in the mid-nineteenth century around resource-based economies reliant upon Indigenous lands and the mass influx of Asian and European labor.[27] In these contexts, segregation occurred as part of a colonial project to remove the Indigenous inhabitants and establish the city as a pure space of white domestic life.[28] As Asian and European migrants, many of them single men, arrived to work in extractive economies, spaces such as reserves and slums served to contain Indigenous and racially mixed populations and mark them as unruly, troublesome, and antithetical to modern urban life. As sociologist Renisa Mawani has discussed in the case of Vancouver, settlers relied upon a racially mixed workforce to build the economy but also feared the possibility of the interracial solidarities and alliances this mixing could generate. She calls this the "deep paradox" of a colonial society rooted in both capitalist accumulation and racial purity.[29] In Seattle, the north-south spatial orientation served to smooth over this tension between, on one hand, racial heterogeneity as demanded by capitalist accumulation and the ever-expanding search for labor and, on the other, racial purity as envisioned by white settlers. It allowed settlers to maintain an exclusionary white district while also accommodating an Indigenous and racially mixed labor force.

Comprehending Seattle's racial past requires an expansive framework—one that takes into account the intersections and overlaps among the various groups dominating the labor force during this period. Studies of Seattle history haven't fully captured this dynamic. Scholars in recent years have made great strides in uncovering a more diverse Seattle history: Shelley Lee and Dorothy Fujita-Rony, for instance, have both situated Seattle within a transpacific context, showing the importance of Asia to the city's urban development.[30] Quintard Taylor has examined the long history of African Americans in Seattle, from the city's earliest days through the late twentieth century.[31] While these and other books have done crucial work in contesting the long-held image of Seattle as an exclusively white city, they remain grounded in their respective community histories.[32] *Seattle from the Margins* builds on this scholarship, widening the scope to explore the heterogeneous and constantly shifting nature of the regional workforce and urban population. The historical experiences of one group were entirely dependent upon the others, in terms of their daily lives and social encounters as well as their shared marginalization within the city. This is not to equate Indigenous dispossession with other forms of uprootedness experienced by non-Indigenous migrant laborers; the dispossession of the first peoples of the region remains ongoing, not an unfortunate event that occurred long ago. But bringing all of these groups together within one framework helps to emphasize the colonial foundations of Seattle's economy and spatial organization, which created a structure of exclusion that persisted well beyond the city's founding and laid the groundwork for later forms of racial segregation.

Returning to Seattle's origins is the only way to really understand the persistence of segregation over time. Segregation was not something imposed on the city by the federal government; instead it evolved from the first days of Seattle's founding in the mid-nineteenth century. White settlers established the north for the purposes of wealth accumulation via land and private property, then sought to protect this space through violence, policing, and municipal law. They dispossessed and displaced the Duwamish, rendering them outsiders in their own lands, then excluded others deemed racially undesirable, including Asian migrants, interracial families, and single men. As Black workers began to arrive in growing numbers during World War II, they entered a racial geography that had already hardened around the division between white and nonwhite, north and south. Though Seattle's Black community predated the war, Asians and Indigenous peoples outnumbered them in the city and the regional workforce. This changed during the war years, as the economy shifted and African Americans became the most dominant nonwhite group.[33] Their growing presence in the city provoked renewed hostility and violence, and Black residents found themselves restricted from the same northern white districts. Seattle's enduring division into north and south shows the layers of colonialism and racism that were woven into the city's foundations—forces that continue to structure socioeconomic inequalities into the present.

AUTONOMY AND INTIMACY ON THE MARGINS

Seattle is fascinating from a historical perspective because of the messiness and complexity of urban life, and the fluid social worlds forged among the city's poor and working classes. But excavating a history of movement, disruption, and uprootedness is a complicated project. Seattle's dynamism and constantly shifting urban population is precisely what makes the city a challenging case for historians—and also why, I suspect, Seattle has remained off the radar for urban history as a field. As scholar Nayan Shah has pointed out, historians have long privileged permanence over transience, tracing people's lives and relationships according to stable communities rooted in place. The archive plays a role in shaping this bias toward permanence. People who remained stationary have a much stronger presence in the archives, as they tended to accumulate a long paper trail: property deeds, leases, marriage certificates, and payroll records.[34] People on the move often circulated outside of the official realm, leaving historians with little evidence of their presence in urban areas.[35]

This bias has also skewed historical scholarship toward middle-class and elite perspectives, particularly among the marginalized. In communities facing diminished access to resources and more economic and racial barriers to stability, individuals who lived in single-family homes or secured stable jobs were comparatively privileged. Because their voices appear more often in institutional and community archives, they receive more attention and their experience becomes understood as a universal experience among that group, excluding the migrants, the poor, and the transient working class from historical memory.

With this class bias also comes a gender bias toward nuclear families and normative domestic life. Moving around on the migratory labor circuit brought people together in ways that did not conform to traditional family structures. Shah refers to this as "stranger intimacy": the fleeting encounters between transient men and the diverse forms of kinship, including inter-racial relationships, that flourished along the migratory routes of the American West.[36] These migratory laborers included married men and men with children who worked in seasonal jobs, in agriculture or canning, that took them away from their families for months on end, or required them to move from place to place with their families. Single and married women also worked as migrant laborers, particularly in Puget Sound agriculture. In these cases, too, the picture of settled family life does not accurately capture the social realities of many laboring people at the time.

To piece together this history, *Seattle from the Margins* turns to the built environment as an archive containing alternative stories of migration and labor in the Pacific Northwest.[37] It looks at the worksites, residences, and leisure establishments that popped up in and around Seattle to serve the mobile workforce and facilitate their seasonal migrations. These sites— labor camps, lumber towns, lodging houses, hotels, and so-called slum districts—played a crucial role in the functioning of the urban and regional economy; they also brought together a diverse and constantly shifting work-force. Through the guest book of a hotel, we can see the heterogeneity of the urban population as well as the different waves of migration that passed through Seattle over time. Floor plans, building descriptions, and photo-graphs reveal living and working conditions. These sources help repopulate the historical record with new actors, illuminating a view of urban life that does not take the settled middle-class experience as universal.

The sites that served this itinerant workforce also provoked reactions among elites and other powerful people who viewed them as hotbeds of labor radicalism and racial disorder. Of particular concern was the possibil-ity of interracial alliances among laboring populations that could destabi-lize the functioning of an economy rooted in racial hierarchy and division. Companies, city leaders, urban planners, and others spent considerable time and effort policing and reforming these spaces. They sought to trans-form housing and work environments as a form of labor discipline and control. The single-room occupancy hotel (SRO), for example, emerged in the early twentieth century to separate workers into their own rooms.[38] Before this, laborers and migrants occupied smaller wooden lodging houses that lacked clear room divisions and could be easily altered from inside. SROs were constructed with more durable materials and planned in a uniform style that could be more easily inspected. In this case and others, building design served to separate workers and give them less autonomy in their interactions with each other.

The built environment, then, reflects tension between the economic necessity of these spaces and the problems they posed to the city's ruling order. Despite their efforts to police, regulate, and reform sites like lodging houses and labor camps, company owners and city authorities couldn't fully control what the workers were doing and how they chose to live their lives. Even after city officials embraced the SRO-style hotel as an attempt to impose order onto unruly urban populations, residents responded by altering the interiors to suit their own needs.[39] They created social worlds that existed outside of official or elite knowledge and continued to inhabit these spaces on their own terms. It was precisely this pursuit of autonomy that so confounded and disturbed municipal authorities, industry leaders, reformers, and urban planners. In these and many other ways, migrants, laborers, and other "undesirables" played a far greater role in shaping the urban environment than previously acknowledged.

URBAN HISTORY UNBOUND

This book attempts to reexamine Seattle's history from the margins, focusing on people and places deemed unworthy and undesirable and tracing the social, economic, and political processes by which they were rendered as such. Doing so, however, requires bending, and even completely breaking, many of the rules by which urban histories are often written. For one thing, much of the book's action takes place outside of the city. Out of the six chapters, only three occur within city boundaries, while the remaining chapters focus on outlying areas around Puget Sound, including the Puyallup and White River valleys, the Puget Sound lumber towns of Port Gamble and Mukilteo, and Bainbridge Island. The choice to zoom in and out throughout the text is deliberate. As a city, Seattle's urban development was linked inextricably with the broader economy of the Pacific Northwest. Focusing only on the city proper would not convey the full story of how this economic system came to be, nor how it was lived and experienced by the workers who made it possible. Much of the urban labor force did not reside in Seattle permanently, and confining Seattle history to the city's official boundaries would render these workers invisible. By playing with scale, from the hyperlocal to the regional and transnational, this book is able to connect the history of migratory labor with the history of urbanization in a way that also attends to the lives and labors of those on the ground.

Another unconventional feature of the book is that it doesn't follow one group of people over time. It doesn't even follow two groups of people and their interactions with each other over time. It focuses instead on the rise and eventual decline of the extractive and seasonal economy, and how the demand for migratory labor shaped Seattle's urban landscape. Not every community, organization, movement, or event will be covered in these pages; rather than offering a comprehensive view of Seattle's social history, the book will focus on the groups most dominant in the workforce at particular moments, examining the specific anxieties they provoked among the city's elites, industry leaders, and officials.

Seattle's working-class population was not static but shaped through multiple, ongoing waves of migration that reflected local, regional, and transpacific spheres of power. As immigration laws transformed the workforce via successive prohibitions on labor migration, first from Asia and then globally, employers embarked on an ever-expanding search for low-wage labor. Given Seattle's Pacific connections, the book focuses in particular on Asian migration, and Asian laborers' interactions over time with Indigenous and European laborers; it also draws specific contrasts between Chinese, Japanese, and Filipino residents, who arrived at different historical moments and within varying geopolitical contexts that greatly shaped their experiences and opportunities—even as they shared a racial status as perpetual foreigners and disposable laborers.

The book begins with Seattle's founding in the 1850s and traces its early economic and geographic development through the 1880s. The first chapter sets the stage by establishing the city's racial geography as rooted in the dispossession of the Duwamish and their containment to the southern district for the purposes of labor. This southern district, in turn, served to segregate the Chinese as they began to arrive as workers in the 1860s and 1870s, joining the Duwamish in powering the urban economy. The significance of the south end only grew as Seattle transformed into a hub of labor migration for the Puget Sound region's first major agricultural industry, hop cultivation.

The second chapter follows Indigenous and Chinese workers, concentrated in Seattle, who became the backbone of the agricultural workforce from the 1860s through the 1880s, as growers organized their farms around the Sound's maritime networks. This chapter looks specifically at the intersecting histories of Chinese and Indigenous labor, examining how the expulsion of Chinese people from the region through mob violence and immigration restriction impacted Indigenous agricultural workers throughout and beyond the Puget Sound.

The third and fourth chapters move from the 1890s through the 1920s as Seattle began to extend its reach into the broader region and across the Pacific. While the Puget Sound hop-growing experiment was rather short-lived, it laid the foundation for Seattle as a labor migration and recruitment hub that other industries, notably lumber, utilized. Chapter 3 examines how the industry drew on a growing foreign-born population in Seattle, one that included Japanese and Northern European migrants, to create a highly exploitative employment system of constant turnover and disposability—a system that also became unmanageable in the face of worker discontent and the possibility of interracial solidarity. Chapter 4 looks at the role of Japanese business operators in sustaining the housing industry in the form of hotel management. Hotels housed much of the urban working-class population in Seattle and became the city's most dominant housing form during the early twentieth century; sociologist Norman Hayner found that Seattle had the second highest concentration of hotel rooms per resident in the entire country by the 1920s.[40] As Japanese hoteliers grew more dominant in the industry and began to expand beyond the south end, city officials deployed the fire and building departments to police and harass them.

Chapters 5 and 6 discuss the decline of the resource-based economy beginning in the 1930s, as Seattle turned to aerospace and airplane building in a shift that transformed the labor force and urban landscape. With immigration restrictions cutting off the flow of labor from Asia and much of the globe, Filipino migrants became a desirable labor source for agricultural, canning, and other industries. As colonial subjects of the United States, which had annexed and colonized the Philippines following the Spanish-American War and Philippine-American War, Filipinos could legally enter the country, but the timing of their arrival in the 1920s and 1930s coincided with the onset of the Great Depression and a surge of nativist hostility that left many struggling economically and forced to travel great distances in search of jobs. Chapter 5 focuses on Filipino laborers' employment by Japanese farmers and their relationships with Indigenous agricultural workers, many of them young Coast Salish women from Canada.

These Japanese farms represented some of the last areas of agricultural activity around Puget Sound; much of the industry had moved over the Cascade mountains to the eastern half of the state, reflecting a broader decline of resource extraction as the foundation of the urban and regional economy. Chapter 6 concludes the story of migratory labor in Seattle by examining the slum clearance projects of the late 1930s and early 1940s that targeted migrant neighborhoods for demolition, including Seattle's Hooverville, a shantytown near the waterfront, and Profanity Hill, a racially integrated area of single male laborers, Japanese and interracial families, and female-headed households. These demolition projects made way for a new workforce and a new city.

The book ends with World War II, when Seattle's economy shifted away from resource extraction and toward manufacturing, propelling acts of displacement against the migrant laborers and others who had once powered the seasonal industries. The expulsion of Japanese Americans from Seattle following the bombing of Pearl Harbor on December 7, 1941, is also part of this story. Though Japanese people had played a crucial role in running many of the small businesses that catered to the region's itinerant working-class population, they were no longer as useful to the city by the late 1930s. Wartime hysteria unleashed after Pearl Harbor created a flashpoint within a longer economic transformation that had rendered Seattle's Japanese population expendable. Later, Black migrants who arrived during and after World War II would face similar patterns of restriction and exclusion as previous populations who helped build the city—demonstrating how much Seattle's early history continued to reverberate into the postwar period and far beyond.

CHAPTER 1

The Sawdust

THE NAME OF THE SOUTH-END DISTRICT CHANGED MANY TIMES over the years, but in Seattle's earliest days, it was known as the Sawdust. In 1853, settler Henry Yesler opened a sawmill at the edge of a lagoon. The lagoon frequently spilled over and covered the ground with water and mud, leaving the area nearly impassable by foot for long stretches of time. Yesler, along with other settlers, began to dump sawdust from the mill into the lagoon and surrounding marsh.[1] The sawdust grew so compact that it formed into land, killing off marine life and permanently altering the shoreline. A new commercial and industrial district of bunkhouses, shops, and saloons soon emerged on top of this dumping ground. It was here that Seattle's first segregated district came into being.

Settlers formed the Sawdust as a place to contain the workers they needed to build the town, starting with the Duwamish, the first people of the lands that would become known as Seattle. Settlers relied on the Duwamish for most everything—their knowledge of the currents and tides, their familiarity with the thickly forested terrain, and their labor. Duwamish workers powered the sawmill, cooked and cleaned for settler families, and constructed the first buildings. But their continuing presence and persistence within the city also complicated settlers' efforts to claim and occupy Duwamish lands.[2] This tension drove settlers to create a bounded area around the Sawdust to segregate the Duwamish, while still making them available as labor.[3] Soon joining the Duwamish were the Chinese, the city's second workforce. Settlers confined Chinese residents to the Sawdust as

A group of Indigenous workers stand in front of the cookhouse at Yesler's sawmill in 1866. University of Washington Libraries, Special Collections, UW 5870.

well, drawing on the same municipal codes and policies they had developed to manage and control Duwamish mobility.

Creating the Sawdust was not only about segregating the Duwamish and Chinese workforce, however. For settlers, it was also about claiming and protecting a space of their own, a residence district on the northern edge of the city. Located on the high ground, away from the mud and dust, the residence district housed white families and came to embody everything the Sawdust wasn't: homogenous, stable, and permanent. Mill Street, later renamed Yesler Way, served as the dividing line that split the city into two distinct, and opposing, territories. This north-south division would continue to structure Seattle's racial geography well into the twentieth century, as the city grew and changed and new workers arrived and unsettled existing hierarchies.

dᶻidᶻəlalič (A PLACE TO CROSS OVER)

Seattle formally came into being on May 23, 1853, when three settlers, Arthur Denny, Carson Boren, and David "Doc" Maynard, filed two plat maps with King County that created the "Town of Seattle." These maps played a crucial role in the town's legal formation by demarcating official boundaries and property lines.[4] Together, the two maps covered approximately 160 acres and showed the town neatly organized into a grid pattern, with all the streets running at right angles and all the parcels of land divvied up into identical units. But these maps painted a deceptive picture. During the 1850s and 1860s, Seattle looked nothing like its official depiction in these two plat maps, which represented the point of view of their creators more than anything else. Though settlers may have imagined an orderly town with clear divisions, they found it difficult, if not impossible, to bring this plan into fruition.

Denny, Boren, and Maynard came to the Pacific Northwest as part of the larger project of US territorial conquest. For much of the early nineteenth century, the United States and Great Britain had battled over the control of Oregon Territory, a vast area that stretched from present-day Northern California to British Columbia. The 1846 Oregon Treaty established the boundary line between the United States and British North America and granted the United States control over the southern portion of Oregon Territory (now the present-day states of Oregon and Washington). But within Oregon Territory at the time lived colonists from both sides who had flooded the region in the 1830s and 1840s and developed their own independent governing structure. In 1843, they formed a territorial legislature and approved land patents of up to 640 acres for the colonists who had shown up and violently asserted their claims over Indigenous lands. As the United States settled the boundary dispute with Great Britain, the issue of what to do with these lands and the colonists who occupied them sparked a debate within the federal government, which led to the passage of the Oregon Donation Land Claim Act of 1850. This act enshrined Oregon's land policies into federal law, which retroactively granted land rights to the existing settlers and extended those land rights to future settlers who would arrive between 1851 and 1855.[5] The act made legal the existing pattern of land theft of the past two decades; as scholar William G. Robbins puts it, the legislation "served to add the final validation to land already occupied by settlers in Oregon country."[6]

Seattle's early settlers actively participated in this land grab. The Donation Land Claim Act induced a mass migration west with the promise of free land and easy riches. As Denny put it, "The object of all who came to Oregon in early times was to avail themselves of the privilege of a donation claim."[7] Denny and Boren were among the first group of white settlers to establish a permanent presence in Seattle. They left from Illinois in April 1851 and headed west with the initial goal of filing a donation land claim in the Willamette Valley. Along the way, they changed their minds after hearing about Puget Sound country and diverted north, arriving in the area that would become known as Seattle in November 1851. Maynard came a bit later, in spring of 1852, after traveling between Olympia and California in pursuit of business opportunities. An acquaintance in California told him of the great forests that blanketed Puget Sound country and urged Maynard to cash in. "You'll soon be rich," the associate declared.[8] Together, Denny, Boren, and Maynard claimed three adjoining parcels of land along the shoreline of Puget Sound and drew up the plat maps that would lay the foundation of this new town.

But these settlers were not entering an empty land where they could simply arrive and impose their will. Their ignorance about the area's terrain and maritime environment, as well as their low numbers, made them reliant upon the knowledge and labor of the Duwamish and other Indigenous peoples of the Puget Sound region. This gave Indigenous peoples the upper hand—for a while, at least—and produced an early urban society characterized more by coexistence than outright domination.[9]

The Duwamish, the first people of Seattle, had inhabited the lands and marine spaces of the lower Puget Sound for thousands of years. *Duwamish* is an anglicization of the Lushootseed word *dxʷdəwʔabš*, meaning "people of the inside." They lived in loosely autonomous, permanent villages along the watersheds and river drainages of the Puget Sound during winter, while in the summer months they moved around for resource gathering and socializing. The nutrient-rich waters that surrounded them fostered abundant marine life—salmon, flounder, shellfish—which they supplemented with berries and game. As maritime people, they traveled primarily by canoe, which brought them into contact with people beyond their villages and even language groups.[10] Though the Duwamish maintained a distinctive territory (and within that territory, divisions remained), they were also linked with other Coast Salish peoples through what historian Alexandra Harmon has described as "far-reaching networks of family ties and social relations."[11] The most immediate networks were those around the lower Puget Sound, among other Lushootseed-speaking peoples; other networks extended northward along the Northwest Coast.

By the time of Denny's arrival in 1851, the Duwamish and other Coast Salish peoples had already experienced tremendous change. There is ample evidence that infectious diseases and other epidemics spread by European and American fur traders and naval expeditions had reached the shores of the Puget Sound long before Denny and his party, ravaging Indigenous societies and contributing to significant loss of lives.[12] Indigenous oral histories also conveyed the horrific impact of these epidemics. In the 1890s, a Squamish elder recalled the "great misfortune" that had befallen his people along the Fraser River. "Men, women, and children sickened, took the disease and died in agony by hundreds," he said, "camp after camp and village after village was left desolate." Critically, however, the elder also stressed their survival and resilience, noting that "little by little the remnant left by the disease grew into a nation once more."[13] While the epidemics took a devastating toll on Coast Salish societies, still they managed to rebuild and adapt.

In many ways, Denny and the early settlers had to integrate themselves into these existing societies. Indigenous peoples vastly outnumbered Denny and his small party of two dozen. When Denny first landed on Alki Point in Seattle, he recalled "over a thousand [Indians] in our midst."[14] Two years later, in 1853, the settler population had barely crossed one hundred. Numbers aside, settlers also depended upon Indigenous knowledge of the land and sea. The Seattle area then consisted of densely forested, hilly terrain surrounded by an interlocking network of lakes, rivers, inlets, and lagoons, as well as the Sound itself. With the land virtually impassable, settlers moved around by water and hired Indigenous guides for their familiarity with the currents and tides as well as the broader geography of the Puget Sound. "Navigation was not to be thought of by ordinary boats or by white men," recalls settler Catherine Leighton, "and was possible only by canoes."[15] Indeed, when Denny and his party first set out for Seattle from Olympia, they hired two Suquamish guides who helped them scout for a place to land and, later, loaned them canoes when they needed their own transport.[16]

Even in their selection of the town center, settlers appropriated Indigenous place-knowledge. After their party's arrival in November 1851, Denny and Boren turned their attention to building a sawmill, which would help clear the land and also provide a commercial foundation for the town. Again, however, the terrain proved challenging. The settlers struggled to find a parcel of land flat enough for a sawmill and also close to the shoreline.

According to early Seattle historian Clarence Bagley, they found such a place after spotting "an Indian house, no longer inhabited, partly overgrown with wild rose bushes," which led them to a "low wooded flat but a few feet above tidewater."[17] The Duwamish called this area dᶻidᶻəlalič, or "little crossing-over place." A promontory that encircled a small bay and marshland teeming with flounder and other marine life, dᶻidᶻəlalič served as an important site of fishing and social gathering for the Duwamish and other Puget Sound Coast Salish peoples.[18] A trail ran from the shoreline east to Lake Washington (then known as Duwamish Lake), which offered a source of freshwater and a connection to the interior. The features that made dᶻidᶻəlalič an ideal site for the Duwamish—a protected bay, easy access to the sea, flat and open terrain—also made it valuable to the settlers, who selected this spot as the location of the sawmill and town center.

The sawmill itself opened in 1853. A year earlier, Henry Yesler had visited Seattle in search of a place for his lumber business. Yesler had bounced around out West, moving from California to southern Washington and, finally, to the Puget Sound region. He did not find Seattle all that appealing at first, but changed his mind once Maynard and Boren, eager to lure a sawmill to the town, offered him a strip of land between their two claims.[19] The strip originated at tidewater, a point where the shoreline sloped downward from forty feet to zero. Yesler built the steam-powered sawmill at the slope's base, which opened into a deepwater bay ideal for large cargo ships and tugboats carrying log booms and transporting lumber. From the shore, Yesler's strip continued inland, running east toward Duwamish Lake, where he established a second claim in his wife's name. This strip of land became known by settlers as Mill Street, for its use by ox teams as they pulled recently felled trees down to the waterfront to be sawed into lumber and transported by ship around Puget Sound and to California.[20]

Indigenous peoples figured centrally in building the early foundations of the town. They helped Denny and the other settlers construct their first log cabins and other structures including the sawmill itself. They also formed the core of the sawmill workforce; they swept sawdust, felled trees, stacked lumber, and managed the log booms while the women cooked and cleaned for the workers, as well as for the town at large. So critical were Indigenous workers to the lifeblood of the town that settlers trod carefully in their dealings with them. In one case, a group of Duwamish built their own houses on a plot of land Denny and his group had cleared for themselves. "Although

SEATTLE

Madison St
Broadway
1st St
Boren's Tract
Yesler Way (Mill St)
Yesler & Co. Mill Site ■
Elliott Bay
Maynard's Tract

N   0   0.5 Mile
     0   0.5 Kilometer

Seattle, showing the split between north and south, with Yesler Way (Mill Street) as the dividing line.

they seemed very friendly towards us," Denny recalls, "we did not feel safe in objecting to their building thus near to us for fear of offending them."[21]

Denny's remark underscores the fluidity of early Seattle society. The spatial boundaries Denny and his party had so carefully delineated on a map meant little when it came to actual conditions on the ground. Historians Alexandra Harmon and Coll Thrush have shown that the lives of white settlers and Indigenous peoples across the Puget Sound region were deeply intertwined. They lived and worked in close proximity, interacting frequently. Settler accounts abounded with stories alluding to this spatial intimacy—and revealed that these social relations did not result in a harmonious or equitable society. In 1854, for example, white missionary

Catharine Blaine described the "miserable Indian shanties scattered all about" in a letter to her family in New York. "We have now become so used to things," she noted, "that they do not seem strange to us."[22] Settlers held deeply contemptuous views of the region's Indigenous peoples and believed them to be uncivilized and racially inferior. But their reliance on Indigenous knowledge and labor meant the settlers had to contend with the Duwamish and other Indigenous peoples as part of their everyday lives.

THE MILL STREET DIVIDE

In the 1860s the sawmill increased production, and the town grew and expanded. Though even at its peak Yesler's mill did not match the output of other area sawmills, its arrival in the Puget Sound region dramatically transformed Seattle. By offering a local market for logs cleared on settler claims, it quickened the pace of land clearance and induced further settlement. Property values correspondingly rose. The wharf Yesler built attracted more maritime traffic, and ships began to enter Elliott Bay with greater frequency. The mill, which housed the region's first steam-powered saw, emitted a loud whistle at the start and end of each work shift, orienting the entire town around the industrial schedule.[23] Next to the mill stood a cookhouse; there, workers ate their meals and people gathered for meetings, lodgings, parties, and even court cases.[24] Perhaps the biggest change came when Yesler began dumping the mill's overflow of refuse into the surrounding marshlands, creating "the Sawdust" and destroying what was once an important Duwamish site for fishing and resource gathering.

With the tidelands covered with compacted sawdust, the area surrounding and south of the mill was transformed into a commercial district. Located on Maynard's original land claim, the southern part of town's orientation toward commercial activity already reflected Maynard's own financial interests. Using Indigenous labor, Maynard had built the first town store even before Yesler arrived to Seattle; there, he sold the "necessities of pioneer life . . . clothing, hardware, groceries, tools, ship chandlery."[25] Once Yesler's mill was up and running, Maynard secured its first contract in order to furnish logs from his cleared land, which he then subdivided and sold to friends and acquaintances as town lots.[26] One of the town's first hotels appeared on a Maynard lot: the Felker House, operated by Mary Ann Conklin, an Irish immigrant who acquired the nickname Madame Damnable for her ability to curse in multiple languages. Conklin arrived in Seattle in 1853, supposedly abandoned by her husband, a ship captain who had fled to Alaska. The Felker House was a two-story prefabricated building purchased by Captain Leonard Felker, who enlisted Conklin to operate the business.[27] Her first customers included seamen and ship captains passing through Puget Sound.

The expansion of the sawmill's labor force brought new workers to the region and helped further shape this area into a commercial and entertainment district. In its first years, the mill had employed mostly Indigenous men and a handful of white settlers residing in the town. Yesler did not provide rooms, only board in the cookhouse, as many of the workers lived nearby. This changed as more workers arrived and Yesler looked to expand the mill's operational capacity. Though Indigenous people continued to provide the bulk of the labor powering the mill, they were joined by other workers, many of them single men from outside the United States—Germany, Scotland, Peru, India.[28] In the late 1860s, Yesler constructed a new sawmill that could produce more than double the amount of board feet. The workforce correspondingly expanded, reaching nearly one hundred by 1870.[29] More workers meant a greater need for supplies, housing, and leisure spaces. An 1871 Seattle directory lists three hotels, nine saloons, seven general stores, three druggists, two breweries, and six cobblers clustered along Mill and Commercial Streets, joining dozens of other small businesses.[30]

As the area south of Mill Street developed into a center of commerce and town life, settlers began to move to the northern part of the city, which remained decidedly more residential. In part, this reflected the individual preference of the land claimants. Unlike Maynard, the other original claimants—Boren, William Bell, and Denny—did not as readily clear and sell off plots of land. Strict religious men and teetotalers, the trio did not approve of the kinds of trade that Maynard welcomed, which included sex and liquor, preferring instead to sell to families and those with more "respectable" intentions. In addition, they had selected terrain that they viewed as more desirable for permanent settlement. Though Yesler had filled in portions of the tidelands, the area surrounding the mill remained a muddy, sopping mess, particularly during high tide or following periods of rain. Located at a higher elevation, the residents north of Mill Street did not deal with the muck and dirt that covered the Sawdust. Denny family member Sophie Frye Bass, who grew up in Seattle during the 1860s, describes the

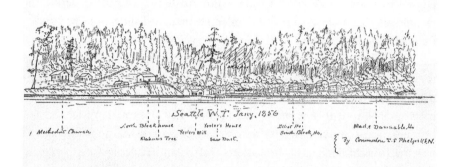

Skyline drawing of Seattle, 1856, showing the early division of the town into north and south. The residence district was located on the high ground; Yesler's sawmill and the surrounding commercial district lay at the shoreline. University of Washington Libraries, Special Collections, UW 41154.

streets north of Mill as being "lined with trees, homes, and old fashioned gardens . . . with white picket fences to keep stray cattle out."[31] Writer Edith Sanderson Redfield similarly recalls the mix of ornate mansions and more modest cottages, each with neat gardens, near her house on the corner of Third and Seneca.[32]

Mill Street thus reflected a growing division in the town of Seattle. On one side, the high ground, single-family homes and gardens stretched over spacious landscapes dotted by the occasional farm or pasture. The other side was characterized by water, mud, dust, workers, seamen, immigrants, Natives, the whirring of machinery, and the sharp call of the mill whistle. These did not represent only physical differences, or the simple split between commercial/industrial and residential areas. Ideological associations became attached to these territories—one superior, one inferior—and these in turn impacted inhabitants' lives, access to resources, and ability to move freely throughout the town. In particular, the cultural narratives about race and sex that shaped the area south of Mill Street—the Sawdust—emerged around the simultaneous containment and displacement of the Duwamish and their transformation from Indigenous inhabitants to unwelcome outsiders.

On February 7, 1865, the newly incorporated town of Seattle passed its first series of ordinances. Appearing in the local newspaper, Ordinance 5 concerned the "removal of Indians" and read: "No Indian or Indians shall be permitted to reside or locate their residences on any street, highway, lane, or alley or any vacant lot in the town of Seattle, from a point known as the South side of Chas. Plummer's ten-acre lot to a point known as the south side of Bell's land claim." This ordinance officially expelled the Duwamish from the area described, which encompassed the northern district through the southern boundary of the town square. There was one exception, however. The ordinance contained a second clause that directed those who employed Indigenous workers to "provide lodgments or suitable residences for the said Indians during the time of said employment."[33] That town leaders felt compelled to pass such an ordinance reflected the persistence of Indigenous people within the growing town of Seattle and their continuing presence among the settlers. But it also marked a shift in how leaders approached relations with them. Moving away from the more fluid social world of the past decade, the ordinance served to harden racial and gendered boundaries around the north and south, while still allowing for the necessity of Indigenous labor.

Ordinance 5 remained officially on the books for only four years. Washington's territorial legislature dissolved the city government in 1867, then approved its reincorporation two years later, at which time town leaders did not reinstate the removal ordinance. Still, the law formalized existing sentiments about the Duwamish and reflected the opinions of city leaders about Indigenous peoples' presence and future within Seattle society—and these conditions did not go away when the law ceased to exist.

Puget Sound's town leaders and municipal authorities of this period impacted Indigenous lives far more than the federal government did. This had to do in part with the regional economy and the demand for Indigenous labor, which pulled many out of the reservations and into the surrounding towns and cities. In 1854–55, Puget Sound tribes signed three treaties with the US government: the treaties of Point No Point, Medicine Creek, and Point Elliott. In them, Indigenous signatories ceded large swaths of land in exchange for reservations and annuity payments. They also reserved the right to fish and hunt "at all usual and accustomed grounds and stations."[34]

Seattle historian Matthew Klingle points out that "the reservations in Puget Sound were designed less to contain Indians than to keep them accessible for labor and to permit them to subsist for themselves."[35] During the 1850s and 1860s, area reservations remained severely underfunded and sparsely populated, as many Indigenous people chose to live off-reservation and pursue wage work and other subsistence activities.[36] Town leaders developed local laws to gain power and to manage the regional conditions that brought settlers and Indigenous peoples into frequent contact.[37]

In Seattle, settlers explicitly rejected the federal government's efforts regarding "Indian affairs." In 1866, nearly all the settlers in King County signed a petition against the creation of a Duwamish reservation along the Black River in south Seattle. Hundreds of Duwamish people had rejected the terms of the Point Elliott treaty, which created the Port Madison reservation across the Sound on Suquamish territory, and called for their own reservation located on their ancestral homelands near the fork of the Duwamish and Black Rivers. With backing from the Indian agent of Washington Territory, George Paige, the federal government appeared ready to move ahead with the Duwamish reservation when the settlers got wind of the plan and moved to squash it. As Paige noted in a report, "The white settlers in the neighborhood desire to have [the Indians] remain among them, that they may avail themselves of their labor, yet at the same time they are unwilling they should have a reservation where they are, because they, the white men, want to appropriate the valuable bottom land which they occupy."[38] In other words, settlers desired Duwamish land and Duwamish labor, and the involvement of the federal government in the form of a reservation threatened both.

In the absence of federal control, town leaders, many of them settlers and prominent landowners who occupied government positions at the local and county levels, took on the role of managing the Indigenous presence in Seattle. They did this primarily through segregation and other modes of containment. Though boundaries had been imposed during the previous decade in the form of land claims and town plats, these remained just scribbles on a piece of paper, abstract lines that meant little in daily life—particularly in the 1850s and early 1860s, when settlers were outnumbered, ill equipped, and reliant on Indigenous knowledge and labor. By the mid-1860s, however, the balance had shifted, and settlers had gained more power, in numbers as well as through the creation of the municipal state. The removal ordinance was passed on the heels of Seattle's official incorporation and coincided with the founding of the city police, the election of the first mayor, and the construction of a new courthouse; trials until that point had been held in Yesler's cookhouse. And while the ordinance simply formalized a spatial division that was already taking shape by 1865, the town now had an apparatus of enforcement to police these boundaries and punish those who transgressed. Ordinance 5 would be one of several passed during the next decade that restricted the movement and residency of Indigenous peoples in Seattle, serving to criminalize their very presence in the town and further legitimize white settler claims to the land.

Municipal efforts at containment focused on the Sawdust, the area that surrounded Yesler's mill and comprised the southern fringes of the city. The measures, which ranged from public health quarantines to vagrancy laws, sought to limit Indigenous peoples to the Sawdust area while also allowing for their labor at the sawmill and other business in the commercial district and at the waterfront. These ordinances did not just involve segregating Indigenous peoples, but also worked to define the city itself as the exclusive domain of white families. Critically, the ordinances overwhelmingly targeted Indigenous women, who bore the brunt of municipal enforcement; throughout the United States and Canada, settlers attempted to diminish the power of Indigenous nations by specifically undermining and controlling Indigenous women.[39] In the Pacific Northwest, the Donation Land Claim Act allowed white men who married Indigenous women to claim double the amount of land until 1855, which made intermarriage and mixed relationships materially beneficial to white male settlers. By the 1860s, however, when much of the land had been appropriated and more white women had migrated to the region, the fluidity of early Puget Sound societies gave way to a social order more rigidly structured around race and gender hierarchies, and a hardening division between whiteness and nonwhiteness.

In June of 1872, the steamship *Prince Albert* left San Francisco with a young boy carrying smallpox. Upon arrival in Victoria, British Columbia, authorities established a quarantine zone near the harbor, where the nearly one hundred passengers remained for nine days before being sent back to San Francisco. Officials in Port Townsend, Washington, the main port of entry into the United States at the time, reacted by enforcing "strict quarantine regulations," while Seattle authorities halted all maritime traffic. In addition, Seattle leaders passed an emergency health measure, Ordinance 30, which required residents and business owners to report signs of contagious disease to the city's health officer, who would then attach a yellow flag to the building that housed the sick person. The ordinance also established a board of health to oversee the implementation of these new regulations, along with a "pest house" to which the sick would be confined until released by a physician.[40]

Though no smallpox reached the Puget Sound region that year, a group of settlers used the episode to argue for stricter and permanent public health quarantines around the Sawdust. They circulated and signed a petition calling for a yellow quarantine flag to be placed on the Illahee brothel. The establishment was operated by John Pinnell, who had relocated from San Francisco in the early 1860s and gained a fortune running a network of businesses including brothels, dance halls, and refreshment stands. The Illahee operated in the Sawdust commercial district alongside a handful of other brothels, and employed mostly Indigenous women who had come with Pinnell from California. Deeming the brothel a "sink of pollution," the petitioners demanded the city council protect the "safety and purity of society" by taking preemptive action against "this evil in our midst." In addition to identifying the brothel as a site of contagion, the petitioners urged the city council to apply a section of Ordinance 30, seeking to prevent those with a known disease from walking in public areas, to the Illahee's workers and customers.[41]

As the petition episode illuminates, the leading white settlers of Seattle who circulated and signed it viewed Indigenous women as a threat to public health and safety. That they targeted only the Illahee, and not other brothels that employed white women, underscores the connections the settlers made between race, sex, and disease. Though it placed direct blame on the owner, John Pinnell, for bringing a hazard into their midst, the settlers' petition also pointed to Indigenous women as the real problem, for carrying hypothetical diseases and spreading them via their own freedom of movement, as well as that of their white male customers. Public health legislation such as the emergency ordinance allowed settlers both to contain Indigenous women to the Sawdust and to identify Indigenous women's bodies as diseased and thus a threat to white settler families' health and safety—and by extension to the town's survival.

Vagrancy ordinances operated in a similar way. In 1873, the city council passed Ordinance 42, designating Indigenous women walking in public after 9:00 p.m. as vagrants and subjecting them to monetary penalty.[42] Though not directly related to the smallpox scare, this vagrancy ordinance played on the same fears and sought the same results as the quarantine action: marking Indigenous women as a disturbance to the general public and criminalizing their mobility. The ordinance also granted the police a great deal of discretion in how they carried out the law, and which areas they targeted for enforcement.

Laws, however, are best understood within the particular cultural context that shapes their meaning and gives them power. In passing these ordinances, settlers drew on the prevailing view of the north and south as distinct, oppositional territories. Settlers referred to the north as the "residence district," which implied family, stability, and permanence, while the Sawdust conjured images of waste and dirt, a useless byproduct and nuisance to be abated. The legal concept of the Indian as a threat to public health and safety was linked inextricably with Indigenous people's confinement to the Sawdust, which itself acquired racialized and gendered associations that marked its inhabitants as morally deficient, uncivilized, and incapable of existing within modern society.[43]

These associations revealed themselves most clearly in two terms used by the general public to describe Indigenous people: "sawdust women" or "sawdust Siwashes."[44] *Sawdust* referred most directly to the area surrounding Yesler's mill, the former tidelands Yesler filled in with actual sawdust from his lumber operations. Over time, however, *sawdust* began to carry a double meaning, alluding to the southern commercial district where sex work, in particular, abounded. "Down on the sawdust" became a popular phrase of the time, linking the area with interracial sex and, specifically, sexual deviancy. Sophie Frye Bass recalled that "anyone who has been here long enough will recall that, after being 'down on the sawdust,' he would be kept busy scratching all the way home, for chodups (fleas) and Indians were close companions."[45] A gendered phrase meant to connote a kind of racialized sexual deviancy, *sawdust* was applied to Indigenous men as well, and used more generally as a descriptor for the Indian in Seattle. Not only did this term ideologically fix Indigenous peoples to the southern district of the city, it also implied they were unsuitable to inhabit any area outside the Sawdust. Language worked in tandem with laws, ordinances, and other forms of policing to segregate Indigenous peoples and further legitimize white settler claims to the land.

These structures of segregation and containment had already formed by the time Chinese migrants began to arrive in Seattle in the mid-1860s. Though Chinese people tried to spread throughout the city, opening small businesses and laundries in the northern "residence district," they found themselves facing the same kinds of restrictions that had targeted Duwamish and other Indigenous people. Settlers responded with hostility as Chinese residents tried to establish autonomous communities outside of the Sawdust, even as Chinese labor became increasingly vital to the functioning of the urban and regional economy. The experiences of Chinese people in Seattle during this period were thus critically shaped by ongoing Indigenous dispossession and the efforts of white settlers to occupy lands only recently brought under their control.

A SHIFTING CITY

The first Chinese people to set foot in the Pacific Northwest arrived aboard two British vessels that left China in 1788. A former captain of the British Royal Navy, John Meares, had organized the voyage; the journey was part of the early transpacific traffic in otter pelts, which were traded primarily for metals, guns, and cloth with coastal Indigenous communities, including the Nootka and Haida, then sold in China where the furs, considered finer and more luxurious than beaver, commanded high prices.[46] Though a British subject, Captain Meares planted a Portuguese flag on both ships as an effort to circumvent licensing fees imposed by the East India Company, which monopolized trade in the Pacific. The Chinese subjects aboard the vessels, numbering roughly four dozen, had backgrounds as "handi-craft men," smiths, and carpenters; some were sailors "who had been used to the junks which navigate every part of the Chinese seas."[47] In May the ships landed in Nootka Sound, Vancouver Island, where the crew constructed a building and sloop and traded with the Mowachaht before leaving in September.

A more substantive wave of Chinese migration to the Pacific Coast of the United States occurred over a half century later, in a more direct consequence of Western imperialism. Eager to control trade in Asia and to force open new markets, the British and other Western powers waged two wars with China known as the Opium Wars. The first was fought from 1839 to 1842 and the second from 1856 to 1860. China lost both wars and was forced into a series of unequal treaties that opened ports to foreign commerce, ceded Hong Kong and other territories to Western control, and granted extraterritoriality to British subjects and their allies operating in China.[48] Alongside the domestic upheavals and political turmoil sweeping China during these decades, the treaties created conditions and structural linkages for mass emigration. At the same time, the discovery of gold in Australia, in California, and along British Columbia's Fraser River lured many migrants, Chinese included, to try their luck in the mining business.[49]

The open flows of transnational migration made possible by these treaties clashed at times with the protectionist impulses of local governments and their white settler constituents. In Washington Territory, this tension played out during the 1860s as the legislature passed a series of exclusionary laws to preemptively discourage Chinese migration. Though millions had left China during the mid-nineteenth century, very few had ended up in Washington Territory. The federal census recorded its first Chinese resident in 1850: Ah-Long, a nineteen-year-old man who worked as a servant at Vancouver Barracks, a US Army outpost built in 1849.[50] Some Chinese migrants passed through Washington Territory during the 1850s, on their way to gold mines in Canada, while others temporarily settled at mining sites abandoned by whites along the Columbia River basin. In 1860, the census again recorded just one unnamed Chinese person in Washington Territory, thought to be Chun Ching Hock. Chun had made his way to Seattle from San Francisco that year; he would eventually open the Wa Chong Company, one of the most lucrative Chinese merchant businesses to operate in the Pacific Northwest.[51]

Despite its tiny Chinese population, Washington's territorial legislature passed a "police tax" in 1864 that required all Chinese residents over the age of eighteen to pay an annual fee of sixteen dollars.[52] The tax had originally included Black residents, but they did not appear in the final legislation; one newspaper attributed this to the potential for interference by abolitionists and other sympathetic parties.[53] During the next four sessions, the legislature amended the act twice, and even extended the police tax to "Kanakas," or Indigenous Hawaiians, who had come to the Pacific Northwest to work in the fur trade and continued to pass through Washington Territory as sailors and seamen.[54]

The demands of industrial capitalism, however, disincentivized territories like Washington from maintaining exclusionary anti-Chinese laws. Washington Territory officially repealed its police tax on the Chinese

Group of Chinese men standing at the doorway of the Wa Chong Company, c. 1905.
Wing Luke Museum.

population in 1869, with the legislature declaring that "any laws or parts of
laws which levy a police tax discriminating against persons of the Mongo-
lian race, or natives of the Sandwich, Society or other islands of the Pacific,
residing in this Territory, be and the same are hereby repealed."[55] The most
immediate cause of this change of course was the 1868 Burlingame Treaty,
which established relations with China, allowed for the free movement of
Chinese people into the United States, and offered nominal protections to
Chinese citizens residing in the country. A gift to industry leaders and big
business, the treaty provided unfettered access to Chinese labor following
the end of the Civil War and the expansion of the industrial economy, which
included railroad construction and agriculture. But even without the Burlingame Treaty, Washington Territory would likely have repealed the tax
anyway. Territorial leaders desperately wanted to expand Washington's
industrial economy and looked to the transcontinental railroad, in particular, as key to the region's economic future. The police tax and other laws
curtailing Chinese migration directly undermined this goal.

Within this context, employers increasingly looked to Chinese laborers
to drastically expand their manual workforce. While Indigenous men and
women continued to labor throughout the region, particularly in the salmon

canning, fishing, and agricultural industries, Chinese workers became preferred in the low-wage sector. This had to do with the particular structure
of Chinese labor contracting and the role of Chinese merchants in organizing a transpacific labor network created for projects like railroad-building.
Historian Kornel Chang discusses Chinese labor contractors who worked
on both sides of the Pacific to funnel Chinese laborers to the United States
and into the low-wage workforce. In a form of outsourcing, employers paid
Chinese labor contractors to serve as intermediaries, responsible for recruiting and overseeing large, independent teams of Chinese laborers who would
perform the most dangerous and physically taxing work. Labor contractors'
ability to manage this transpacific workforce made them highly valued by
industrialists, railroad barons, and other employers in Washington Territory and throughout the American West.[56]

Patterns of Chinese migration into the Seattle area reflected these
broader legal and economic shifts. The first Chinese residents arrived in the
city in the mid-1860s and consisted of a handful of individuals who opened
laundries and cigar shops south of Mill Street, in and around the Sawdust.
These establishments were clustered along Commercial Street, then the
nucleus of Seattle's burgeoning business district; later Commercial became
the southern portion of First Avenue. These early residents, who numbered
less than ten, faced a mix of hostility and fascination. Anonymous vandals
demolished a "Chinese wash-house" in 1864 and attempted to burn down
a "cigar manufactory" the next year; the latter act was condemned in a local
newspaper, whose editor called for the "miscreants" to be brought to justice.[57] Though clearly a vulnerable population, the Chinese residents also
appeared as objects of local curiosity. Nearly the entire town turned out to
witness the wedding of Chen Cheong to Gin Came in March 1867. One local
observer called it a "novel affair" and admired the bride's traditional gown
for its "feminine taste and skill in needle-work."[58]

One of these early residents was Chun Ching Hock. Born in Taishan, a
village located in the southern Chinese province of Guangdong, Chun had
sailed to San Francisco in 1860 at the age of sixteen, then headed north to
end up in Seattle, working as a cook in Yesler's mill. Chun managed to save
some money; in 1868, after a short trip back to China, he opened a store just
south of the mill, naming it the Wa Chong Company.[59] Operating out of a
small frame building, Wa Chong in its first few years served as a general
merchandising business, selling cigars, tea, sugar, fireworks, and a small

array of Chinese goods. During the early 1870s, Chun brought on Chin Gee Hee, a new partner, after the death of his original partner, Chun Wa; Chin Gee Hee worked to develop Wa Chong's employment services. As the first labor-contracting business to operate in the expanding Seattle area, Wa Chong furnished temporary and seasonal laborers to regional employers—salmon canneries, coal mines, sawmills, local and transcontinental railroad projects—and for city contracts grading streets and digging canals.[60]

As Wa Chong's fortunes grew, so too did its impact on the local urban landscape. With profits from its lucrative labor-contracting business, the company invested in real estate, buying up pieces of property south of Mill Street and forming the foundation of a growing Chinese district.[61] By 1876, a city directory recorded over two hundred Chinese residents in Seattle. New businesses, including eight laundries and three grocery stores, opened up along Washington and Main Streets, joined by the old cigar shops and washhouses that had once operated next to Yesler's mill.[62] The headquarters of Wa Chong stood at the corner of Third Avenue and Washington; a three-story brick building housed its store and offices, with dwellings for laborers and employees located next door and in the back.[63] As one of only three brick buildings south of Mill Street, Wa Chong's headquarters looked very different from the surrounding landscape, which consisted mainly of one- and two-story wood frame buildings, occupied by Chinese and non-Chinese alike. Considerably more expensive than building in wood, the use of brick signaled Wa Chong's wealth and status as well as the company's prominent place within Seattle's emerging urban landscape.

Though Chinese merchants, laborers, and small businesses clustered along Washington Street, constituting the city's first Chinese neighborhood, non-Chinese men and women lived and worked there as well. Washington Street served as the center of an Indigenous diasporic community that included Indigenous families from British Columbia and Alaska as well as four interracial couples, white or European men and Indigenous women from Washington Territory.[64] An 1884 Sanborn map lists at least one "Indian structure" along Washington Street, nestled among dwellings that housed Chinese laborers. In addition, Washington Street had by this time become a district for commercial entertainment and leisure, with seven saloons and Smith's Bijou Theater across the street from Wa Chong's headquarters. The city government also maintained a presence along Washington Street through its jailhouse and livery, the location of these operations suggesting the district's continued undesirability despite its bustling commercial traffic and growing residential population.[65]

A more strident anti-Chinese hostility spread through Seattle in the 1870s, replacing the tolerant curiosity that had once characterized local public views. A financial panic in 1873 and an ensuing depression made the Chinese easy scapegoats in a time of economic troubles. While city elites and businessmen including Henry Yesler continued to support Chinese entrepreneurs like Chun Ching Hock and Chin Gee Hee for their networks of transpacific labor, these opinions clashed with the anti-Chinese sentiment brewing both locally and along the Pacific Coast. As Seattle pursued a railroad project, the Seattle to Walla Walla line, newspaper editors began to comment on the threats posed by Chinese labor. "No Mongolians," shouted a headline in the *Puget Sound Dispatch*. "It is to be hoped that the management of the Seattle to Walla Walla Railroad Company will from the very start adopt the rule of employing only American or European labor."[66] Other papers featured articles about the anti-Chinese movement in California, using those reports to sound alarm bells on the growing Chinese presence in Seattle. The *Seattle Post-Intelligencer*, for example, published a letter describing the anti-Chinese riot that swept San Francisco in 1877, urging local readership to consider the "ugly question of Chinese importation and labor as a disturbing element in this community."[67]

To regulate the Chinese presence in Seattle, city officials began drawing on measures previously imposed on Indigenous women in order to control where Chinese residents lived and constrain their ability to form autonomous communities. Though newspapers published dire warnings about the supposed threat of Chinese labor, the actual anti-Chinese policies implemented by the city targeted neither the laborers nor the system of contracting that brought them to Seattle. Instead, city measures sought to contain the growing presence of permanent Chinese inhabitants and small business operators. As many in Seattle well knew, the city and region's economic viability was linked to the transpacific flow of highly mobile labor, organized by companies such as Wa Chong. The territorial legislature had abolished the police tax for essentially this reason, just as Henry Yesler, Doc Maynard, and others invested in the city's economic growth had welcomed the transpacific connections Wa Chong brought to Seattle. The laborers who worked under Wa Chong maintained a temporary presence in Seattle, often staying only a few days before being sent out to worksites on the outskirts of the city or in the surrounding region. Those not involved in the contracting business, but who nonetheless signaled their intention of establishing a permanent presence in the town, became subject to restrictive laws.

The movement to segregate Chinese migrants was not unique to Seattle. San Francisco, Los Angeles, Vancouver, and other Pacific Coast cities implemented similar laws seeking to restrict Chinese mobility through public health ordinances, property discrimination, and policing. These efforts are frequently portrayed as a form of xenophobic action, targeting a minority group long considered racially inferior and incapable of assimilation. But an underexamined aspect of this history is the context of Indigenous dispossession and the creation of these cities as white settler societies. Chinese migration to the Pacific Coast coincided with the mass displacement of Indigenous peoples in emerging urban centers, and the rapid conversion of Indigenous lands into private and public property. Segregating Chinese people served as one avenue of restricting their access to this newfound property and wealth, while also making them available as low-wage labor.[68] The anti-Chinese ordinances are thus linked with the displacement of Indigenous peoples and the creation of the city itself as a space of white domestic life.

In Seattle, the bulk of these ordinances focused on segregating Chinese laundries to the area south of Mill Street. Like other cities and towns, Seattle saw Chinese workers enter the laundry business with greater frequency than any other occupation. Laundries required little start-up money and had low operating costs, while also doubling as sleeping quarters for operators and staff. Considered domestic work and thus unsuitable for the white male producer and wage earner, laundries occupied a niche that did not directly compete with white labor. As historian Mary Lui has shown, the work of laundry operation became strongly associated with the Chinese, and the businesses were racialized as unhygienic and dangerous to public health and safety.[69] In Seattle as well, Chinese laundries bore the brunt of local laws that cast them as hazardous to the public. Echoing similar concerns around the mobility of Indigenous women, municipal regulators targeted the businesses under the guise of public safety and restricted them to the Sawdust.

Though Chinese laundries did not pose an economic threat to white Seattleites, they did take over an occupation long dominated by Indigenous women. Early settlers had relied almost entirely on Indigenous women for

View of Mill Street, 1876, showing Hop Sing laundry among the businesses. University of Washington Libraries, Special Collections, UW 5835.

domestic work, including washing clothes. Missionary Catharine Blaine employed Indigenous washerwomen; a biography of Doc Maynard and his wife Catherine recalls Kikisoblu (called Angeline by settlers), daughter of Chief Seattle, "[assisting] the women of the town in their laundry work."[70] Indigenous women also performed these services for Yesler's mill and other logging camps around Seattle. Historian Tera Hunter has discussed this dynamic in the case of Black washerwomen in the South who found themselves in competition with Chinese laundries after the Civil War.[71] In Seattle, the record remains less clear about how directly Chinese laundries competed with Indigenous women, but the broader story points to a shift in the early 1870s away from the individual labor of Indigenous washerwomen and toward the Chinese-run laundry business. This underexamined story of economic competition speaks to the complicated status of Chinese migrants in early Seattle society. Many chose to enter the laundry business because it was the only occupation available to them outside of the harsh, physically perilous world of manual labor. And yet, in doing so, they also closed off one of the few avenues of subsistence for Indigenous women within the settler economy.

City authorities used the danger of fire as a pretext to segregate Chinese laundries. On August 8, 1877, a fire broke out in Olympia, Washington's territorial capital, and damaged a significant portion of the city. Allegedly originating in a "Chinese wash-house," the Olympia fire gave newspaper editors an occasion to caution the public about the danger posed by Chinese laundries, which one report described as "generally tenanted by a class of laundrymen who keep lights burning at all hours and smoke opium incessantly." The article called for Seattle to limit the particular location in which such businesses could operate; such measures existed in California towns and cities, where Chinese laundries were "restricted to a particular locality and forbidden to put a building outside that limit."[72] Seattle, of course, had reason to fear the spread of fire. Like other cities of the time, its built environment consisted overwhelmingly of wood. It also lacked reliable access to running water and a working fire department. But Chinese laundries did not differ considerably in construction from the other businesses south of Mill Street; the neighborhood's laundries, restaurants, saloons, theater, and hotels were all one- or two-story wood frame buildings. By calling attention to the Chinese laundries, and not the other structures, the author connected the problem of fire with the Chinese presence in Seattle.

In 1882, the city passed an ordinance to "restrain and regulate" laundries operating within the fire zone.[73] Two years before, city officials had taken heed of public demand and delineated an area that was subject to inspection and regulation for the prevention of fires.[74] Located along Mill Street and to the south, the fire zone essentially drew a boundary around the Sawdust, the so-called troubled district where loggers and sailors mingled in saloons and brothels and Chinese and Indigenous laborers moved around the streets. Though the 1882 laundry ordinance did not name the Chinese specifically, it did not need to—they operated nearly all the laundries in the city, all of them situated south of Mill Street.[75] For businesses already established, the ordinance required a positive report from health inspectors in order to continue operation, while those who wished to open a laundry had to gain permission from the city. In its immediate impact, the ordinance put five Chinese laundries out of business.[76] It also created a legal precedent that enabled the harassment and policing of Chinese laundries and other businesses, a practice that continued into the 1890s and beyond.[77]

In other ways, however, the city struggled to implement the ordinance, largely because Chinese laundry operators devised strategies to circumvent the restrictions. Some operated clandestine laundries or ones that deliberately evaded city regulators. Fire Chief Gardner Kellogg complained that "two of three of those prosecuted have established themselves in the basement of Hop Sing Wash House between 2nd and 3rd St. on Mill."[78] Others opened laundries outside the fire zone, north of Mill Street, sparking a furious response by a group of white residents who filed a petition requesting a total prohibition of laundries in the city.[79] This prompted city officials to amend the laundry ordinance in 1886, expanding its reach beyond the fire zone and into the entire city of Seattle.[80] Municipal records show that the city consistently rejected Chinese requests to open laundries north of Mill Street.[81]

The laundry ordinance joined a series of other municipal laws passed in the early 1880s, including an opium ban and a cubic air ordinance, which all worked in tandem to render the Chinese unfit for inclusion into urban society, a hazard to be abated and controlled.[82] As with the "sawdust women" before them, the relegation of Chinese laundries south of Mill Street further marked these businesses, and those who operated them, as an undesirable and threatening presence. At the same time, these ordinances helped reinforce the city's racialized boundaries between white and nonwhite, further protecting the northern district as the exclusive domain of white domestic life.

Yet exceptions remained. A handful of Chinese men and Indigenous women did reside north of Mill Street during the 1870s, complicating the city's racialized divide. They worked as servants in the homes of Seattle's most prominent and wealthy families, living with them permanently. Records from the 1880 census list eight Chinese men and three Indigenous women in the "residence district" north of Mill Street.[83] Henry Yesler secured the services of a Chinese servant, Ah Ty, as did Bailey Gatzert, who served as mayor of Seattle from 1875 to 1876. Lois Hilderbidle, the daughter of a German father and a Duwamish mother, worked in the home of physician Herman Bagley, who lived with his wife and children in a Victorian mansion on Fourth Street across from the territorial university.[84] Domestic service had a long history in the region, with settlers employing Indigenous women to perform labor in their home and to cook for workers at the mill sites. As with laundry work, it appears that Chinese laborers competed with Indigenous women in this particular occupation, though by the early 1880s both groups continued to perform domestic labor for wealthy Seattle families.

The employment of Chinese men and Indigenous women in the homes of the very same leaders who deemed them threatening to public health and safety may seem contradictory. But the logic of segregation was never about total containment. The city's ordinances sought to carve out a spatial order rooted in white racial supremacy, but that order also remained flexible and responsive to the settler economy's material demands. Chinese servants and seasonal laborers did not threaten the status quo because they remained economically dependent. Chinese laundries, on the other hand, operated independently, outside the realm of white settler control. The laundry business signaled Chinese economic mobility and the intention of permanent settlement within the city. For Indigenous women, the work of domestic service functioned differently. White women viewed the employment of Indigenous women in the home as a project of assimilation, imparting lessons about "modern housewifery" in order to civilize Indigenous servants through the imposition of bourgeois gender norms.[85] In both cases, domestic service filled an economic role while also offering symbolic capital particularly for white settler women, who could remove themselves from the drudgery of household labor.[86] The employment of Chinese and Indigenous servants was not incompatible with the prevailing racial geography of the city and the northern residence district's constitution as the exclusive domain of white families.

The role of Mill Street as a boundary marker would only grow more critical as the resource-based economy expanded and brought new migrants and laborers through the city. It served to sort out the desirable from the undesirable, protecting the north as a place of permanent white residence while making available the labor of nonwhite migrants. As the case of the Duwamish illuminates, Seattle's rise as a city was made possible by the dispossession of its Indigenous inhabitants. White settlers appropriated Indigenous land, then created a municipal state to control and delegitimize Indigenous claims to that land. Though at first an abstract division, the Mill Street boundary was actualized through the formation of a municipal apparatus—laws, courts, police, inspection teams—that monitored the use of space by the Duwamish and criminalized those who transgressed. A similar logic fueled the actions against Chinese migrants as they arrived in Seattle and unsettled its emerging racial geography.

And yet the preponderance of restrictive ordinances city leaders passed from the 1860s through the 1880s reveals the porousness of these boundaries.

Laws kept appearing because Mill Street did not stand as an impenetrable barrier. People on the ground challenged the top-down vision of Seattle by pursuing their own agendas and navigating the landscape on their own terms. These challenges would continue to pose problems not just for city officials, but for employers and industry leaders who drew on Seattle's concentration of Indigenous and Chinese labor to power the regional economy. Hop farmers, in particular, utilized maritime networks traversed by Indigenous and Chinese workers to access a highly mobile labor force needed for the short three-week picking season. As the farmers soon came to realize, however, the mobility of the workforce and its concentration in Seattle made their industry possible but also created the conditions for the industry's potential undoing. In that way, sawdust was an apt metaphor for Seattle's first segregated district: a waste product used to lay the foundations of the city, the literal ground around which Seattle developed, but one that was, in the end, not so solid after all.

CHAPTER 2

Urban Roots of
Puget Sound Agriculture

THE HISTORY OF HOPS IN THE PACIFIC NORTHWEST BEGINS WITH water. Though agriculture is often understood as a solely land-based endeavor, Puget Sound waterways played a crucial role in the emergence of this particular regional industry. The Puget Sound basin covers over sixteen thousand square miles of water and land, carved out over several millennia by a retreating glacier. Flowing north, it converges with the Strait of Georgia, and west, with the Strait of Juan de Fuca, forming the body of water known today as the Salish Sea.[1] Though the Puget Sound provided the cities and towns dotting its shoreline with access to the Pacific Ocean, its rivers and tributaries served an equally useful purpose, linking small inland towns with coastal communities across Western Washington.

Seattle stood at the heart of this vast marine space. Situated at the convergence of multiple rivers, the lands that would become known as Seattle served as a crucial hub of Indigenous migrations.[2] Though located within Duwamish territory, other Indigenous peoples up and down the Northwest Coast also had a presence in Seattle, whether for travel, resource gathering, or connecting with extended family. These migrations did not stop with the arrival of white settlers and the disruptions of urban displacement. Seattle's role as "the place where one crosses over" persisted into the late nineteenth and early twentieth centuries and beyond.

Chinese histories in the Pacific Northwest also revolved around water. Many of the early Chinese migrants came to Seattle through Vancouver, traversing the waters of the Salish Sea as they crossed into the United States from Canada. Chinese laborers also worked aboard steamships that sailed through the Puget Sound, including those that carried lumber to markets around the region and down to California.[3] Though their connection to the Salish Sea was very different, they shared with their fellow Indigenous migrants a maritime world that brought them frequently to Seattle.

The concentration of Indigenous and Chinese migrants in Seattle established the city as an early hub of labor migration. Their maritime mobility and accessibility made them a desirable source of labor for employers across the region, which lacked a railroad system until the late nineteenth century. Hop growers, many of them settlers who established farms on the rivers and tributaries of the Puget Sound, utilized these urban-based maritime networks, often traveling up to Seattle to hire their seasonal workforce. Hops, the main ingredient used for flavoring beer, arrived in the Pacific Northwest in the 1860s and soon emerged as the region's first major agricultural industry, in large part because of the availability of Indigenous and Chinese labor. Though the Klondike gold rush of 1897 looms large in local historical memory as the key event that shaped Seattle's regional connections, the miners and adventurers who passed through the city on their way up north were traversing routes that had long been established by Indigenous and Chinese migrants.[4]

The concentration of these two groups in the same city, within the shared space of the south end and waterfront district, appealed strongly to employers. Chinese and Indigenous migrants had a presence in many different urban coastal areas across the Pacific Northwest during this time, but it was only in Seattle that the two were pushed so closely together.[5] In Seattle, employers had access to both groups and could hire one or the other or both at the same time. This gave hop growers, in particular, the flexibility they needed to accommodate the unpredictable nature of the hop harvest. It also allowed them to exploit divisions between the two in order to depress wages and maintain a profit margin. Though scholars tend to treat Indigenous and Chinese laborers as inhabiting almost separate worlds, their proximity and interconnection made the regional economy possible.[6]

This city-based employment system, though, did not always work as growers anticipated. The maritime world of the Puget Sound allowed for a kind of autonomy among the workforce that continually undermined grow-ers' expectations of a smoothly functioning industry. It brought people together in unpredictable ways, leading to new forms of sociability and leisure as well as conflicts and violence. As Seattle's role as a hub of labor migration expanded, this unpredictability intensified; it would plague employers, industry leaders, and politicians well into the twentieth century. In this way, the hops industry set the stage for future industrial expansion, while also exposing the system's inherent fragility and the stark limitations of settler power.

HOP FARMS AND THE SALISH SEA

In her memoir, *Tulalip, from My Heart*, Tulalip elder Harriette Shelton Dover recalled her mother's seasonal migrations down to the hop fields. Together with extended family in "six or eight canoe loads," her mother traveled each year from Guemes Island near Anacortes to the Puyallup Valley. Over several days, the group "would come along the Sound" and camp at night, stopping and eating lunch during the day. Then, "they would go up the Puyallup River to where Ezra Meeker's hop fields were."[7] With this story Dover illuminates a crucial aspect of the Puget Sound hop industry: the farms were oriented around major rivers. The eastern side of Puget Sound is surrounded by rivers: the Nisqually down by Olympia; the Puyallup and Duwamish; the Snohomish, Skykomish, and Stillaguamish; and the northern Skagit and Nooksack. Puget Sound Coast Salish peoples had traversed these rivers since time immemorial, moving around the region in "beautiful" canoes.[8]

In the 1850s, hop farms began to pop up along these waterways, claimed by some of the first settlers in Washington Territory. Ezra Meeker, who would later achieve worldwide recognition as "hop king" of the Pacific Northwest, first spotted the location of his Puyallup Valley hop farm on a canoe trip through the southern half of Puget Sound. Born in Ohio, Meeker had made his way west along the Oregon Trail, lured by the promise of free land through the Donation Land Claim Act. He arrived in 1853 and spent the next several months along the water, scouting potential sites for farm-land. Reluctant at first to pay for Indigenous guidance, Meeker and his brother attempted to sail the waters of the Puget Sound in a homemade skiff, only to find themselves lost and struggling against the strong current. At that moment, in Meeker's telling, a group of Puyallup men passed by and towed them right into Commencement Bay at the mouth of the Puyallup River. Meeker recalls that after that mishap "we secured the services of an Indian and his canoe to help us up the river and left our boat at the Indian's camp near the mouth."[9] From there, Meeker explored the Puyallup River valley, birthplace of Puget Sound hop culture. He would later operate one of the era's largest hop farms.

Following Meeker's lead, other settlers arrived in the 1850s and established farms in the fertile lands surrounding Seattle, including the valleys of the Puyallup and White Rivers. Running along the southeastern side of the Puget Sound basin, the two rivers formed a maritime highway that cut through thirty miles of land between present-day Seattle and Tacoma. Both rivers flowed into Puget Sound; the Puyallup River drained into Commencement Bay on the southern end, while the White River joined the Duwamish River just south of Yesler's mill in Seattle. These rivers offered settlers a water-based transportation network as well as rich alluvial soil ideal for growing crops. According to Seattle historian Clarence Bagley, "The only farms of the district in those days were along the banks of rivers."[10]

As was the case in Seattle, these early settlers acquired farmland through donation claims and benefited materially from the dispossession of the region's Indigenous peoples. Though settlers like Meeker focused on farming instead of building a town and commercial center like Denny and Maynard, their occupation of the Puyallup and White River valleys constituted a parallel movement made possible by the same legal structures their urban counterparts utilized. The Donation Land Claim Act itself predated the ratification of the three Puget Sound treaties—those of Point Elliott, Medicine Creek, and Point No Point—and allowed settlers to claim unceded Indigenous lands, amounting to an "invasion of white settlers," in the words of Muckleshoot elder Joe Bill.[11] Another Puyallup elder recalled, "There were a lot of white people then taking lands . . . yes, they took their possessions, took their homes, they took cleared lands."[12] Even after the three treaties' signing and ratification, settlers continued their land grab irrespective of treaty terms setting aside reservation lands. Settlers also expressly ignored the reserved rights of Indigenous peoples to their traditional fishing and hunting grounds. Individual settlers and industrial firms like railroad companies continued to take and occupy the most valuable lands, including those within reservation boundaries, without penalty, even after legal protest and violent resistance by Puget Sound tribes.

Situated on prime agricultural land, this group of white settlers began to establish farming businesses. Hops had been brought to the United States from Europe in the seventeenth century, spreading first into New England and then New York, which emerged as the center of global hop production by the turn of the nineteenth century. Hop cultivation followed the movement west and became popular along the Pacific Coast beginning in the 1850s. In Washington, Ezra Meeker's father, Jacob, first received hop roots from an acquaintance in Olympia. From these first roots, the Meekers planted and harvested one bale of hops in 1865 that sold for eighty-five cents per pound, "more than had been received by any of the settlers in the Puyallup Valley."[13] Impressed with these profits, Meeker's neighbors, including L. F. Thompson, E. C. Meade, and J. P. Stewart, ordered a barrel of hop roots from California, planting four acres and sparking a craze that would eventually spread throughout the valley. Growers sold hops locally to brewers in the Pacific Northwest; as production increased they expanded sales into California, and then into Europe by the early 1880s.

In the early years, growers faced significant hurdles. Hop production involved heavy startup costs, including investments in equipment and facilities. After securing the land, growers planted the hop roots, which grew in vines around tall wooden poles during spring and summer. Once ripe, hop cones produced pungent-smelling resin containing the chemical compounds used to flavor beer. As a child, Dover spent time on the hop fields and recalled that "even within a few yards you can smell them."[14] In order to preserve the resin's flavor and color, growers dried the hop cones in a process known as curing, baking the hops in a kiln over low heat for several days. In the 1860s, New York farms churned out almost ten million pounds of hops per year in large-scale industrial drying plants, while in Washington curing occurred in barns or even living rooms around the stove.[15] Workers moved the cured hops to a separate shed or barn to be pressed, bagged, labeled, and either stored or shipped. Growers sold directly to beer brewers, whose agents visited the fields in early summer to negotiate a fixed price, or to merchants who bought and sold hops independently.

The unpredictable ripening process of the hop plant made finding pickers a particular challenge. Growers required pickers for only a short period, typically two to three weeks in the late summer. The timing of picking season depended upon temperature, climate, and humidity; even a handful of chilly or rainy days could delay the harvest. "We will not finish hop picking until the first of next week," one grower lamented. "The rainy weather damaged the hops more than I thought it would."[16] Once fully ripe, the hops had to be picked within a short window or the cones would start to rot, forcing growers to sell at lower prices. Though not as physically taxing as other forms of agricultural labor, hop picking nonetheless required many dexterous hands to detach the cones, sticky with resin, from the vines. Growers hired foremen to oversee and pay the workers, typically seventy-five cents to one dollar per box, as well as inspectors to grade the quality of the picked hops. In the beginning, growers looked locally for help with the harvest. They enlisted their wives and children as well as Indigenous pickers from the surrounding Puyallup and White River areas, including men, women, children, and the elderly.

In the early 1870s, growers quickly realized that their industry's expansion depended upon labor. Without enough workers to come harvest, Puget Sound hops would never exist as anything more than a local specialty. But procuring the thousands of temporary workers needed for the profits they envisioned was complicated. Individual growers depended more than others on existing transportation infrastructure to bring workers to the fields. Logging companies, for example, built service railroads to move workers and timber from the forests to the sawmills, while the Northern Pacific Railway Company commanded its own fleet of steamers throughout the Puget Sound.[17] Only one passenger railroad operated in Western Washington at the time—a spur line from Kalama, a cannery town along the Columbia River, to Tacoma. Growers initially considered Columbia River salmon canneries as a promising source of seasonal labor, since the salmon-canning industry offered a concentrated pool of unemployed workers whom growers could access at a convenient time. Cannery schedules followed the salmon runs, which tapered off in July and August, just in time for the hop harvest.[18] Cost, though, remained an issue. The Kalama line could funnel cannery workers directly from the Columbia River Valley into southern Puget Sound, but the railroad company refused to lower its rates, forcing growers to look elsewhere for pickers.

At this point, growers consciously decided to utilize Puget Sound's maritime networks to move large teams of seasonal workers in the absence of land-based transportation. According to one local newspaper report, growers specifically looked for "the Indians and Chinese of Washington Territory . . . and from the same class of people in Victoria [and] New Westminster" because they were accessible by water. Growers dispatched agents "on the boats" to every coastal community and industrial site, which included all of the Puget Sound reservations.[19] As discussed in the previous chapter, few Indigenous peoples had relocated to reservations in the 1850s and 1860s. Severely underfunded and disorganized, reservations held little attraction for those who could live on the outside and pursue seasonal wage work. But in the years following the Civil War, federal Indian policy grew more punitive, doling out harsher punishments to those who did not accept forced assimilation programs. Further, increasing white settlement during this period pushed more and more people off their land and onto reservations. The reservation borders remained fluid, however. The wage economy pulled many Indigenous people off the reservations seasonally, while others continued to live and work among settlers in local towns and cities.[20] While the reservation system functioned as an important feeder into the hops workforce, growers were capitalizing on the residents' existing mobility.

In addition to the reservations, growers looked to British Columbia's canneries, where they found concentrations of Indigenous and Chinese workers along the Fraser River. Though Chinese laborers dominated the US cannery workforce, Indigenous workers played a far bigger role on the Canadian side in the late nineteenth century and beyond.[21] The broader Pacific Northwest's salmon canning industry began in earnest during the 1870s, when newly constructed plants along the Fraser and Columbia Rivers attracted large teams of seasonal workers. In northern Oregon, Chinese crews provided the bulk of the labor, occupying almost every spot in the cannery hierarchy, from skilled positions as butchers, tinsmiths, and can testers to semiskilled and manual labor. During this period cannery owners utilized informal methods of labor contracting, typically relying on individual Chinese employees to recruit and oversee their Chinese-speaking workforce.[22] In British Columbia, employers enlisted Indigenous fishers, primarily men, whose knowledge of salmon migration and fishing technology proved invaluable during the canning industry's early years. Indigenous women and children worked on the shore mending nets and in the plants as fish cleaners and can fillers.[23] While Canadian cannery owners also hired Chinese teams to perform factory work, they relied more on Indigenous labor than their American counterparts did.

By focusing their recruitment strategy on the maritime environment of the region, growers hoped to ensure a steady stream of workers who could travel to the fields by water. Unlike the salmon canneries dotting the Columbia River, the British Columbia plants along the Fraser River allowed for fast, cheap water-based travel to the hop fields. Indigenous workers leaving from Victoria, Vancouver, and the Northwest Coast could travel by canoe through the Strait of Georgia, down into the Puget Sound, and up the Puyallup and White Rivers, while those coming from Puget Sound communities simply had to journey across the Sound. Chinese workers could also move quite easily by boat, which remained the cheaper, more practical option for transportation. Steamships and smaller ferries made frequent trips around the Puget Sound and across the maritime border between the United States and Canada.

To assemble this massive team of seasonal labor from all around the region and effectively respond to unpredictable harvest conditions, hop growers needed easy access to a consolidated workforce. Seattle again emerged as a critical hub of labor: a stopping-over place for workers as they passed to and from the hop fields, and a site of labor recruitment where growers went to hire workers and negotiate terms of employment. Rather than smoothing over inefficiencies, however, this geography of migration gave workers the upper hand in their dealings with growers, carving out autonomous spaces that consistently undermined the logic of capitalist exploitation and control.

INDIGENOUS AND CHINESE WORKERS IN THE CITY

Seattle in 1870 was still a relatively small city, its population hovering around one thousand residents. With an official incorporation date of 1869, Seattle was also a very new city. At that time, the urban economy still revolved mostly around Yesler's sawmill, which sold cut timber to other settler communities around Puget Sound as well as California. The commercial and entertainment district surrounding the mill, known as the Sawdust, provided another source of economic activity, attracting people from beyond the city itself and generating revenue from customers far and wide. Indigenous and Chinese laborers constituted the bulk of the urban workforce at that time, toiling in the sawmill and construction projects as well as performing domestic labor such as laundry and housekeeping. As discussed in the last chapter, Seattle remained stratified by race, reflecting settlers' efforts to claim and occupy Indigenous lands by creating a northern

residential district for white families and policing racial and gender boundaries through municipal regulation. These practices also consolidated
workers in one geographic area, which benefited employers, including hop
growers, who could more easily access this pool of labor. Seattle's urban
context of racial segregation and displacement thus played a key role in
Puget Sound hop growers' employment practices, as well as the city's growth
as a regional hub.

Seattle's position within the marine space of the Puget Sound made it
an ideal place for Indigenous workers to converge before the harvest season.
Seattle had long served as a "crossing-over place" for Puget Sound Coast
Salish peoples. As more Indigenous people from along the Northwest
Coast, including Alaska, joined the hop-picking workforce, they included
a stopover in Seattle. Sightings of their canoe fleets signaled the start of
hop-picking season and were widely covered in the Seattle press. In 1879 a
local journalist noted, "The bay and its shores were dotted and lined with
their canoes, while the store fronts and sidewalks downtown were thick
with the Indians themselves."[24] Another report described the waterfront
during hops season as "crowded with rudely constructed tents and other
hastily built habitations."[25] Many camped along the shore for days, often
with their children and families, cooking and socializing with one another
before heading out to the harvest. Though some commentators described
these multitribal waterfront gatherings as "strange" and "striking," Indigenous movement through this area had long predated the city itself and
would continue even after the decline of the hop industry.[26]

In addition to social gatherings, Indigenous workers used their time in
Seattle to shop and engage in other commercial activities. Before the harvest, they often focused on purchasing food, clothing items, and other supplies for the three-week picking season, while after the harvest they indulged
in less practical goods to take back home, such as cuff links and handbells.[27]
Their presence and purchasing power created a legitimate sensation among
local businesses and shopkeepers. Not confined to the shore and waterfront
camps, Indigenous shoppers ventured into the commercial district, purchasing "anything which may attract their attention in store windows,"
according to one account.[28] Other vendors and merchants came directly to
them, like one "enterprising" salesperson who "spread his goods on boxes
outside, and has done on the sidewalk a rushing business with Indians
returning flushed with money from the hop-yards."[29] Front Street (now First

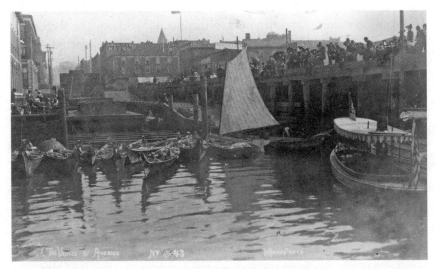

Indigenous dugout canoes docked at the foot of Washington Street in Seattle, c. 1891. Washington Street served as an early workers' hub. Indigenous and Chinese labor networks converged in one shared space within Seattle's south end; Wa Chong's main building was located just two blocks east of this waterfront location. University of Washington Libraries, Special Collections, NA 897.

Avenue), which ran along the waterfront near Yesler's sawmill, received the most traffic. Its shops offered goods and services ranging from banking to billiards, jewelry to tailoring, cigars, hardware, and candy.[30] Indigenous hop pickers also took the opportunity to vend their own goods to local Seattle-ites. One newspaper described the popularity of "woven baskets and large rugs" being sold by Indigenous women in the commercial district.[31]

It was during this time that hop growers traveled up to Seattle to recruit pickers camped along the waterfront. Once growers had decided to scale up and look beyond the local towns for their workforce, hop picking took on a life of its own among Coast Salish and other Northwest Coast Indigenous communities, becoming one of the most popular forms of wage labor. "The reservation has been quite deserted during the last month," wrote a missionary on the Tulalip reservation in 1882, "the Indians nearly all gone hop picking."[32] Local authorities in Canada reported similar migrations. On Vancouver Island, one government employee estimated some "six thousand British Columbia Indians are now crowding to the hop fields of Washington Territory."[33] Growers no longer had to recruit directly from the reservations and canneries; they could simply show up to Seattle in advance of the picking season and negotiate directly with workers. For their part, Indigenous workers came prepared. Each group of pickers selected a labor negotiator, or "Boston man," to deal directly with growers and settle in advance issues such as payment and the number of pickers required.[34] After agreeing on the terms of employment, the pickers dispersed, traveling by canoe up the rivers and to the various farms where they camped during the harvest, returning to Seattle again at the season's end.[35]

On one hand, the highly mobile workforce allowed growers to increase their profits and expand their farms' capacity. Puget Sound growers saved on transportation costs by relying on Indigenous pickers, who provided their own transportation in the form of canoes. In New York, by contrast, growers carried local pickers to and from their homes each day in wagons, and paid train fares for those coming from out of town.[36] In Puget Sound, recalled Meeker, many of the Indigenous hop pickers traveled "long distances, some of them three hundred miles in their canoes . . . all by the inland channel and among the islands of the Puget Sound."[37] But as growers cast a wider geographic net to satisfy their need for a larger workforce, their operations grew more and more unpredictable. Growers often had no idea when their pickers would arrive or how many would show up in any given year, an issue that Indigenous negotiators became adept at exploiting. "They are masters of the situation," grumbled one employer, "quick to . . . profit by [our] anxiety."[38] Another grower complained bitterly about "tricky and sly" Indians who drove a hard bargain, withholding their labor until the last possible minute in order to secure better terms.[39] While the concentration of Indigenous workers made the hops industry possible, it also created the conditions for collective action and bargaining.

As Indigenous pickers gathered in the city for the hops harvest, a regional hub of Chinese labor and commercial life flourished nearby. Most Chinese businesses during the 1870s were situated on Washington Street, just a short walk away from waterfront. Though the census counted only thirty-three Chinese residents in King County in 1870, this number increased steadily during the next few years, growing to over two hundred in 1876.[40] The Wa Chong Company stood at the heart of Washington Street and accounted for much of this population boom. When the company moved from its initial location by Yesler's mill to its permanent spot a few streets over on Washington, the owners bought up parcels of land surrounding their headquarters to create a Chinese commercial district. They

WA CHONG & CO.,

China Tea Store,

Briok Store, Corner of Washington and Third Sts., Seattle.

DEALERS IN

RICE, OPIUM AND ALL KINDS OF CHINESE GOODS,

Chinese Landscape Pictures, Oil Paintings, also for Sale

Contractors, Mill Owners and others requiring Chinese help will be furnished at short notice.

THE HIGHEST PRICE PAID FOR LIVE HOGS.

Advertisement for the Wa Chong Company (also referred to as Wa Chong & Co.), 1879. Note the location of the building on Washington Street, just steps away from the waterfront and common docking area for Indigenous migrants. University of Washington Libraries, Special Collections, UW 539.

leased out the property to laundries, shops, restaurants, and other Chinese businesses.[41] While much of Wa Chong's business model focused on labor contracting—they furnished Chinese labor to sawmills, railroads, city construction projects, and the Puget Sound mosquito fleet—the company also operated an import-export business and sold Chinese goods including tea, opium, fireworks, and paintings to local Seattleites.[42] Washington Street thus served as a key node in the transpacific circulation of people and goods; like Indigenous consumption and labor, this south-end city block helped shape Seattle's commercial life and role in the regional economy.

During the early years of the hop industry, growers directly recruited Chinese workers from the canneries in British Columbia, hiring laborers left unemployed at the end of canning season. As the industry expanded and its connections with Seattle grew stronger, growers traveled to the city and negotiated with Chinese labor contractors along Washington Street. Because hop growers only needed pickers for a short period, three weeks at the most, the labor contractors often diverted workers from other projects for the harvest season. The Wold brothers in Issaquah, for example, engaged the services of Quong Chong & Co. in 1885 to provide three dozen Chinese workers to pick hops for ninety cents per box. The company agreed to send two teams from the coal mines in Newcastle to the Wold brothers' hop farm just a few towns over.[43]

Hop growers relied less on Chinese labor than they did on Indigenous labor. Because of the overwhelming popularity of hop picking among Coast Salish and other Indigenous peoples, growers tended to employ Chinese pickers only during harvests with unusually high yields, or if they faced other kinds of labor shortages. Growers also turned to Indigenous pickers with more frequency because, in the words of a Puyallup Valley hop farmer, "they are more likely to return another season" than the Chinese.[44] Contrary to their caricature as robotic tools of the capitalist class, Chinese laborers made strategic choices about where and when to work. For growers, this complex system of labor recruitment and employment laid the groundwork for the industry's massive expansion during the 1870s and early 1880s.

A SPECTACLE IN THE VALLEY

The 1877 Puyallup Valley hop harvest stands as a prime example of how growers managed their vast hop-picking workforce. This particular harvest is notable from a historical perspective because it was the first time growers put into action their plans for utilizing maritime networks and recruiting workers regionally. As a result, that season nearly three thousand Indigenous and Chinese pickers from British Columbia and around Puget Sound flocked to the fields, constituting the largest hop-picking workforce assembled at the time.[45] Because of the size and heterogeneity of the workforce, local newspapers devoted extensive coverage to the Puyallup Valley harvest—the *Seattle Post-Intelligencer* had a designated hops reporter that season—and revealed an unusual level of detail about the industry and its workforce. One local reporter declared, "A drive through the Valley will . . . furnish one of the most industrious and interesting spectacles to be seen anywhere, and such a one as few who have the opportunity can afford to lose."[46]

The workers who arrived in the Puyallup Valley that season encountered a farming community of approximately eight hundred residents. As the center of agricultural production in the Pacific Northwest, Puyallup developed primarily around the hops economy, with over thirty growers farming hundreds of acres throughout the valley.[47] In 1870, Puyallup's population was approximately three hundred, the majority consisting of white,

American-born farmers—many of them early settlers, along with their families and employees.[48] By 1877, however, the town was diversifying. Still dominated by farming, Puyallup was also attracting a scattering of skilled tradespeople as well as professionals and day laborers. Though most occupied the farmlands spread along the banks of the Puyallup River, a central town had also popped up with several general stores, a school, and a hotel. Chinese people maintained a presence in the region, with several dozen serving as laborers, farmhands, and cooks.[49]

A portion of the workforce that year also included Puyallup tribal members, whose displacement from their ancestral lands had allowed the first hop farms to emerge and the industry to expand throughout the valley. The name "Puyallup" comes from the anglicization of the Lushootseed word *spuyaləpabš*, meaning "people from the bend at the bottom of the river," although over time the word also came to mean "generous and welcoming to all who enter our lands."[50] In 1854 the Puyallup had signed the Treaty of Medicine Creek, which created the Puyallup reservation near the present-day city of Tacoma. Dissatisfaction with the size and location of the reservation land, which was heavily forested and cut off from their pretreaty subsistence grounds, led some Puyallup tribal members into armed conflict with settlers and Indigenous allies in 1856. To smooth over tensions, the federal government agreed to greatly expand the reservation boundaries to include much of the Puyallup's pretreaty lands. In the ensuing years, however, white settlers and railroad interests encroached upon these lands without penalty, leaving the Puyallup with very little beyond a poorly resourced reservation that encompassed only a tiny slice of what the government had promised them.[51] Hop picking therefore provided a crucial means of survival and subsistence for the Puyallup, as it did for other Indigenous peoples, during a period of intense upheaval and impoverishment.

As the 1877 harvest approached, growers arranged their workers' housing by race. Indigenous and Chinese pickers inhabited separate encampments located next to the hop fields. In the encampments, tents housed single families or groups of two or three; separate space was designated for cooking and leisure activities. Pickers stayed within the boundaries of their camps every day except Sunday, when they traveled into the town of Puyallup to socialize or trade with other pickers. White workers, on the other hand, boarded with growers and their families, or in facilities provided by growers. Though conditions varied by farm, white workers also ate meals in separate facilities, often prepared by the grower's wife or a hired cook.[52] On Ezra Meeker's hop farm, for example, white workers received their housing for free, but paid for meals, which Meeker deducted from their paychecks at the end of the season.[53]

The racial stratification of workers' housing served a critical function in the broader agricultural economy. By not offering permanent shelter to Indigenous and Chinese employees, growers saved money and also were better able to justify a racialized division of labor that relegated Indigenous and Chinese pickers to low-wage, temporary work. Unlike the salmon canneries, which employed nonwhite workers in a variety of positions in the labor hierarchy, on hop farms only whites held skilled and managerial roles, ranging from dryers and balers to ticket bosses, foremen, and firemen. Growers used the expense of housing as an excuse to not hire white pickers, whose so-called standards of living would require better accommodations. One grower declared that he "could not take care of white men even if [he] could afford to hire them," adding, "The season is too short to warrant any outlay for that purpose, while Indians and Chinamen take care of themselves."[54] The temporary encampments further guaranteed that hop pickers left town at the season's end, while white workers could stay on after the harvest or find work in the surrounding community. Housing functioned as a physical marker of race as well as a method of exploiting and shaping a racialized labor force.

Though growers had their own reasons for organizing the workforce this way, it does appear that Indigenous and Chinese pickers made the most of these encampments, at least during the 1877 harvest season. As historian Vera Parham argues, hop picking allowed Coast Salish peoples to work in the wage economy "without giving up their historical lifestyles"—seasonal migration, canoe travel with family, setting up camps, and conversing in their own languages.[55] They could also earn a wage while pursuing fishing, whaling, and other economic endeavors. The encampments additionally offered pickers opportunities to engage in aspects of their culture deemed uncivilized by missionaries and government agents.[56] "There are acres of Indian camps scattered through the hop fields here," one local news report stated. "The bright fires blazing in every direction, Indians . . . and children lying around them. . . . Here and there amongst them their Indian game is in progress."[57] Here, Indigenous people could relax and socialize outside of the reservation and the constraints of colonial suppression.[58]

Indigenous encampment on a Puyallup Valley hop farm, c. 1870s. 1995.0.45, Washington State Historical Society, Tacoma (Wash.).

For Chinese pickers, the hops harvest and the relative autonomy of the encampments also appealed. Located far away from the industrial centers, hop farms offered a decent wage without the punishing kind of physical labor Chinese workers typically performed. Hop picking did not require standing for long periods, moving heavy loads, or handling machinery. Workers often sat on the ground or on chairs or wooden crates while picking the hop cones from the vines. The encampments, too, provided a protected space away from the foremen and labor contractors who controlled every aspect of their jobs in settings such as railroads or canneries. Chinese pickers did work under foremen in the hop fields, but their encampments remained free of the managerial surveillance that pervaded the factory system. A local observer toured the Chinese camps at night and described a relaxed and peaceful scene: "They are sitting around their camp-fires smoking and quietly chattering in their native tongue, and some are in their tents sleeping, the bright moon shining in on them through the open ways."[59]

Though growers tried to maintain order by segregating and containing their workforce, the divisions fell apart on Sundays when all the pickers left the fields and joined local townspeople for a day of recreation and amusement. "Every hop yard is like a little boom town," one hop foreman stated. "Tents pitched all around, bakers wagons, butcher carts, watermelon and fruit peddlers visit the yards."[60] Another noted, "The atmosphere literally buzzes with excitement, business is booming and money plentiful."[61] In Puyallup, these gatherings took place across the river from the main town, in an open field missionaries dubbed the Devil's Playground. Visitors accessed the Devil's Playground by ferry, which proved a "great source of revenue to its owner." Horse racing, the main event, attracted mixed-race crowds as large as three thousand people a week. Indigenous pickers pooled funds to construct a dance hall that hosted weekly balls, while a group of white townspeople ran a refreshment stand that offered cider and root beer.[62] Indigenous pickers also traded and sold goods including woven baskets, shells, and mats, which one newspaper described as "very durable for kitchen use."[63]

Perhaps unsurprisingly, missionaries and government agents loathed the hops industry for pulling so many Indigenous people off the reservations and into areas outside of their purview. Myron Eells, a missionary on the Skokomish reservation, summed up the feelings of many in his position when he stated that the hops harvest "has not . . . always been a healthy place for their morals, as on Sundays and evenings, gambling, betting, and horseracing have been largely carried on."[64] Missionaries like Eells viewed Indigenous people as childlike and thus susceptible to the influences of "corrupt white men" like those who visited the Devil's Playground and other hop-related festivities.[65] Another concern involved Indigenous children who traveled with their parents down to the hop fields. Colonial programs of assimilation focused on Indigenous children, forcing them to abandon connections to their culture and families through religious instruction and schooling.[66] Indian agents and others who oversaw reservation schools throughout Puget Sound often discussed separating children from their families as a key objective. One official plainly stated, "In order to make an Indian school successful the children must be taken from the influence of their parents."[67] Hop picking thus undermined colonial control. But as much as missionaries disliked the hops harvest, there was very little they could do. Hop growers formed an influential class in Washington Territory and their economic interests far outweighed any other concerns.

The wild success of the 1877 harvest marked the beginning of a legitimate hops craze and thrust Washington Territory into the national spotlight. By the early 1880s, tales of abundant land and fantastic profits circulated from coast to coast. "The profits in the business beat anything in the farming hire that I have ever heard of," marveled Charles Ayer, a visitor from Connecticut.[68] Articles began to appear in national and international publications declaring Washington "the coming hop producing country."[69] For Washington boosters and territorial officials, hops represented an opportunity to lure capital and people to the Pacific Northwest. Further, they exploited this national interest to market hops as a symbol of the region's agricultural potential. In 1884, Governor Watson Squire appointed Ezra Meeker as commissioner of Washington's delegation to the New Orleans world's fair. As Meeker later boasted to his investors, the "remarkable [growth] has been entirely due to the favorable conditions found to exist here for the development of this branch of agriculture."[70]

Low-wage labor was crucial to hops' expansion during this period. Flush with cash, growers expanded their agricultural holdings and invested in drying and baling facilities. By 1884, Puyallup Valley hop farms alone covered over two thousand acres of land, up from five hundred in 1877. Ezra Meeker's hop empire swelled during this time. Equipped with ten industrial dryers, his Puyallup farm boasted "one of the most elaborate layouts in the Pacific Northwest."[71] He also became the region's largest agricultural employer, hiring more than one thousand hop pickers at peak season. With his own personal wealth quickly ballooning, Meeker and his wife replaced their old log cabin with a seventeen-room Victorian mansion.[72] Meeker later credited this hop boom with a blight that swept Europe in 1882, enabling Puget Sound growers to "[command] unheard-of prices."[73] While the failure of the European crop certainly drove up demand for Washington hops, Meeker and others profited from a mobile, racialized, and undercompensated labor force of Indigenous and Chinese workers. As Meeker himself admitted, Puget Sound growers cultivated hops at a lower price than any other region in the world.[74]

But the bubble would not last. The first inkling appeared in the fields as Indigenous pickers began to express dissatisfaction with their working conditions. During the early 1880s, several low salmon runs on the Fraser River caused the near collapse of British Columbia's salmon-canning industry.

Because their livelihoods depended largely on fishing, Indigenous workers turned to hop picking, among other work, to supplement this lost income. One government official on Vancouver Island noted, "Most of them are away to the American side for the hop picking . . . there being little work and low wages at the canneries in British Columbia."[75] With hop wages increasingly important for their survival, Indigenous pickers fought every effort by growers to reduce their pay. In 1883, a group of Indigenous pickers threatened to walk off the fields midseason to protest attempts by growers to undercut their wages. That next year, workers employed by Meeker staged a two-day strike, demanding a wage increase from $1.00 to $1.25 per box.[76] Downplaying the incident, local newspapers declared rumors of a strike "entirely groundless!"[77] Yet growers could not deny this growing discontent, which would explode into violent conflict in a few short years.

RAILROADS, RACE, AND LABOR

The mid-1880s was a time of transition in the hops industry, driven largely by changes in transportation. In 1884, the Northern Pacific completed a line from Tacoma to Seattle that gave the city its first connection to the transcontinental railroad. Investors had also funded a regional railroad line, the Seattle & Walla Walla, that linked Seattle with Newcastle and the outlying areas to the east. The railroad expansion transformed the hops industry in two major ways. The first change involved labor. Rail transportation untethered the industry from its reliance on the waterways of the Puget Sound and allowed growers to cast a much wider net in their procurement of labor. This dealt a devastating blow to Indigenous workers. Not only did they face new competition over precious hop-picking jobs, but they also lost a key point of leverage in their negotiations with growers. No longer dependent on maritime routes, growers had no reason to bargain with Indigenous pickers and could simply move on to other options in the case of strikes or demands for higher wages. While Indigenous workers continued to participate in the industry, their clout diminished.

The proliferation of railroads also shifted the geography of the hops industry. Instead of concentrating solely in Puyallup and White River valleys, growers began to enter the hops market and open up farms in new areas. The town of Squak (known today as Issaquah) and its surrounding valley emerged as a major hop-growing center largely because of the railroad.

In the early 1870s, Seattle settlers had banded together to fund the Seattle & Walla Walla railroad line as a response to Northern Pacific's decision to locate its western terminus in Tacoma. The work progressed at a snail's pace and was headed for disaster when Henry Villard, a railroad baron and financier, decided to buy the company and rename it the Columbia & Puget Sound Railroad. Villard's interest in the line stemmed from his ownership of the Oregon Improvement Company, which operated several highly profitable coal mines east of Seattle. With Villard's financial backing, railroad construction diverted to the coal mines in Newcastle, with the Columbia & Puget Sound line soon offering both freight and passenger service to Seattle and back.[78] Though this cut into the profits of the Puyallup and White River growers, Meeker capitalized on this new business by opening a brokerage firm that bought and sold Puget Sound hops to merchants in San Francisco and London.[79]

Situated approximately twenty miles east of Seattle, Squak Valley in the mid-1880s was a farming community with strong ties to the coal industry. Settlers came to Squak later than Puyallup or White River valleys, reflecting the new availability of railroad transportation. In 1880, the settler population hovered just under fifty residents, all European families whose primary occupation consisted of coal mining or farming.[80] Hops had first arrived in the region in the late 1870s, planted by Inglebright and Lars Wold, brothers from Norway who had heard tales of Puget Sound hops and moved to Seattle to try their luck in the business. By 1880, the Wolds owned twenty acres of farmland; they expanded their holdings to thirty-five acres just two years later.[81] Though this paled in comparison with Meeker, whose farm spread across five hundred acres and two counties, it nonetheless made them leading hop producers in the area. By the mid-1880s, other growers had begun to flock to Squak Valley—including George Tibbetts, who also owned the general store.[82]

In 1885, the Wold brothers sparked controversy around the valley when they hired sixty-five Chinese workers to pick hops for the season. Though growers had employed Chinese workers during the 1870s, anti-Chinese sentiment had spiked dramatically in the ensuing years. The federal government had passed the Chinese Exclusion Act in 1882, limiting Chinese immigration to all but the elite classes. In places like Washington Territory, however, the legislation had little immediate impact.[83] With the government expending few resources on immigration control, the border remained essentially untouched during the latter part of the nineteenth century, allowing Chinese workers to enter the United States through Canada. The Canadian government passed some restrictions, including a head tax on all Chinese immigrants, but this did not end the entry of Chinese laborers into Canada. Territorial officials in Washington publicly denounced the "hiving hordes of Chinese" at every turn, but took little further action.[84] The economy of the Pacific Northwest continued to depend on a flexible labor force; without the Chinese and their system of labor contracting, area industries risked depression or even failure.

The proximity of Squak Valley to Seattle made Chinese workers a convenient source of labor, particularly as railroad transportation expanded. Washington's Chinese population had jumped from 253 in 1870 to over 3,300 just a decade later.[85] No longer organized primarily around the Columbia River canneries, Chinese residents by 1885 were laboring in road construction crews, logging camps, and coal mines across the territory. Seattle's coal industry had grown into a particularly lucrative enterprise, and Squak Valley was located in the center of this mining activity, adjacent to Newcastle, the second largest mining operation in Washington. The Oregon Improvement Company, owners of the Newcastle mines, employed a large Chinese workforce; the sixty-five Chinese pickers who arrived in Squak to work for the Wold brothers came from Newcastle, diverted temporarily for the three-week harvest.[86]

These shifts in labor and geography enabled growers like the Wold brothers to undercut Indigenous demands. Though they denied it, the Wold brothers brought the Chinese workers to Squak Valley during a dispute with their Indigenous labor force. A few days earlier, a group of Indigenous pickers working for the Wold brothers had rejected a proposed wage cut from the standard payment of one dollar a box to seventy-five cents.[87] The price of hops had plummeted that year and decreasing wages allowed the Wolds to maintain their profit margin. In the face of growing protest, they turned to Chinese labor contractors in Seattle, where they recruited sixty-five workers and agreed to pay them ninety cents a box.[88] The Chinese contracting system had emerged to fill the demand for large-scale seasonal labor in the railroads and lumber mills; contractors provided a critical service by organizing and supplying temporary workers who could be both quickly assembled and easily dismissed, a necessity for employers facing perennial labor shortages during the peak summer months. As intermediaries, contractors organized networks of labor on both sides of the Pacific, recruiting workers from China and funneling them into various seasonal jobs in the United States and Canada.[89]

The first team of thirty-five Chinese pickers arrived on Saturday, September 6, from the mines at Newcastle and set up camp in the Wolds' orchard. Known as the "China Camp," their sixteen tents stood isolated from the rest of the farm, located on a "little peninsula formed by a creek" and encircled again by a fence.[90] Workers slept two to a tent on wooden boards and brought with them tin cans and coffeepots. The next day a group of residents intercepted the second team of Chinese workers on the road leading to Squak, forcing them to turn back to Newcastle. Fearing for their safety, the Chinese workers already camped out on the farm made motions to leave, but "were told that everything would be all right and they could go to work tomorrow." On the evening of September 7, 1885, a group of white and Indigenous men walked over from George Tibbetts' general store, climbed the fence separating the Wold brothers' hop farm from the main road, and opened fire on the tents scattered in the orchard. Three Chinese workers were killed and three wounded in a spray of bullets so intense that, according to one survivor, it "sounded all same China New Year." One man attempted to burn down the entire camp, but the fire failed to spread, leaving the orchard littered with bleeding bodies and tents "thoroughly perforated and almost riddled with bullets."[91] With no cover or place to flee, many of the Chinese pickers jumped into the creek and waited there until dawn.

News of the attack spread quickly, and the next day, authorities in Seattle dispatched the sheriff, coroner, and prosecuting attorney to investigate. By the 1880s, Seattle's influence had spread well beyond the borders of the city itself and into the surrounding areas. The sheriff's office and court system extended to Squak Valley and beyond, showing the broad reach of the municipal state that had formed in the 1850s to police and manage the mobility and autonomy of Duwamish and, later, Chinese residents in Seattle. The Seattle-based team conducted a preliminary investigation and decided to charge five white men and two Indigenous men with murder. The Seattle newspapers had reacted with shock to the Squak Valley massacre, as it became known, though not out of empathy for the victims. In fact, reporters agreed with the sentiments fueling the violence. As one editorial put it, "The people of King County may be said to be unanimous in their recognition of the evils entailed by the employment of Chinese contract labor." The writers objected instead to the "unmanly" and "unnecessary" display of physical violence, which reflected poorly on the city of Seattle and could potentially damage Washington's bid for statehood.[92] In their eyes, a trial was crucial in upholding respect for the laws such vigilantism openly flouted. As it became clear, the outcome of the trial did not matter as much as the appearance of justice it represented. Despite testimony in which one man admitted to the shooting, the jury acquitted all parties, a verdict overwhelmingly supported by the Seattle public.

Though depicted at the time as a fight between the white workingman and the degraded Chinese laborer, the real issue concerned rival hop growers and their efforts to stoke racial tensions for financial gain. A depression in the hop market that season had driven down prices around the globe, hitting newer growers particularly hard. George Tibbetts had recently opened a hop business with his partner George Hill, former Indian agent at Neah Bay.[93] Their first substantial harvest occurred in 1885, and things did not go well for the newcomers. In a letter to Hill, Tibbetts lamented, "The hops will fall far short of my expectations."[94] With such a low yield, Tibbetts worried they would not fulfill the terms of their contract with a San Francisco hop merchant. Though authorities never formally charged Tibbetts—his status in the community shielding him from blame—the trial transcripts show that he spearheaded the effort against the Wolds and their Chinese pickers. He assembled the perpetrators just before the murders, firing eight shots into the air as a signal for the group to gather in his store, and provided them with guns and ammunition. Several of the accused also worked for Tibbetts, including an employee of his general store and the foreman of his hop farm.[95] With the Chinese gone and the Wolds' harvest destroyed, Tibbetts could eliminate a major competitor.

All of the involved parties exploited racial fears of Chinese labor that were circulating across the Anglophone settler world. The Wolds capitalized on racial divisions to discipline Indigenous laborers; George Tibbetts and his associates mobilized to rid the area of the so-called Chinese menace. In doing so, they drew on racial discourse about Chinese labor that stretched back to the Civil War. Historians Alexander Saxton and Moon-Ho Jung have argued that opposition to Chinese laborers, cast as slavelike and thus a threat to the white worker, allowed white supremacy and capitalist exploitation to flourish in the era of emancipation. The notion of the Chinese as inherently cheap labor had nothing to do with actual Chinese workers, who desired and fought for decent wages as much as everyone else. Growers in the Pacific Northwest had in fact stopped relying on Chinese laborers in the late 1870s because they had become too unpredictable, often choosing to stay in occupations that offered better wages and job security. But the image of the "coolie" proved a powerful method of fragmenting the workforce along racial lines as well as justifying the actual exploitation of Chinese workers, relegated to manual labor and other low-paying jobs.[96]

The role of Indigenous men in the massacre against Chinese pickers remains less clear. In the aftermath of the shooting, Seattle newspapers sensationalized the violence between the two groups, declaring it a "war of the races."[97] Tensions did exist between Indigenous and Chinese workers; in this case, the decision by the Wold brothers to hire Chinese pickers directly threatened the livelihoods of Indigenous pickers who relied on hop picking as a means of survival. This distinguished them from the white perpetrators, none of whom worked as hop pickers or even manual laborers. And yet transcripts from the murder trial hint at a more complicated story. The Indigenous men involved in the violence did not come from far away to pick hops, but lived in and around Squak Valley and personally knew the white men who spearheaded the massacre. Those who testified at the trial reported that the white men had burst into their homes and coerced them into joining, threatening that "if the Indians did not come that they would be shot."[98] Another spoke about how he remained in the back of the group and "got frightened and ran away" when he heard the gunfire.[99] Both speculated that the white men wanted Indians involved so they could blame them afterward for what happened.[100] While Indigenous hop pickers did have real grievances about the presence of the Chinese that harvest season, their responses were also shaped by the local context of Squak Valley and their own vulnerability to white settler violence.

The Squak Valley massacre pushed the issue of Indigenous labor into the public spotlight. As anti-Chinese hostility and violence exploded around Puget Sound, Indigenous people became the desirable workers, praised for the very qualities supposedly lacking in Chinese labor. In 1879, a White River valley hop grower, for example, explained his preference for

Indigenous pickers in terms of Chinese foreignness. "Farmers think it more politic to employ a class that will empty their earnings into the coffers of the country," he declared, "than to pour the thousands into the lap of some long-tailed celestial in the Flowery Kingdom."[101] Statements like this stressed pickers' Indigeneity not to recognize their status as sovereign peoples, but rather to bolster calls for Chinese exclusion while still maintaining a population racially suited to agricultural labor. In 1884 Governor Watson Squire noted in a report on the hops industry, "Indians appear to excel the whites in their ability for picking."[102] Hop growers, politicians, and those involved in agriculture drew heavily on the colonial idea of the Indian as inherently premodern; Indigenous peoples' connection to the land, seen as natural and thus evidence of their inability to live in modern times, justified their relegation to agricultural forms of labor.[103] This thinking aligned with federal assimilation efforts of the time. Just two years after the Squak Valley case, the US government would pass the Dawes Act of 1887, which sought to break up tribally held communal lands to sell off to settlers and push Indigenous people into farming.[104]

Squak Valley marked the beginning of a sustained effort to purge the Chinese from industrial labor and remove them completely from the region. After the massacre, the violence spread to the coal mining center in Newcastle, where white town residents threatened Chinese workers and burned down their housing. In response the Oregon Improvement Company, which operated the mines, discharged its Chinese workforce. By October, agitation had spread to Tacoma; it erupted in early November when white mobs expelled the entire Chinese population from the city. Seattle followed suit a few months later. On February 7, 1886, a group of white men rounded up the city's Chinese residents and forced them onto a ship leaving for San Francisco. Governor Watson Squire declared martial law the next day, and federal and state troops stormed the city. By the end of 1886, not a single Chinese person remained in Pierce County, and many of those living in King County had fled to other regions.[105] The Chinese did not disappear completely from the Pacific Northwest; in the words of historian Chris Friday, Chinese workers who decided to stay "became more valuable assets to canners and contractors and accordingly demanded and received better wages."[106] Even so, the Chinese community in Washington never fully recovered, and by the turn of the century, employers throughout the region had begun to turn to other sources of labor.

The expulsion of the Chinese from the Pacific Northwest created a vacuum in the agricultural industries, and hop growers faced labor shortages. Unlike the canneries, hop growers did not hire Chinese workers again, fearing another outburst of violence would further damage their profits and long-term prospects in the region. The labor shortfall was exacerbated by the success of the British Columbia fishing industry, which had rebounded from its near collapse earlier that decade. Healthier salmon runs meant fewer Indigenous workers coming down to the Puget Sound hop fields. In 1888, scouts returned from British Columbia in advance of the hops harvest with dire news, reporting "pickers harder to get this year."[107] The Fraser River salmon runs had occurred much later than usual, and many Indigenous workers had decided to stay on the Canadian side and fish. "I expected to employ British Columbia Indians," remarked White River hops grower C. P. Hayes, "but some pressure was brought to bear on the Indians on the other side . . . as it was feared the fisheries on the Fraser River would suffer."[108] Advertisements for hop-picking jobs in the Puyallup and White River valleys flooded the local newspapers, and growers proclaimed the labor situation "very serious." "I am in sore distress this year," admitted a grower, "and will lose thousands of dollars if more pickers cannot be obtained very shortly, as the hops are now ripe and must be picked this month."[109]

Though no longer physically present, the mere threat of Chinese labor still proved quite useful in serving the interests of the grower class. As picking season approached, rumors began to spread around the valleys that growers were bringing teams of Chinese workers from as far away as Vancouver, sending townspeople around Puget Sound into a panic. In the city of Tacoma, residents organized committees to investigate each aspect of the labor problem and devise solutions that would prevent the "re-introduction of Chinese into Pierce County." The mayor and his team negotiated successfully with the Northern Pacific Railway to lower its rate and furnish a special train that would leave Tacoma every morning at 6:00. Though the mayor declared the rate change a victory for anti-Chinese politics, profits most likely drove the rail company's decision. The hop business was a potentially lucrative source of revenue for the railroad, which had just completed work on its transcontinental line. Committee members in Tacoma convinced local schools to extend summer vacation so white children could pick hops alongside their parents. Though missionaries and Indian agents had demon-ized Indigenous parents for taking their children to the hops harvest, accus-ing them of negligence and using it as further justification of parental unsuitability, authorities applauded white parents' and children's efforts to save the harvest and respond to these "emergency" circumstances.[110]

White women also flocked to the fields that season, offering growers a new source of temporary labor. Though the literature on Pacific Northwest history has focused overwhelmingly on men, white women established a significant presence in Washington, first as missionaries and pioneer wives, then in greater numbers as teachers, nurses, domestics, secretaries, and professionals. In the 1880s, with railroad transportation expanding and their population increasing, they became a viable alternative to Chinese or Indigenous labor. Washington's overall female population rose from 29,000 in 1880 to 131,000 in 1890; in Pierce County alone the number of women jumped from 1,300 to 18,700.[111] Greater numbers, however, did not neces-sarily translate into more jobs. Women faced limited employment options in the Pacific Northwest, where the economy revolved primary around the labor of male migrants in seasonal industries.[112]

Hops proved the exception. By the 1890s white women occupied a sig-nificant part of the hops workforce. Seattle again served as a hub of white women's labor, as it had with Chinese and Indigenous workers. Hop growers recruited white women pickers primarily through the Seattle Public Employment Office, a free city-run service that connected workers with temporary and permanent jobs in the region. The City of Seattle established this office in 1894 as a response to the growing influence of private employ-ment agencies, which charged all work seekers a fee and thus incentivized high turnover. Records from the office's first year in business show that most requests for workers came from hop growers during the late summer months. That year, demand for white women pickers nearly doubled that of white men, and only increased during the following year. By the end of the nineteenth century, hop picking was one of the most common forms of employment for white women in Seattle, second only to housework, and the only nondomestic form of labor the public office offered white women; all other positions involved cooking, cleaning, or nursing.[113]

The numbers at the employment office reflected the popularity of hop picking among white women. But for hop farmers, the growing reliance on white women pickers created new problems. Until that point, hop picking had largely been considered "Chinaman's work, Indian's work," racialized labor deemed unsuitable for white people and especially white women.[114] The entire industry's organization relied on the racial distinction between temporary pickers and permanent employees. With the introduction of white women, growers began to shift their language around hop picking, presenting it more as leisure than as actual work. With white women in the fields, hop picking became a "time of festivity, as the vintage is in wine growing countries." One commenter stated, "Shop girls consider it a good way to put in a vacation; some for fun, some for money, and some for their health."[115] Hop picking certainly did appeal to white women, just as it did to other groups; it offered a decent wage with minimal time commitment, and its communal organization allowed single women to go to the fields with friends and married women to bring along husbands and children. But portraying these women as solely seeking leisure or festivity erased their role as laborers while using their presence to promote hop picking as a less stigmatized occupation—in Washington territorial governor Eugene Semple's words, "clean and respectable."[116]

It's notable as well that despite this discursive shift, white women encountered the same low wages and rough conditions their Chinese and Indigenous counterparts did, at least in comparison with white male employees in managerial or permanent positions. As white women began arriving in the fields for the first time, growers initially tried to build them permanent housing "suitable for white peoples to live in."[117] Ezra Meeker built a separate facility for up to one hundred white pickers, while a grower in the White River valley "made hasty preparations for white people," which included food and shelter.[118] But apart from Meeker and a handful of others who could afford the cost of construction, food, and materials, most growers provided rough shacks with no amenities or housed women and children in tents. James Hunter Shotwell, a hop grower in Olympia, noted that his fields "were overflowing with women and children. They are camped in the orchard and all about."[119] When filled with Chinese or Indigenous pickers, these accommodations were physical markers of racial inferiority; with white women, they represented a fun adventure or festive activity.

Some local residents welcomed the arrival of white women, believing they would bring respectability to their towns during the harvest. Interracial sociability had become a point of contention among local townspeople. Though some looked forward to the harvest and the money it

Indigenous family on a Puget Sound hop farm. University of Washington Libraries, Special Collections, NA 4189.

generated, others viewed the Sunday gatherings as a nuisance. "Horse racing and gambling were carried on regularly every Sunday," declared a Puyallup resident, "and the business was in no manner neglected during the week, despite our severe law for its prohibition."[120] Another resident complained about the unknown outsiders and other undesirables drawn to the harvest festivities, telling a newspaper "a lot of the roughest and dirtiest looking men that has ever been in the valley are hanging around here at present."[121] Because harvest gatherings figured so centrally in stimulating local economies, residents had little authority to stamp out these activities. Communities therefore welcomed white women pickers, believing their presence would bolster their towns' declining standards of respectability and help transform the gatherings from spectacles of vice into decorous affairs. "I wish [the grower] would hire all white pickers instead of Indians," one white hop worker lamented. "Then we could have dances in the warehouse and have some pretty good times."[122]

Hop picking's transformation from work to festivity depended upon projecting a wholesome family atmosphere, which involved not only white women but also Indigenous workers, who remained a vital force in the hops industry during the 1880s and beyond. Unlike the all-male teams of Chinese laborers, Indigenous pickers arrived in the fields as families; fathers, mothers, children, and even grandparents worked together during the harvest. This family structure made Indigenous pickers more easily assimilable into the quaint image of the hops industry growers and townspeople alike hoped to construct, and placed them apart from the Chinese, whose deviation from normative family life was used to justify their continued exclusion. In an 1888 report Governor Semple stated, "Hop growers will doubtless next year be better prepared to accommodate white labor . . . as there is now an apparent assurance that women and children will not come into contact with Chinese coolies."[123] Here Semple conjures the figure of the Chinese laborer as threatening to the white family, making its violent expulsion from the industry a necessary precursor to the employment of white women and the transformation of the hops business into a respectable, family-oriented affair. This new vision of hop picking—a harmless, leisurely pursuit, undertaken by festive townspeople on small family farms, devoid of the violence and power structures that created the industry—required the erasure of the Chinese. It also relegated Indigenous pickers to an imagined, premodern past, stripping them of their status as autonomous workers and presenting them as mere extensions of the landscape itself.[124]

THE DECLINE OF PUGET SOUND HOPS

In 1892, a hop lice epidemic swept the Puget Sound region, infesting the soil and foliage of the hop vines just before picking season. Ezra Meeker recalled, "I walked down to the yards, a quarter mile distant, and there I saw the first hop-louse. The yard was literally alive with lice and [they] were destroying."[125] Farmers in Puyallup Valley alone lost over $100,000 that season. "We do not now expect to see a recovery from the present decline," Meeker lamented as the meager profits trickled in.[126] The hop louse inflicted far more than just physical devastation. It also damaged the region's reputation as an ideal agrarian landscape. The Puget Sound was now marred by the same diseases that had wiped out crops in Europe. The "richness of the soil" that had served as a prime selling point for the area's hops industry no longer worked to attract investors and commercial buyers. After a few more disappointing harvests, Meeker shut down his farm. "I quit the business," as he put it, "or, rather, the business quit me."[127]

Though Meeker describes the end of Puget Sound hops as "a clap of thunder out of a clear sky, so unexpected," the louse infestation only accelerated a process already underway.[128] With the expansion of railroads and land-based transportation, the centers of agricultural production began to shift from the Puget Sound region. The Eastern Washington town of Yakima surpassed Puyallup in hop cultivation even before the lice epidemic hit. During the early twentieth century, Yakima was transformed into a major hop-producing region; today it continues to grow the majority of hops in the United States.[129] Many hop growers in the Puyallup and White River valleys, like Meeker, sold off their land and moved on to other business pursuits.

Hop growing continued to some extent in the Puget Sound region, but it took a very different form into the twentieth century. The proliferation of railroads allowed greater access to Seattle and the surrounding areas, giving rise to a thriving tourist industry. Some hop growers shifted their focus from commercial production to tourism as their farms became magnets for white visitors eager to catch a glimpse of what Paige Raibmon calls the "authentic Indian."[130] The town of Snoqualmie, located near the foothills of the Cascade Mountains, became a tourist hub that revolved around the hop harvest and its predominately Indigenous workforce. Tourists and photographers, both professional and amateur, snapped thousands of images, which depicted the hop harvest as a romanticized view into an imagined past.[131] These images made their way into local historical societies and archival collections, forming the bulk of today's primary source materials on the history of hop production in the Puget Sound region. Tellingly, only a handful of photographs in the major repositories of University of Washington and Washington State Historical Society depict Chinese hop pickers.[132]

The decline of Chinese and Indigenous labor in the Puget Sound hops industry went hand in hand with the marginalization of these groups within the city itself. While Coast Salish and other Indigenous hop pickers and workers continued their seasonal migrations through Seattle,

Chinese hop pickers and encampment in Puyallup. 2010.0.345, Washington State Historical Society, Tacoma (Wash.).

Duwamish people endured further displacement and destruction of their homelands. Municipal projects such as the construction of the Lake Washington Ship Canal served as a major driver of Duwamish dispossession, along with individual acts of violence against local Indigenous communities.[133] In 1893, for example, a white settler burned down a group of Duwamish homes in West Seattle, forcing them to flee "in large numbers . . . with their canoes and belongings."[134] They relocated to Ballast Island, a small patch of land in Elliott Bay formed by the ballast dumped from passing ships. Until that point, Ballast Island had served as a temporary camping ground for Indigenous hop pickers as they made their way to the fields in late summer. This group, along with others who joined them, formed a permanent community on Ballast Island until the early twentieth century.

Seattle's Chinese population also experienced intense marginalization during this period through both anti-Chinese violence and immigration restriction. Some Chinese did remain in Seattle following the 1886 anti-Chinese mob attack, but their role in the seasonal economy diminished significantly through legislation that sought to curtail Chinese immigration into the United States. While Seattle's Chinese community did grow over time and remained a crucial presence, their economic impact would never reach the heights it did before Chinese exclusion. With immigration restriction in place, the transpacific movement of labor was no longer possible, and many Chinese merchants and labor contractors either returned to China or transitioned to other business pursuits.

The 1890s saw the end of Puget Sound's hops industry and the urban networks that sustained it. But the industry's impact was far-reaching. Hop growing helped establish Seattle as a regional and transnational hub of labor, setting the stage for future industrial expansion and migration. Lumber companies, in particular, built on the hop industry's foundation, turning to Seattle on a much larger scale to recruit and hire workers—specifically foreign-born workers from regions including Japan and Northern Europe. As Seattle became more deeply entwined with the regional and global economy, lumber company owners and managers found themselves confronting the same issues as hop growers: an inability to control or contain their workers, and a rising labor militancy fostered by the very conditions that made the industry possible.

CHAPTER 3

Race, Radicals, and Timber

IN 1909 THE *INDUSTRIAL WORKER*, A PUBLICATION OF THE INDUS-
trial Workers of the World (IWW), published an article about the particular
form of labor exploitation that propped up Washington's lumber industry.
The author called it the rule of the three gangs. "They work it as follows,"
he explained. "The bosses run a camp; in connection with this last is the
employment office; a sign is posted, 'men wanted for x camp'; the men buy
the job and go, at their own expense to the camp." The boss then fires the
men already working at the camp and replaces them with this "fresh batch
of suckers." These discharged men, "now hoboes," return to the employment
office to see about other jobs. And the cycle continues. "So," the author
concluded, "each camp requires three gangs: one coming, one going, and
one working."[1]

As this article makes clear, migratory labor was not just the domain of
agriculture; it played a key role in the lumber industry as well. By the early
twentieth century, Seattle's south-end district had transformed considerably since its early years as a hub for agriculture and the hops industry. The
neighborhood now served as home base for a broader regional employment
system that drew a much wider range of workers, including ones from Japan
and Northern Europe. Lumber companies utilized the networks previously
established by hop growers to cultivate a mobile and disposable labor force.
This constant stream of labor allowed the Northwest's lumber industry to
expand massively. By 1910, lumber employed two thirds of the workers in

Washington State.[2] If hops had laid the foundation for Seattle's role in the regional economy, the lumber industry cemented the city's status as "the main clearinghouse for the migratory labor hordes" of the Pacific Northwest and far beyond.[3]

But the lumber industry differed from hop farming in one key aspect. Its mobile labor force consisted of many more white and foreign-born European men. Hop growers had relied mostly on the seasonal labor of white women, Chinese men, and Indigenous families. White men on hop farms had worked in managerial roles or as foremen, stable jobs that did not require them to move around as much. This racialized and gendered division between stable work and mobile work had, up to this point, been central to the structure of the entire regional economy. What happened when white and European men entered into this multiracial world of itinerant labor?

This question consumed local officials, reformers, social scientists, and businessmen who grew increasingly alarmed at the "hordes" of white and European men roving around the region without stable jobs or traditional families.[4] Their concerns crystallized around Scandinavians, the "best class of foreigners" who had fallen from their chosen path as farmers, landowners, and the future backbone of Pacific Northwest settler society, integrating themselves instead into the world of Seattle's south end and coming dangerously close to their fellow Japanese workers in the lumber industry.[5] Things came to a boiling point when the IWW arrived in the region, bringing its militant call to overthrow the capitalist system and create a multiracial workers' movement.

What came next is well known: backlash, government repression, and the decade-long decline of the Pacific Northwest labor movement.[6] But less understood is the urban dimension of the story. Lumber companies and federal officials viewed rising labor militancy among the workforce as an urban issue and initiated sweeping changes that cut off the industry's reliance on Seattle as a hiring center. They did so specifically to integrate the wayward Scandinavians and other Europeans more firmly into the stable white workforce and away from Japanese laborers and the mixed world of the Sawdust. While Seattle's multiracial urban networks had fed the lumber industry's expansion, they also laid the groundwork for new kinds of solidarity and political imagining. This moment in Pacific Northwest history is a story of labor struggle and reform. To a greater extent, though, it is a story about the power of whiteness in fragmenting a diverse workforce and reasserting capitalist dominance during a period of severe disruption.[7]

ONE COMING, ONE GOING, ONE WORKING

The industry's demand for a mobile workforce originated in the early twentieth century, when changes in transportation dramatically shifted the geography of lumber production. Before this, lumber companies had operated much like hop farms, clustering along the shores of Puget Sound to access a maritime network before the railroad's arrival. Without land-based transportation all aspects of lumber work, including logging and timber processing, were tied to areas with navigable water. Logging crews, initially dependent on animals to move timber and supplies, never strayed far into the forest. They felled trees along the tidewater, and teams of oxen pulled logs to the shore along "skid roads" greased with whale or dogfish oil. Tugboats pulled these log booms to neighboring sawmills, where they collected in mill ponds until space opened up inside on the chains. Businessmen, primarily from California, had established these early sawmills in places like Port Blakely, Port Gamble, and Seattle; those locales' deep-water ports could accommodate the steamships that hauled piles of raw and processed timber down to California and across the Pacific to China, Australia, and Hawaii.[8] As a result, lumber work remained largely stationary and geographically dispersed around a patchwork of Puget Sound operations.

Settlements—early company towns controlled by the owner or hired manager—sprouted up around these sawmills. They typically consisted of worker housing, a cookhouse, and a shop for clothing and supplies. Though most loggers operated independently, they relied on sawmills for food and other necessities, and many resided in or around these towns. Port Gamble, one of the first such lumber settlements in Washington, was founded by Andrew Pope and William Talbot, two childhood friends from Maine who had dabbled in California's lumber business before moving north in 1852. They brought lumber, sawmill machinery, and other building materials from New England, along with a team of white workers from their hometown of Bangor, Maine.[9] The white laborers first resided in bunkhouses with an adjoining cookhouse, though the company later moved them into "neat little frame houses" once they married.[10]

S'Klallam workers also labored at the sawmill. However, they did so because the lumber company displaced them from their land, forcing them to find jobs to support themselves.[11] Port Gamble was located within S'Klallam territory and known among the S'Klallam people as Teekalet.[12] Once Pope and Talbot, along with their associate Josiah Keller, selected the site for the sawmill, they demanded that the S'Klallam living there relocate across the bay to Point Julia.[13] As a S'Klallam elder recalled, "The mill people came along and sent the Indian over across the Bay, on the Spit."[14] They agreed to move in exchange for jobs as well as lumber and supplies to build houses. However, the conditions were poor, and the site often flooded during winter.[15] After signing the Point No Point Treaty in 1855, which created the Skokomish reservation, some S'Klallam refused to leave again and remained in Point Julia. They worked at the sawmill, while supplementing their wages with hop picking, fishing, and other economic activities.[16] By the early twentieth century, Point Julia (now called Little Boston) had transformed into a permanent community. In 1936, S'Klallam leaders successfully petitioned the federal government to recognize their status as a sovereign nation and to create the Port Gamble S'Klallam reservation on 1,200 acres around Little Boston.[17]

As logging intensified during the late nineteenth century, deforestation along the tidewater prompted companies to seek forms of transportation that would allow access to new sources of timber. Larger, well-capitalized firms began to invest in logging railroads and steam locomotives, which could push further inland than horses and oxen. The first logging railroad, appearing in 1881, ran from Tenino to Olympia, while the Port Blakely Mill Company built another on Bainbridge Island in 1888. These developments coincided with the arrival of the Northern Pacific Railway in 1883 and the Great Northern Railway in 1893, untethering the industry from its reliance on maritime routes and opening up East Coast markets for the first time. Washington's connection to transcontinental railroad lines sparked the interest of lumber barons in the Great Lakes, on the hunt for new investments following the near total depletion of the region's white pine forests. Companies like Weyerhaeuser bought up over a million acres of Washington timberland and began construction on new sawmills and logging railroads around Tacoma and Grays Harbor. By 1905, Washington had emerged as the country's largest supplier of raw timber and a global center of lumber processing.[18]

The industry's financial and geographic expansion transformed the structure of labor and daily life. No longer concentrated within small mill settlements along the Puget Sound, workers fanned out across the region. Loggers moved deep into the forests, and smaller sawmills sprang up along railroad lines. Demand boomed for manual laborers to construct and maintain railroads, unload train cars, haul lumber, and sweep sawdust. Corporate owners, meanwhile, began to consolidate the branches of lumber production. Independent loggers, unable to afford the equipment and machinery needed to compete with well-financed corporations, were absorbed into larger firms. Logging crews subsequently bloated from an average of fifteen men in 1870 to two hundred or more by the 1890s. Mechanization created new positions even as it rendered others obsolete. The many duties of a logging crew boss, for example, once had included recruiting and overseeing workers, tending to the animals, keeping the books, and ordering new supplies. Now these tasks were divvied up between multiple discrete jobs—timekeeper, bookkeeper, railroad engineer, foreman, and fireman, among others.[19]

The mobility and segmentation of the workforce combined with increasingly centralized corporate ownership gave rise to a new system of hiring. Local connections or word-of-mouth recommendations were supplanted by private employment agents who worked for profit. These agencies contracted with lumber companies to fill open positions at all levels—from manual labor to higher-paid logging and engineering positions. Agencies charged a fee to apply for jobs, typically one to two dollars a person, and issued a ticket that lumber companies or contractors required for employment consideration.[20] The services provided by employment agencies proved an ideal fit with the changing demands of a workforce in which jobs had become both more numerous and more expendable. Agents offered companies a steady stream of workers, which guarded against strikes or any other show of labor unrest. As a representative from the International Union of Timber Workers stated, "I think the fact that the employer knows by merely telephoning to an industrial center he can get other men on the next train it makes him less patient with the men for any reason, be it frivolous or important, and he discharges the men because he knows he can get more to take their place very readily."[21]

Lumber companies turned to Seattle as the "main clearing house" for this increasingly nonpermanent workforce.[22] Before the railroad's arrival, hop growers had utilized Seattle's position along the Puget Sound to access

THE ENDLESS CHAIN—EMPLOYMENT SHARK, THE TRANSPORTATION AGENT AND THE BOSS—FLEECE THE WORKERS.

A 1909 cartoon from the *Industrial Worker*, the newspaper of the Industrial Workers of the World, showing the cycle of high turnover and disposable labor cultivated by the lumber industry during the early twentieth century.

the city's concentration of Chinese and Indigenous labor. Much had changed, however, in the intervening years. The discovery of gold in Alaska and the Yukon in 1896, known as the Klondike gold rush, further built up Seattle's physical landscape and infrastructure to accommodate people on the move. Seattle served as the primary stopover for miners and prospectors heading north; some thirty to forty thousand migrants passed through the city during the peak years of the gold rush (1897–1900). Businesses sprouted up primarily in the southern half of the city to accommodate this flood of travelers and other short-term residents. The number of hotels and lodging houses, for example, shot up from 139 in 1896 to over four hundred in 1905.[23] Seattle's port dramatically expanded regional operations, offering daily steamship service to and from Alaska as well as other major Pacific Coast ports, including San Francisco, and across the Pacific. The gold rush also jump-started the employment business in Seattle, due to the sheer number of people entering the city in search of work and other opportunities.[24] "Seattle has gradually become the center of the labor market," a state official noted in 1899. "From all over the state of Washington, Seattle is looked to as the supply point for skilled and unskilled labor of all kinds."[25] Lumber companies therefore found in Seattle an urban economy and geography built to facilitate the movement of people, ideal for the kind of expendable itinerant workforce their new corporate system demanded.

But Seattle's significance to the lumber industry surpassed its role as a regional clearinghouse for labor. During this period, Seattle emerged as a different kind of hub: a global city and destination point for foreign-born migrants who would become a dominant force in the industry, comprising nearly two thirds of the workforce by 1910.[26] Lumber's reliance on foreign-born workers, particularly those from Japan and Northern Europe, came as the direct result of Seattle's expansion beyond the regional sphere.

"GATEWAY TO THE ORIENT"

The wave of overseas migration that reached Seattle during the late nineteenth and early twentieth centuries must be understood in the context of the city's growing prominence as the "Gateway to the Orient," a connection point that linked US and Asian markets and enabled the flow of commodities in a lucrative transpacific trade.[27] Officially, this era began in 1896 with the arrival of the Japanese steamship *Miike Maru* in Seattle's Elliott Bay, a much-celebrated event that inaugurated formal trade relations between Seattle and Japan. The Pacific Northwest region had long sparked the interest of railroad barons and industrialists specifically for its proximity to Asia; driven by desire for access to Chinese markets, many looked to the Pacific Northwest as a place for unfettered capitalist expansion.[28] For much of the nineteenth century, however, Seattle had largely flown under the radar. Despite the efforts of Henry Yesler and other early settlers and boosters, investors had bypassed Seattle in favor of neighboring cities Tacoma and Vancouver, BC. Seattle did emerge as a hub of Chinese labor contracting and commercial trade in the 1860s and beyond, but much of its traffic came filtered through Vancouver and Victoria, as Seattle lacked a direct shipping route to China and the rest of Asia.

Things changed in the 1890s, when James Hill, a railroad executive and so-called "empire builder," began to eye Seattle as a potential gateway to Asia.

Hill was, in the words of historian Kornel Chang, "infatuated with the myth of boundless China markets" and he invested in the Great Northern Railway to realize his dream of a transpacific commercial empire.[29] Working with local elites desperate for a leg up in their competition with neighboring cities, Hill announced Seattle as the terminus of the Great Northern Railway in 1890. With construction completed in 1893, Hill turned his attention to shipping; he formed the Great Northern Steamship Company, which offered both freight and passenger service between Seattle, Yokohama, and Hong Kong. He also negotiated a contract with the Japanese shipping company Nippon Yusen Kaisha (NYK) that promised discounted rates in exchange for exclusive use of Great Northern Railway lines. Japan had entered its own period of expansionism, and NYK was on the hunt for an entry point into inland US markets. Hill's deal appealed to NYK executives because northern Seattle's shipping route was about one day faster from Yokohama than the routes of other Pacific Coast cities, giving the company an advantage against its competitors.[30] In 1896, NYK established Seattle as the sole location of its North American headquarters; that fall it began regular operations between Japan and the Pacific Northwest. By the end of the decade, NYK's Seattle fleet included fourteen steamships that had carried more than fifteen million dollars' worth of goods to Japan and the rest of Asia.[31]

Seattle's position as a nexus between Japan and the United States transformed the city into a destination for overseas migrants. Greater access via steamship and railroad opened up new routes of migration and pulled new populations into the city for the first time. The city's Japanese population jumped from 125 in 1890 to over 2,200 in 1900 and to nearly seven thousand by 1910.[32] Most Japanese migrants during the earlier period had consisted of students, seamen, and a handful of enterprising individuals who came to the city in search of opportunity. Kihachi Hirakawa, for example, left Yokohama for Seattle via Vancouver in 1890 to join an uncle who had established a hotel business in the city. Frustrated with the harsh demands of his father, Hirakawa had fled Japan for a fresh start, looking to take English classes and continue his education.[33] Another early resident, Masajiro Furuya, was a trained tailor who had developed an interest in the United States during a stint in the Japanese military. Furuya arrived in Vancouver in 1890 and soon made his way down to Seattle, opening a tailor shop and mercantile business that specialized in Japanese products.[34]

As Seattle established more direct channels to Japan and the rest of Asia, the economic focus of the city's Japanese community shifted. Prominent Japanese residents including Furuya and Charles Tetsuo Takahashi, founder of the Oriental Trading Company, began expanding their businesses to include labor contracting and other employment services. Immigration restriction had cut off the flow of labor from China, driving the Pacific Northwest's Chinese labor-contracting business to near extinction. Railroad companies and other industrial firms sought other sources of low-wage labor, and Furuya, Takahashi, and others were eager to fill the void. The Japanese labor contractors worked much like their predecessors, funneling laborers from across the Pacific and into the manual workforce.[35] In managing and organizing this highly mobile workforce, they provided the valuable service of shielding companies from involvement or responsibility. Furuya, in particular, enjoyed huge success, accruing enough wealth to open up company branches in Yokohama, Portland, and Vancouver, and to fund the construction of a brand-new headquarters building on Second Avenue and Main in Seattle.[36] The success of Furuya and other labor contractors transformed Seattle into a hiring and recruiting center for Japanese workers. By 1909, a government report recorded seventeen Japanese employment businesses in Seattle: "Domestics, bar and restaurant employees, farm, sawmill, cannery, and railroad hands—in short all kinds of laborers—are supplied to employers who have need for them."[37]

Though Japanese labor contractors are best known for their association with the railroad companies, the lumber industry came to rely heavily on their services as well. Before the 1890s, some Japanese laborers worked in lumber, but they did so haphazardly and without any form of organization. The Port Blakely Mill Company was one of the first sawmills to hire Japanese workers: a motley group of seamen and other travelers. One Japanese migrant who began work at Port Blakely in 1890 observed twenty-three fellow Japanese laborers, all "sailors who had landed from sailing ships . . . used to carry cargos of lumber to all parts of the world."[38] After the corporatization of the lumber industry created new demand for hiring and employment services, lumber companies began relying on Japanese contractors like Furuya to fill the most physically dangerous and high-turnover positions: section work on logging railroads, hauling lumber at the mills, feeding timber into the mechanized sawblades.[39] Japanese labor contractors were appealing in their ability to quickly mobilize labor and to ensure a steady

Japanese laborers working at a loading ramp, Pacific National Lumber Company, early twentieth century. Though their position on top of the cut timber implies that they are loggers, Japanese laborers were excluded from logging, which was considered "skilled" work and reserved for white and European men. University of Washington Libraries, Special Collections, C. Kinsey 2609.

flow of workers. As the owner of the Pacific National Lumber Company put it, all his employment needs were taken care of by simply "phoning to Seattle to M. Furuya Co."[40] The number of Japanese lumber workers rapidly increased; by 1910 Japanese laborers accounted for 7 percent of the state's lumber workforce, despite being less than 1 percent of the total population.[41] Lumber work was one of the most common occupations for Japanese migrants upon arrival to the United States; an academic study conducted in 1924 estimated that nearly a quarter of all Japanese residents in the Pacific Northwest had once worked in lumber.[42]

Japanese labor contractors held an ambiguous position within Seattle's early Japanese society. As business leaders and prominent individuals, they maintained connections with the city's white elite and contributed to the founding of many Japanese cultural and religious institutions, including the Nippon Kan Theater, which still stands today. But their wealth and prominence were achieved through the direct exploitation of their fellow countrymen. Contractors charged various fees and commissions from the laborers they procured—first an initial fee for job placement, then a monthly fee paid to the company via a foreman who managed the workforce.[43] Contractors also charged workers for food and supplies, which often came directly from their own mercantile or grocery businesses. Furuya developed a particularly lucrative trade supplying Japanese labor camps around the region with Japanese food products and other items imported from Japan. The end result was a highly coercive system of economic dependency that was, in the words of one Japanese lumber worker, "no good for the working-man, just good for the boss."[44] The contractors benefited tremendously from this exploitative system, which in turn allowed them to establish these cultural and institutional foundations.

By the early twentieth century, Seattle's economy and status as a city had grown considerably. As "Gateway to the Orient," Seattle finally had a direct connection to Asian markets and the shipping and railroad infrastructure to support that connection. But as the Japanese population in the Pacific Northwest grew, so, too, did Hill's anxieties about the future of his transpacific empire. Railroads required local markets—settlements of people to use the lines and make them profitable. In the face of declining westward migration, had he opened up the Pacific Northwest to the wrong kind of foreigner? Though Japanese workers had laid the foundation of his wealth and prosperity—building his railroad and extracting the raw materials he shipped around the world—Hill never saw them as settlers or permanent members of society. For this, he turned to Scandinavians. These "good for-eigners" became targets of a recruitment effort by Hill and his Great Northern railroad company. Hill did not anticipate, however, that Scandinavians would enter the workforce in large numbers, turning away from farming to become another source of labor, alongside the Japanese, for the rapidly expanding lumber industry.

"THE BEST CLASS OF FOREIGNERS"

In the late nineteenth and early twentieth centuries, European migration to Seattle looked much different than it did to other regions of the United States. In New York, Chicago, and other non-Western cities, the European population was much larger and more diverse, representing many different regions and nationalities. While earlier nineteenth-century European migration had consisted largely of Northern Europeans, including a substantial number of Irish, the later wave brought Southern and Eastern Europeans to US urban centers. In 1920, for example, eight hundred thousand Italians and 1.5 million Jews, many of the latter from Eastern Europe, called New York City home. Together, these two groups alone made up over 40 percent of New York City's total population.[45] Similar patterns played out in cities of the East Coast and Midwest, where Europeans comprised the backbone of the industrial working class.

In the Pacific Northwest, though, Europeans who arrived during this period were mostly Scandinavians, recruited directly by Hill and the Great Northern to become landowners. This type of colonization scheme was common in regions across the American West, as railroad companies sought to populate areas surrounding their lines with white settlements. The companies played a direct role in shaping patterns of migration and settlement. Using land granted to them by the federal government—as massive subsidies to induce railroad construction—rail companies resold parcels to settlers in order to create the local markets needed to ensure their lines' future profitability. Historian Jason Pierce has shown that companies favored some settlers over others, and spent considerable time and money recruiting those they considered the most desirable.[46] Scandinavians were among the groups frequently targeted by railroad companies for permanent settlement. The Northern Pacific, for example, "became one of the most aggressive lines" in attracting Scandinavians to Minnesota, sending promotional materials and recruiters back to Europe to emphasize similarities in climate as a key regional selling point.[47] As a result Minnesota's Scandinavian population grew into one of the largest in North America.

Scandinavian migration to Seattle and the Pacific Northwest followed a similar trajectory. Swedish historian Jorgen Dahlie notes that Hill, concerned about the decline of westward migration during the 1890s, believed the future prosperity of his commercial empire in the Pacific Northwest "depended on the settler."[48] Hill viewed Scandinavians as the "best class of foreigners," and created an immigration division within the Great Northern to recruit them as settlers.[49] The Great Northern advertised the Pacific Northwest in the Scandinavian press and other venues, selling the region as a place of cheap and abundant land. "Homeseekers have come to realize," a Great Northern pamphlet boasted, "that in the Northwest are the best sites of good farms that can be purchased by men of small means."[50] The company also relied on Scandinavians in the United States to act as de facto "immigration agents," offering them free passage back to their homelands to spread the word among their compatriots. These overseas efforts bore some success.[51] While the majority of Scandinavians had relocated from elsewhere in the United States, over twenty thousand came to Washington directly from the countries of Sweden, Norway, and Denmark.[52] By 1910, Scandinavians comprised nearly 8 percent of Seattle's total population, by far the largest foreign-born group in the entire region.

Scandinavians did not receive the same degree of nativist backlash as other European groups, who faced widespread hostility and suspicions about their whiteness and fitness for citizenship.[53] In the Pacific Northwest, Scandinavians were readily accepted as white people and as settlers, handpicked to replenish and revitalize white society in an era of declining westward migration.[54] They stood as the "standard bearers" of whiteness, classified by eugenicists at the time as the most racially pure and hence the most desirable based on their heredity as Northern Europeans.[55] This is precisely what Hill meant when he called Scandinavians the "best class of foreigners." He and other railroad barons envisioned the group's seamless transition into farming, property ownership, and the reproduction of a social order rooted in white racial purity and homogeneity.

Positioned as the future of Pacific Northwest society, Scandinavians served as a bulwark against the growing migration from Japan. It's not a coincidence that the Great Northern began its promotional efforts to Scandinavians during the 1890s, a period that witnessed the most rapid expansion of Seattle's Japanese population. Unlike Scandinavians, Japanese people were viewed as inherently foreign and racially incompatible with whiteness. They faced an entire legal apparatus, including restrictions on citizenship and property ownership, that prevented their permanent settlement and ensured they would remain in the United States only as expendable, alien laborers.[56] This further differentiated the Japanese from other Europeans who worked as laborers and endured xenophobic attacks but were not subjected to the same restrictions and legal forms of racialized exclusion. The Europeans could become naturalized US citizens, and thus had a future and a security in the United States that the Japanese did not.

The high hopes that Hill had for Scandinavians in the Pacific Northwest did not really pan out. Though recruited to the region as farmers, not

Japanese workers with guns in Mukilteo, Washington, early twentieth century. Japanese employees of Crown Lumber lived in a ravine, which locals derisively called "Jap Gulch." They acquired the guns to protect themselves from white mobs who harassed and threatened them. My great-grandfather, Raisuke Tamura, helped smuggle the guns into the camp. Courtesy of the Mukilteo Historical Society.

laborers, many Scandinavians were too poor to buy land and instead entered the workforce. They worked as laborers on the railroads and docks, as fishermen and maritime workers, and, most often, as loggers. By 1910, Scandinavians accounted for nearly one quarter of all lumber workers in Washington State, with most located in the Puget Sound region.[57] Like the Japanese workers, they viewed lumber as a temporary occupation, allowing them to save money and go into farming or other pursuits. And lumber was familiar work. Many who came to the Pacific Northwest traced their roots back to lumber-producing regions of Scandinavia. Signe Anderson, for example, was born in a small logging town in central Sweden where her father, two grandfathers, and mother all worked for the local sawmill. After losing their jobs following an economic downturn, the family migrated to the Pacific Northwest via Ellis Island to join a relative, and her father soon found work at a logging camp and then a sawmill in Conway, Washington.[58] Anderson's story was not uncommon. Swedish demographers have shown that the majority of Swedish emigrants to Washington State originated from Sundsvall, a "major sawmill district" in Sweden.[59]

As part of the itinerant working class, Scandinavians traversed the same migratory routes as other laborers. Their participation in the lumber workforce brought them frequently through Seattle, where they encountered Japanese workers and other migrants who lived together in the city's south end. The racially mixed world of the Sawdust and the regional networks of migration were what most shaped Scandinavian workers' experiences in the Pacific Northwest, not the insular farming communities Hill and other railroad barons envisioned for them.

THE SAWDUST AT THE TURN OF THE TWENTIETH CENTURY

In 1900, the south-end district known as the Sawdust looked very different than it did in the 1860s and 1870s, when its primary residents were Chinese and Indigenous laborers, mixed-race families, and those associated with Yesler's sawmill. The expansion of the city's port and waterfront area populated the Sawdust with new residents. Japanese laborers and small business operators settled in the south end, which became home to a bustling Japanese district. White and European residents' numbers also swelled in the years during and after the gold rush, which had built up an entire geography in the south end to accommodate people on the move: entertainment venues, brothels, cafés, and other businesses. Employment agencies that catered to white workers set up shop south of Yesler Way to capitalize on the steady stream of unemployed miners returning from Alaska. They joined the Japanese and Chinese labor-contracting firms that had already established a presence on Washington Street. The result was a district constantly in flux, a fluid and heterogeneous space that defied easy categorization.

In the fall of 1903, a Japanese writer named Nagai Kafū vividly captured this social world. Kafū arrived in the Pacific Northwest to immerse himself in the sights and sounds of the region's emerging cities. An admirer of the literary works of Émile Zola, Kafū traveled extensively throughout the United States and France from 1903 to 1907, recording his musings about the gritty realities of urban life for Japanese audiences back home. He spent considerable time in Seattle, where he resided in the raucous working-class district of the city's south end. There, each night, he observed "crowds of menial laborers who had finished their day's work" wandering the district's "lantern-lit alleys" and filling the air with the "distinct odor of sweat and alcohol."[60] From this "tangle" of narrow streets "poured an unending stream of human voices mingled with the sound of gramophones from taverns and shooting galleries and the raucous sound of a circus band."[61] He described the district coming alive in the evening hours, the revelry often lasting until sunrise when laborers stumbled back to their lodging houses or headed to their worksites for another day on the job.

Though he commented on many different topics, Kafū appeared most struck by the heterogeneity of the district. When he first arrived, he noted "both oriental and occidental" laborers frequenting the same cigar shops and fruit stands. Another day, he walked down a single alley and encountered "the haunts of Chinese and Japanese people . . . Caucasian laborers out of work and . . . blacks suffering from poverty and oppression."[62] Particularly noteworthy to Kafū were the moments that showed Japanese residents' integration within the south end and their coexistence with whites and other groups. He recalled hearing the "hard, flat sounds of the *samisen*" next door to a saloon, and white children who yelled "*sukebei*," a Japanese vulgarity that roughly translated into "lecher" or "dirty old man." "It had been used by Japanese prostitutes and came to have special meaning," Kafū explained, "[and] now I found the word circulating among the lower-class people of America."[63] What he conveyed with these writings was integration in the truest sense—not just people living in the same district and working alongside one another, but also the new forms of social and cultural life that emerged from such proximity.

It was from this district that lumber companies procured their workforce, and the integration within the Sawdust posed problems for an industry rooted in racial division and workers' investment in whiteness. Like other industries of the time, lumber was structured around a racial hierarchy between white and nonwhite workers. Companies reinforced this hierarchy in a variety of ways, but mostly through employment and housing. White workers were given access to the highest-paying jobs, which in lumber meant logging, shingle weaving, and other "skilled" positions. Nonwhite workers, on the other hand, were relegated to manual labor. Whites also worked as laborers, but they weren't restricted from occupying other jobs within the workforce. In terms of housing, companies situated white and nonwhite workers in separate accommodations. One's job often determined where one lived; loggers resided in bunkhouses in the woods, for example, which automatically created division within the workforce. Even when white and nonwhite workers occupied the same jobs, companies separated them into different areas for housing purposes.[64]

In the Pacific Northwest, Scandinavian and Japanese workers occupied the two ends of this hierarchy. Companies employed Scandinavians overwhelmingly as loggers. It's difficult to know if this overrepresentation occurred because Scandinavians themselves sought out logging positions due to their backgrounds and experience in woods work, or if companies recruited them specifically for this role. It's also possible that Scandinavians were slotted into logging positions by the Seattle employment agents who recruited workers on behalf of the lumber companies. Whatever the reason, companies grew reliant on Scandinavian loggers and came to justify their employment in highly racialized terms. Consider, for example, a government report explaining the phenomenon of Scandinavian loggers: "They are strong and well adapted to the climate of the Northwest, are industrious, adaptable, and progressive."[65] Here, a connection is made between climate and work ethic in a way that naturalizes whiteness and imbues Scandinavians with desirable traits. Beyond this symbolic association, logging also paid better than other positions and thus gave Scandinavians access to higher wages, allowing them greater economic mobility than other groups. In fact, Scandinavians received some of the highest wages in the industry, second only to US-born whites in skilled positions.[66]

Japanese workers, on the other hand, occupied only manual labor positions in the sawmills and on logging railroads. They received the lowest wages "without exception" in the industry, paid less than all other groups who performed the same kind of labor.[67] Japanese labor contractors played a role in maintaining this wage disparity; they, not the companies, controlled issues around payment. Japanese laborers did not work as company employees, but rather as outsourced labor, organized and managed by the contractors.[68] But the entire structure of Japanese labor contracting operated within a larger context of Japanese disenfranchisement. Unlike Scandinavians and other Europeans, the Japanese could not become naturalized US citizens and thus had few legal protections and rights. Their exclusion from mainstream unions also cut off one of the main avenues for self-protection within the labor force. The system of Japanese labor contracting worked so well for lumber companies and other industries because of Japanese laborers' existing marginalization within US society.

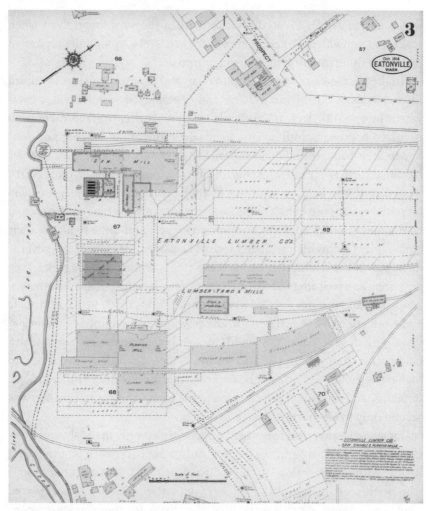

Site map of the Eatonville Lumber Company, 1914. The company's Japanese laborers lived in a segregated encampment located at the bottom left of the map. Sanborn Fire Insurance Map from Eatonville, Pierce County, Washington, 1914.

Employers further entrenched this racial hierarchy by segregating the Japanese from other workers. Lumber companies relegated Japanese laborers to isolated encampments, often deliberately situated near sites of industrial waste or nuisance—creeks that overflowed with refuse, lumberyards filled with sawdust. Japanese laborers who worked for Crown Lumber in Mukilteo lived in a muddy ravine called "Jap Gulch" by local whites. "We

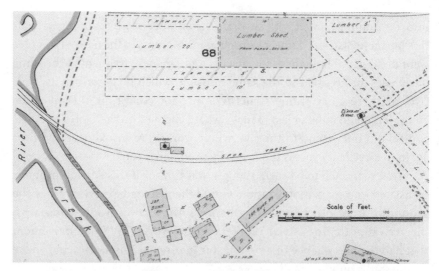

Close-up of the Eatonville "Jap Camp." The map shows the marginalization of the Japanese laborers, who lived in a cluster of buildings encircled by a railroad track, creek, and dam flume. Sanborn Fire Insurance Map from Eatonville, Pierce County, Washington, 1914.

don't like it down here in hollow where it's damp," a Japanese laborer named Kobayashi told a researcher.[69] A visitor to the Walville lumber company noted the location of its Japanese encampment near a creek that served as a dumping ground for garbage, "out of sight but not out of smell."[70] The encampments served not only to physically separate the Japanese workers from the white workers, but also to reinforce their status as disposable labor.

Given the efforts on the part of lumber companies to reinforce and reproduce racial hierarchy in the workforce, the Sawdust posed particular challenges. The Sawdust and the Seattle-based labor networks served as the foundation of the lumber industry's entire employment system. The mobility and constant turnover of the workforce were central to the industry's expansion and profitability, and key factors in guarding against strikes or other forms of solidarity and worker mobilization. But the Sawdust also brought together the very groups that companies tried so hard to keep apart. It fostered a kind of closeness between white, European, Japanese, and other residents that undermined the project of racial division. An observer in

1910, for example, noted with surprise the number of whites living in Seattle's Japanese district, "largely European immigrants of the newer type." He went on to detail how these Europeans and Japanese frequented the same businesses and resided in the same housing, which he described as "one, two, or three-story frame structures in poor condition."[71] And while employers could more or less manage what happened on their job sites, their control did not extend to the city, where workers returned over and over again in a cyclical process the industry itself had created.

What remained to be seen, though, was how or if this spatial intimacy translated into mass mobilization. Could these shared experiences lay the groundwork for other kinds of alliances? The answer would come with the arrival of the Industrial Workers of the World (IWW), a movement that had the best chance of any to foster interracial solidarities and shake up the status quo.

"BORDERING ON ANARCHY"

The early twentieth century marked a time of intensifying labor struggle and militant action in the Pacific Northwest. Because of its dominance in the region and its utterly corrupt and exploitative business practices, the lumber industry emerged as a primary target, with the IWW its primary foe. With members known as the Wobblies, the IWW formed in 1905 in Chicago to unite industrial workers in the United States and around the world in revolutionary struggle. While unions such as the American Federation of Labor (AFL) organized workers according to trade, the IWW focused instead on workers across industries to build a unified movement against capitalism.[72] The preamble to its constitution declared, "There can be no peace so long as hunger and want are found among millions of working people and the few, who make up the employing class, have all the good things of life." The workers of the world must join together, it continued, to "organize as a class, take possession of the earth and the machinery of production, and abolish the wage system."[73] IWW organizers arrived in the Pacific Northwest in 1907 and quickly made their mark with a strike of two thousand sawmill workers in Portland, followed by a mass walkout in a Grays Harbor logging camp in 1912.

The IWW had great success organizing within the particular conditions of the Pacific Northwest lumber industry. According to IWW historians, the group's "guerilla-style, point of production approach . . . proved to be ideally suited to an industry dependent on a multitude of scattered camps and sawmills where order was maintained by a local foreman."[74] They were able to slip in and out of the camps and move around the migratory labor circuit, using to their advantage the very strategies imposed to exploit the workforce and guard against solidarity. Pacific Northwest lumber proved to be what historian Philip Foner calls an "ideal field" for the IWW: a high proportion of its laborers, who included migrants and the unemployed, were ignored by the existing mainstream union structure, and discontent was widespread at all levels of the workforce.[75] This allowed the organization to build a massive base of support across the region.

To access these migratory networks, the IWW established its regional headquarters in Seattle. By the late 1910s, nearly two dozen IWW locals had formed in Seattle, far more than any other city in Washington. Four of those locals focused solely on organizing loggers and sawmill laborers around Puget Sound, and boasted membership numbers into the thousands. Seattle had particular appeal to IWW leadership. As the main regional center of labor and employment, Seattle offered a highly concentrated population of workers, particularly in lumber. This included workers looking for jobs at the employment agencies as well as those passing through the city or residing there temporarily. The IWW located its main office for the first few years (1907–9) along Washington Street, a well-known workers' hub surrounded by "cheap lodgings," saloons, and barbershops. At that time, Washington Street also served as the heart of Chinese and Japanese labor contracting. Across from the IWW headquarters were Chin Gee Hee's main office and Chinese workers' housing, while a Japanese hall and lodgings could be found just two doors down.[76]

It's not a surprise that the IWW selected this neighborhood for the location of its first headquarters. The IWW welcomed Asian members, unlike the most influential union in the Pacific Northwest, the AFL. Led by notorious anti-Asian racist Samuel Gompers, AFL unions restricted membership to whites only and led vicious campaigns against Asian workers.[77] But the AFL was hardly alone in its anti-Asian agitation. Most mainstream labor unions of the time served those they believed to be "legitimate populations"—whites and Europeans—and were deeply hostile to Asian (and other nonwhite) workers.[78] Though the individual sentiment towards Asian workers varied, organized labor as an institution became a vocal proponent of anti-Asian exclusion during this period and, in some cases, led the charge for Asian laborers' expulsion from the United States.

The IWW, though, correctly identified these actions as serving the interests of the powerful rather than the workers. While Gompers agitated publicly for Japanese exclusion, IWW leaders decried this anti-Asian racism as the "same old game of divide and conquer" that pitted workers against one another to the ultimate benefit of employers.[79] The organization understood the role of race in perpetuating capitalist exploitation and viewed Asians as fellow workers and allies in revolutionary struggle. Stories of Japanese and Chinese labor strikes and militant action filled the pages of the *Industrial Worker*. "A yellow skin is to be preferred a thousand times to a yellow heart," declared an article on the Japanese plantation workers' strike in Hawaii.[80] The *Industrial Worker* often framed these articles to refute the racist caricature, espoused by Gompers and other union leaders, of Asian labor as inherently cheap and servile. Reporting on a strike by Chinese steamship workers in the South, the newspaper declared that "the shipowners who employ Chinese crews . . . may yet come to the conclusion that after all, the reliable white seamen are the most economical in the end."[81] In addition to covering Asian labor actions, the IWW published some of its materials in Japanese, including the preamble to its constitution, and raised funds to support efforts by Japanese workers.[82]

The IWW's stance on race and its efforts to appeal to Asian workers quickly caught the attention of city officials and industry leaders. In 1909, police arrested IWW members who were standing on Washington Street, then the heart of Japanese and Chinese labor, and decrying the evils of the employment business.[83] This "free speech" fight was one of the IWW's primary tactics: members spoke on street corners or other public spaces, denouncing capitalist exploitation and urging passersby to join in revolutionary struggle. The IWW openly courted arrest in order to challenge prohibitions on free speech and highlight municipal corruption and hypocrisy.[84] The organization's free speech movement started in 1908, when authorities arrested over two dozen IWW activists in Spokane, Washington, for violating an ordinance against street speeches, passed earlier that year at the request of the city's employment agents. From there, the IWW's free speech movement spread across the American West. The decision to launch a free speech fight on Washington Street represented a direct appeal to Asian workers, and the arrest represented a reaction to those efforts by city authorities.

In the end, though, the IWW struggled to attract Japanese workers. It wasn't for lack of interest, necessarily. According to journalist James Omura, the IWW was a "sensation" at the time, and "the Japanese people, the Issei, talked a great deal about it."[85] Nor was it due to a clash in political leanings. The network of Japanese unions and small business associations in the Seattle area—barbers, shoemakers, railroad laborers—was animated by what historian Dana Frank describes as a "political ferment and thriving intellectual climate" where socialist ideas "were hotly debated."[86] The workers at Crown Lumber, for example, formed a literary club where they read "all the works of Marx" and discussed capitalism and their experiences as laborers.[87]

It appears instead that the IWW didn't prioritize Japanese workers in a meaningful way. The group focused much of its initial local effort on organizing loggers and shingle weavers, two occupations that had traditionally excluded Japanese labor. The IWW also attempted to form a stronghold in Everett, a city well known among Japanese people for having "an anti-Japanese air."[88] A handful of Japanese workers did join the IWW. Labor organizer Daisho Miyagawa recalls meeting "an Issei old-timer who had been an IWW member, an honest-to-Paul Bunyan Wobbly" in the 1930s.[89] Taro Yoshihara, a Japanese communist who migrated to the United States in the early twentieth century, was among IWW leader William "Big Bill" Haywood's close associates. Described by the press as Haywood's "bodyguard," Yoshihara was present during the FBI raid of IWW headquarters in Chicago and was taken into custody along with Haywood and other IWW leaders.[90] But these cases remained few and far between. A wide gulf existed between the IWW rhetoric of revolutionary solidarity with Japanese labor and the organization's actual practices on the ground.[91]

This misstep on the part of the IWW represented a lost opportunity to bring together the two dominant groups in the Seattle-based lumber workforce, Japanese and Scandinavian workers. While the Japanese laborers showed little interest in the IWW, Scandinavians flocked to the organization, forming one its strongest bases of support. Swedish workers, in particular, joined the IWW in large numbers, eventually creating their own IWW local in Seattle and publishing at least one Swedish-language IWW newspaper called *Solidaritet*. Scandinavian laborers' involvement with the IWW, as opposed to the racially exclusionary AFL-affiliated unions, was a promising sign that they were open to interracial alliances. Despite being

A group of white and European loggers in a bunkhouse, 1892. Loggers endured terrible conditions throughout the Pacific Northwest. University of Washington Libraries, Special Collections, D. Kinsey 155A.

pitted against each other, Scandinavians had a lot in common with their fellow Japanese workers. Both groups had frequent encounters in places like the Sawdust; both experienced exploitation at the hands of employment agents and a labor structure that treated them as expendable. Their living and working conditions also mirrored one another. Scandinavian loggers lived in ramshackle, overcrowded bunkhouses where they slept on wooden platforms arranged like horse stalls—no mattresses or bedding, only sacks stuffed with hay. "There were two little windows near the roof you couldn't even see through," recalled a logger, "[and] you were overcome with the odor of drying socks."[92] But in the absence of more sustained attention from the IWW, these shared experiences did not develop into formal alliances.

Still, the massive popularity of the IWW among white and European workers was enough to provoke a response by industry leaders, police, and other officials who believed that nothing less than the future of Pacific Northwest society was at stake. "The IWW is a serious menace here," declared a local businessman, "bordering on anarchy."[93] As the IWW began to match its fiery rhetoric with direct actions, including strikes and walk-outs, authorities imposed an array of repressive measures to blunt the group's momentum. One of the most common strategies against the IWW involved "concerted denial of employment."[94] Companies worked with employment agencies to form blacklists of suspected IWW members and organizers and ban them from working in the industry.[95] Other tactics included harassment and physical violence. The most infamous case in the Puget Sound region occurred in Everett in 1916, when hundreds of armed townspeople, led by Snohomish County sheriff Donald McRae, opened fire on a group of IWW members who had arrived from Seattle to support a local shingle weavers' strike. Over a dozen were killed, and many more wounded, in what became known as Bloody Sunday.[96]

Conflict came to a head in 1917 as the United States entered World War I. Using as leverage the growing demand for timber products in the construction of warships and airplanes, the IWW made the call for a mass strike of lumber workers in Washington State. On June 20, 1917, the Lumber Workers Industrial Union No. 500, a Spokane-based IWW local, became the first to walk out on their jobs, an action quickly followed by lumber workers, both IWW and nonaffiliates, across the region. Despite their revolutionary rhetoric, the vast majority of strikers demanded only simple reforms aimed at improving their material conditions and work environments. These included an eight-hour day, increased pay, better sanitation and bedding in the bunkhouses, and the abolition of the employment industry (in favor of hiring through IWW union halls). By August the strike involved nearly half of the state's lumber workforce and had closed down over 80 percent of lumber operations in Western Washington and Puget Sound.[97] Facing the disruption of wartime productivity, the federal government jumped in, joining local leaders and lumber company owners to crush the strike and rid the country of the IWW once and for all. Government officials used the nationalist sentiment of the war effort to brand the IWW as a treasonous organization; its leaders and members were criminalized, arrested, jailed, and deported. With its leadership decimated and much of its membership in disarray, the IWW called off the strike in September and urged its members to return to work.

The rise of the IWW and other leftist movements sparked changes in federal immigration policy that targeted Europeans for the first time and allowed the US government to deploy immigration enforcement as a way of stifling European dissent and radicalism. US policy had long regulated Asian immigration. One of the first federal immigration laws was the Page Act of 1875, which Congress passed to limit the entry of Chinese women. The government followed with further restrictions on Chinese and then Japanese laborers.[98] Europeans remained relatively untouched in federal immigration matters until the Immigration Act of 1917. This policy's sweeping measures completely cut off immigration from South Asia and imposed the first restrictions on European immigration in the form of literacy tests and other categories of inadmissibility, including political radicalism and pauperism. A year later, President Woodrow Wilson moved to strengthen the preexisting prohibitions in the 1917 act by expanding the definition of anarchism and beefing up immigration authorities' enforcement powers in a renewed 1918 act.[99] This act applied to "alien" Europeans, those who had not yet naturalized as US citizens and who had lived fewer than five years in the United States.

These immigration policies not only regulated who came into the United States, but also allowed the government to arrest and deport those deemed in violation of the law. In the Pacific Northwest, dozens of IWW leaders and members were rounded up by immigration agents and summarily deported back to Europe via Ellis Island. Officials interpreted the parameters of the law quite loosely in order to target those with even a minor IWW affiliation. Immigration agents arrested John Morgan, an Irishman living in Everett, for the simple act of "[distributing] IWW literature at various times" and "[corresponding] with prominent IWW leaders."[100] During the 1918 calendar year alone, twenty-seven aliens were arrested in the Seattle area and deported under the statutes of both the 1917 and 1918 immigration acts, with the most common charge being "advocating or teaching the unlawful destruction of property." Of the twenty-seven deported, eleven were Scandinavian (ten Swedish and one Norwegian).[101]

In this moment, the European emerged as alien. No longer an immigrant or desirable foreigner, the European alien was an irredeemable figure, a troublemaker and agitator who threatened the United States from within. For these Europeans, the state brought the full force of immigration control, in the form of arrest, imprisonment, and deportation. The very mechanisms created to maintain Asian expendability were now deployed against subversive Europeans, deemed an alien menace and expelled from the nation. But then, a new question arose: what should happen to the other European dissidents—those who had become US citizens or who did not fall under the jurisdiction of immigration control? If the IWW had revealed anything, it was that the discontent went far beyond a small group of aliens and agitators and extended to much of the European working population. This required something more than repression; rather, it called for a broad societal response that would bring these "unassimilated citizens" back into the fold of whiteness, or risk further chaos and upheaval.[102]

BUILDING THE SELF-CONTAINED LUMBER TOWN

After the strike, industry leaders, government officials, and local authorities engaged in a period of soul-searching, wondering why the IWW had so attracted Europeans, and Scandinavians in particular. Many were disturbed that these "good foreigners" had fallen so easily under the sway of the IWW, and concluded that something was very wrong to make them abandon their chosen path as good citizens and loyal Americans. From a historical perspective, the case of Scandinavian lumber workers is, indeed, interesting. Their attraction to the IWW over other unions showed a willingness to channel their labor militancy in a way that did not reinforce racial hierarchy or promote racial exclusion. And the surge of radicalism and resistance among these European workers was a response to their material conditions and experiences, which included their participation in the heterogeneous world of migration in and around Seattle.

In order to understand the IWW's popularity, lumber companies commissioned reports by teams of social scientists. The federal government also produced its own accounting of how the IWW had gained such a foothold among lumber workers in the Pacific Northwest. All of these studies pointed to the same root cause: the mobility of the workforce and the "unhealthy social conditions" that stemmed from it.[103] William F. Ogburn, a Columbia University sociologist, identified the lack of stable family life in the lumber industry as the primary cause of labor unrest. He found that only 5 percent of those he surveyed had wives and children present, which he believed contributed to feelings of hostility and alienation from modern society. Ogburn recommended that companies construct permanent housing and amenities as a way of creating "stable conditions for family and community life."[104] Others agreed. "Indeed, it can be truthfully stated," another sociologist noted, "that the present radical attitude of the loggers is the culmination of years of the most inhuman neglect."[105] The Department of Labor put it most bluntly: "Here, nearly everything combines to make them radical."[106]

In these officials' eyes, the issue spoke to a deeper problem with Pacific Northwest society. The lumber industry's demand for a mobile workforce had shaped an entire generation of men without homes, steady jobs, or normal family lives. The conditions of transiency had bred a deep resentment toward authority that the IWW had skillfully exploited, and would continue to exploit until the industry dramatically changed how it managed its workforce. These concerns around transiency were, of course, fundamentally concerns about whiteness, and about who was and was not allowed to be a transient. Asian laborers faced an entire legal and political structure devoted to ensuring their continual movement, uprootedness, and inability to establish autonomous lives. For Europeans, on the other hand, transiency signaled something different: that they had strayed from their path as landowners, heads of home and family, and the backbone of the white settler order. Their individual failures did not reflect on them as a group, but rather on the society that had allowed it to happen.

Lumber companies took this criticism to heart and sprang into action. The first order of business involved cutting off their reliance on Seattle-based labor networks and establishing self-contained lumber towns that revolved around a permanent nonmobile workforce; they saw this as the best way to pacify their workers and guard against future uprisings. The companies moved loggers in from the woods and established housing for them in the surrounding towns or near the sawmills. They invested in new forms of transportation to move laborers to and from their worksites every day. One logging company owner recalled, "We bought steam-heated passenger coaches, which were quite satisfactory for a long time, and took the men back and forth every day by railroad . . . [which] helped to bring a slow change."[107] Companies constructed modern housing facilities with improved sanitation and electricity. They built recreation centers and libraries, to promote wholesome forms of entertainment and prevent lumber workers from visiting Seattle's saloons and brothels after payday each month. The measures mirrored reforms undertaken at the municipal level to rein in corruption and crack down on employment agencies.

Rather than relying on Seattle as they had in the past, employers began to recruit workers on their own. Their top priority involved hiring married workers, whom they viewed as more stable and less likely to rebel. They housed these married workers in newly constructed company homes and granted them the best jobs and highest wages.[108] The Snoqualmie Falls Lumber Company, owned by Weyerhaeuser, designed its housing to attract as many married workers as possible, viewing them as "a much steadier, more reliable lot of men."[109] The company first built a cluster of homes near the railroad tracks known as the "flats," making them available for rent only to married couples or families. Soon, demand for company housing outstripped the available stock, prompting the general manager to write Weyerhaeuser president George S. Long asking to build homes for "at least fifty or sixty more married men."[110] The company quickly constructed a new development along Railroad Avenue. Located on a dead end overlooking a wooded area, these homes were painted burgundy with white trim and offered electricity in each room. Edna Hebner, who grew up in Snoqualmie Falls, remembers moving into her "nice new house" on Railroad Avenue as a young girl. "This was a three-bedroom, red shingled house with a shingle roof," she recalls. "It had a bathroom, kitchen sink with water, pantry between the kitchen and dining room, woodshed out back which was connected to the house by a raised wooden walk."[111]

In this context, Scandinavians became highly desired as workers and town residents, despite their past support of the IWW. Of all the European groups, Scandinavians had the highest rates of marriage. A government report from 1910 found that nearly 90 percent of Scandinavians had wives present in the United States, compared with less than half of Greeks and Hungarians.[112] As such, companies tended to minimize Scandinavian participation in the IWW. A logging camp operator recalled, "These Scandinavian graders, mostly Swedes, were scared to death by this proclamation spieled out by the [IWW] organizer and they all walked over to the office . . . they didn't know why they were quitting, this fellow just bulldozed them into it."[113] In other words, Scandinavians were innocent and easily manipulated newcomers, didn't know any better, and had clearly been coerced by the IWW. It was now up to the lumber industry to provide them with modern homes and community life, to counteract the influence of the IWW and help transform these men into productive citizens.

Single men continued to labor in the logging camps and sawmills, living separately from the married workers. Employers housed single male laborers in company-run boarding homes designed to promote good health and morals. Workers had their own rooms and toilets with shared

New housing constructed for white married workers at the Snoqualmie Falls Lumber Company, c. early twentieth century. After the strikes and militant actions by workers during World War I, lumber companies used housing developments like this one to pacify the workforce and separate married workers from single men. University of Washington Libraries, Special Collections, C. Kinsey 4127.

showers and dining facilities staffed by a company cook. A local visitor described the Snoqualmie Falls Lumber Company boardinghouse as "very modern" and praised its "modern plumbing and hot and cold water in each bedroom."[114] In addition to providing libraries and reading rooms, companies formed baseball teams to encourage respectable forms of leisure and give workers an outlet outside of drinking, which they often did during trips back to Seattle.

The new boardinghouses showed much improvement over the earlier era, when all workers could expect was a broken-down shack with no running water or working toilets. But companies also used the built environment as a form of labor discipline, to control laborers and make them more dependent on their employers than on organizations like the IWW. This control was particularly evident among single men, cast as a potential threat and danger to the wholesome community of married couples and families and who needed to be inculcated with the proper norms of modern life. Companies engaged social workers and health inspectors to visit the boardinghouses and ensure that residents were living properly according to these new standards.

Though these changes targeted all Europeans, efforts clearly diverged with married men and single men. For married men, the end goal was assimilation and integration into white settler society; the company homes and modern recreation facilities were only a temporary arrangement until they could move into the surrounding towns as breadwinners and homeowners. The program for single men, on the other hand, was never really about assimilation, but rather about containing their "destructive . . . radicalism" and preventing their agitation within the workforce.[115] Since they lacked what social scientists believed to be the moderating influence of marriage and family life, companies had to provide it for them in the form of more rigid, controlled environments and programs overseen by social workers and health officials. Their singleness would continue to mark them as outsiders, racialized as other, as not-quite-white.

They shared this otherness with Japanese migrants, also deemed incapable of assimilation and treated as beyond the boundaries of white settler life. In this new era, however, Japanese laborers posed less of a direct threat than white and European single men, partly due to the marginalized status of Japanese migrants and their plummeting numbers within the lumber industry. The Gentlemen's Agreement of 1907–8 had cut off the flow of labor from Japan, and very few new workers were entering the industry. Prohibitions on Japanese naturalization and property ownership also functioned as safeguards, limiting Japanese workers' power and ensuring their expendability. The desirability of Japanese workers, compared to single white and European men, can also be explained by their conformity to marriage and normative family life. Though the Gentlemen's Agreement cut off labor migration from Japan, it continued to allow Japanese women to enter the United States. Many Japanese married couples and families began to inhabit these lumber camps, fitting the new demands of the modern lumber workforce.

Ironically, these developments allowed a degree of social mobility for Japanese families and a relaxing of the rigid forms of segregation that had relegated them solely to segregated encampments. In Mukilteo, Crown Lumber allowed Japanese married workers to move into company homes, though only after those homes had largely been abandoned by European and white families. Japanese children also attended Mukilteo's public school, while Japanese families were accepted into the town's Presbyterian Church. Japanese single men remained completely shut out of these forms of mobility, remaining in the segregated "Jap Camps," but even they had become tolerated by the local townspeople. They fielded two baseball teams that competed against Crown's white teams, as well as those in Seattle, Tacoma, and other lumber towns. Instead of generating tension, these games were highly anticipated and enjoyed by all. Further, a handful of Japanese single men attended an English class taught by a local white woman three evenings a week.[116] The unsupervised interaction between a white woman and Japanese men would have once erupted into controversy, but by the late 1910s, local townspeople did not object publicly.

The Japanese workers, both single and non-single, adhered to these new standards of community life, making them a desirable alternative to single white and European men. A local white woman in Mukilteo declared, "I would rather have those Japs for neighbors than Greeks and other foreigners."[117] But while some Europeans continued to be viewed with suspicion and downright hostility, domestic life created a pathway of assimilation for them that did not exist for Japanese residents, whose participation in the town's social life did not bring them any closer to citizenship and equal standing within the United States. The 1920 Snohomish County census reveals this growing divide: homeowners in Mukilteo included a mix of European and white families, while Japanese people continued to reside in rundown company rental homes and boardinghouses.[118] As Europeans became more fully integrated into white settler town life, the Japanese remained wholly on the margins.

The rise of self-contained lumber towns that relied on permanent and nonmobile workers made it almost impossible for the IWW to maintain its organizing power within the industry. To be sure, the arrests and deportations of the IWW's most active members decimated the leadership of the organization and created new fear and vulnerability among sympathizers. But the IWW had capitalized more than any other union on Seattle's particular structure of employment, using to its great advantage the high turnover and constant mobility of the workforce. It's one of the main reasons the IWW found such success in the Pacific Northwest lumber industry, in particular, despite its failure to fully realize its vision of a multiracial alliance of workers united against capitalism.

In Seattle, though, the story of race, labor, and social order was far from over. There, city authorities faced a different set of problems. Japanese entrepreneurs had ascended to a relatively powerful position within the urban economy, running hotels and lodging houses that served the region's workforce. Though Japanese residents had their own agenda and reasons for pursuing hotel management, Seattle authorities grew alarmed at their influence—and their movement beyond the segregated south end.

CHAPTER 4

Japanese Hotels and Housing Reform

AS LUMBER COMPANIES SOUGHT TO TRANSFORM THE CONDI-
tions of their industry to discipline an unruly workforce, similar changes
were underway in Seattle. City officials had grown concerned about the state
of the rowdy south-end district, now called the Tenderloin. In 1910, sensational tales about Seattle's Tenderloin began to circulate in the national press,
with one magazine calling it a "gambling hell."[1] This unwelcome attention
proved embarrassing to city officials and boosters, who had just hosted the
Alaska-Yukon-Pacific Exposition, a world's fair meant to showcase Seattle's
status as a "modern metropolis."[2] The district's many lodging houses and
hotels came under particular scrutiny. At the time, Seattle had one of the
highest concentrations of short-term housing in the country.[3] Though these
lodging houses and hotels played a critical role in the economy, providing
temporary accommodations to the mobile labor force, authorities began to
see them as a source of the Tenderloin's social problems. The city embarked
on a massive program to reform these buildings and, by extension, the
people who inhabited them.

Japanese entrepreneurs were crucial to these efforts. They operated the
majority of the lodging houses and hotels south of Yesler, as well as many
of the businesses serving migrant workers and other Tenderloin residents.
As the city began to enforce stricter building regulations, order upgrades,

and construct new hotels in the south end, Japanese leaders saw an opportunity to implement their own reform program and, in the process, insert themselves as cocreators of a new and modern Seattle. They joined the city in policing Tenderloin residents and formed a new Japantown that catered to families and other "respectable" people. For a time, their interests aligned with those of city officials. But this did not last.

Japanese leaders had a vision that went far beyond the Tenderloin. They began to expand their hotel business, recruiting Japanese families and married couples to open hotels outside of the south end and in northern white areas. It soon became clear to Japanese leaders, however, that the city did not consider them equal partners in shaping a new Seattle, but accepted them only for their economic role south of Yesler. The movement of Japanese hotel operators into white neighborhoods alarmed city officials, who sent the fire department to police and harass them. The very tools authorities had developed to control rowdy Tenderloin residents were now being deployed against Japanese hoteliers as a harsh and constant reminder of where they really belonged.

"A CITY OF HOTELS"

Seattle in 1910 was in the midst of dramatic transformation. The 1896 discovery of gold had lured thousands of men and women to the Pacific Northwest, where they passed through Seattle on their way to Alaska and the Yukon. The Klondike gold rush boosted Seattle's population; it also raised the city's national and international profile as the gateway to Alaska and the broader Pacific Rim. City leaders and boosters had capitalized on this image with the 1909 Alaska-Yukon-Pacific (AYP) Exposition, which promoted Seattle as a hub of international trade and commerce. In historian Shelley Lee's words, the AYP provided the city with a platform to distance itself from its "frontier past," and embrace its future as a "modern metropolis."[4] City engineers, meanwhile, implemented their own vision of modernity, pursuing a series of regrade projects that widened streets, flattened hills, and filled in tidelands. By the end of 1912, over one hundred million cubic tons of dirt had been moved to make way for the coming urban and commercial expansion.[5] A revamped streetcar system and railroad depot connected outlying areas with the city center, while factories and warehouses settled along the waterfront.[6]

Yet Seattle remained, more than ever, a city built around transient people and the seasonal migrations that guided their travels. Seattle's seasonal population, while always high, exploded with the arrival of gold seekers and adventurers who remained in the city during the winter months. Seattle streets were "thronged with idle men—men who have returned from the Klondike and Nome and who are waiting for spring to get back to those places," a local businessman grumbled in 1901.[7] Frank Bell, a white prospector who had returned from an unsuccessful stint in the Northwest Territories, warned a friend against coming to Seattle in the winter: "I told him that it was hard to get work here in the winter, for there are always a lot of men come out from the north every fall and spend the winter in Seattle."[8] Even after the Klondike frenzy died down in the first years of the twentieth century, Seattle continued to attract what local authorities called the "floating population," those who resided in the city seasonally before heading up north to Alaska.[9]

The need for short-term housing skyrocketed with the influx of Alaska-bound travelers. Existing hotel and lodging house operators found themselves "taxed to the utmost" as people crowded into rooms, onto floors, and inside basements. As demand began to outstrip existing housing stock, hotels, lodging houses, boardinghouses, and private rooms began to pop up around the city.[10] In 1896, one year before the gold rush reached Seattle, the city directory listed 139 hotels and lodging houses. By 1900, this number had jumped to 212.[11] No longer confined to the waterfront or the district south of Yesler, housing spread into many new neighborhoods of the city: Fremont, Capitol Hill, Ballard, Belltown. The gold rush brought other changes to Seattle's economy and geography, such as a booming retail business outfitting miners with clothing, supplies, and equipment, but housing continued to shape the physical landscape even after the craze died down. By 1905, Seattle's hotels and lodging houses numbered over four hundred. "The city lacks neither sufficient high-class hotel accommodations or facilities for handling those who are looking for a cheaper shelter," a local newspaper reported, dubbing Seattle "a city of hotels."[12]

Not all hotels were considered equal. While hotels of this period mostly served working people and those not looking for permanent housing, a range existed in the kind of guests hotels would and would not serve. In Seattle, the difference between "high-class" and "cheaper" accommodations mapped onto existing racial geographies. Yesler Way, the former Mill Street, continued to serve as the boundary line between white areas to the north and multiracial areas to the south. Residents referred to Yesler Way as "the line" or "the divide," reflecting its prominent role as a physical and symbolic border demarcating two distinct, and opposing, territories. Upon returning to Seattle, Frank Bell found a job at a cigar stand in the city's central business district and rented a room at a nearby hotel for $2.50 per week. Later, he moved to a rented room in a residential neighborhood before heading back to Nome, Alaska.[13] As a white man with a job in the off season, Bell could stay in most neighborhoods during this period. Others, however, did not enjoy the same degree of mobility within the city and were largely restricted south of Yesler Way.

The built environment both reflected and reproduced this hierarchical terrain. Much of the property "above the line," including the central business district and waterfront areas, had been rebuilt in the early 1890s following the Great Seattle Fire, which left the city in smoking ruins in 1889. The tragedy of the fire had presented a financial opportunity.[14] Envisioning these areas as key to the city's commercial future, investors from Seattle and San Francisco pumped money into redevelopment efforts, financing the construction of a new cityscape that featured grand four- to six-story buildings made of brick and stone, with up-to-date amenities like steam heat and elevators. Many of these new buildings became hotels that served a decidedly different class of people than those in the south end. Hotel operators marketed these new buildings as "first-class" to distinguish their businesses as physically modern and updated, and also to signal the kind of clientele they wished to attract.

The Diller Hotel, located on First Avenue and University Street, was one of Seattle's original first-class hotels. Built in 1890 by Leonard Diller, who migrated to Seattle from Ohio in 1876, the 80-by-111-foot brick building contained 140 guest rooms, each with private bath, hot water, and a telephone. The Diller also featured a hotel café, complimentary stationary, and an elevator that whisked guests up and down its four stories. A 1906 advertisement touted the hotel as "modern and first-class," situated in a convenient location "readily accessible to the new union depot and to the steamboat landings." Rates ranged from seventy-five cents to two dollars per day for a single room and up to three dollars per day for a larger suite.[15] The all-white clientele included tourists, male professionals, married couples, and individuals with steady jobs and incomes; many worked in the central business district.[16]

The Diller Hotel at First Avenue and University Street, 1905. The Diller was a typical "first-class" hotel north of Yesler Way. MOHAI, Anders Beer Wilse Collection, 1988.33.221.

The south end, on the other hand, looked almost the same following the fire. Though much of the district had also burned in 1889, the area was not considered as valuable commercially. It also did not have building restrictions like the ones implemented within the central business district, where the city had banned wood construction. Smaller and denser than uptown structures, south-end buildings were made mostly of wood and crowded

A typical block south of Yesler, 1905. MOHAI, PEMCO Webster & Stevens Collection, 1983.10.7546.

together on subdivided lots. Unlike the Diller's uniform façade, the buildings consisted of a mix of styles, colors, and materials reflecting the diversity of businesses that operated within—shops, cafés, saloons on the ground floor with guest rooms on the floors above. Walking up South Main Street between Fourth Avenue South and Fifth Avenue South, a newcomer in 1905 could choose from eight lodging houses, two restaurants, three saloons, and a handful of shops; the alley leading away from the street offered even cheaper accommodations, as well as a theater.[17]

The rooms offered in the south end differed greatly from those in the first-class hotels north of Yesler. Most of the south end's accommodations were lodging houses—a type of smaller hotel, often built in wood, with fewer rooms and almost no amenities.[18] Distinct from a boardinghouse, which included breakfast and dinner service, lodging houses offered only a space for sleeping, with the expectation that guests find their meals elsewhere. The price of most lodging houses started at ten cents a night. The "dime-beds" provided a bare cot or bunk bed in a large, windowless room, sometimes even a basement, packed with as many as 150 people. "Those who stayed in the dime-beds," recalled a lodging house operator, "brought their own bedding and slept in these silkworm type racks."[19] For twenty-five cents, a lodger could reserve a single room with a mattress, while fifty cents secured bedding and other furnishings. Most south-end lodging houses averaged fewer than twenty rooms to a building and one toilet per floor. Though room furnishings varied, they frequently consisted of a bed, a chair, and a pitcher of water for washing hands and faces.[20]

Though the loud signs and chaotic façades of the south end suggested a bustling street scene, much of the social, commercial, and sexual activity occurred inside and off the main streets. The district's layout enabled residents to move from place to place without ever going outside. Upper-floor hallways cut through subdivided buildings; doors led from one lodging house to the next. Stairways connected saloons, pool halls, and other ground-floor businesses to sleeping rooms above—a particularly useful arrangement for sex workers, giving them an easily accessible customer base. One south-end resident remembers, "Brothels were usually located in two- or three-story buildings, of which the first floor was occupied by a gambling den, liquor store, pool hall, restaurant."[21] Even the exits emptied out onto alleyways rather than main streets, offering clandestine entry into other buildings.

Lodging houses had become associated with prostitution, in particular. During the first decade of the twentieth century, debates raged in the city about the future of commercial sex work. "Open-town" advocates wanted prostitution to operate legally, within restricted areas, while closed-town advocates wanted it banned completely.[22] For a time, Seattle operated as an open town, with an official red-light district located south of Yesler; the neighborhood became known as the Tenderloin, after a similar district in San Francisco. Critics viewed lodging houses as clandestine spaces where illicit activity could go undetected, even outside of the restricted areas. Partly at issue was the structure of the lodging house, which had open interiors and no barriers between floors. "Stairways exist connecting bar-rooms with sleeping apartments, lodging, and rooming houses," fumed a local resident, "where prostitution . . . is carried on and liquor unlawfully disposed of."[23] Another declared, "A stairway leads directly from the Office Saloon to the floors above . . . and men and boys are allowed to visit the place freely."[24] As concern about Tenderloin crime and prostitution intensified, the lodging house became a focal point in calls for reform.

Historians often locate this era's reform impulse among middle-class white women who gained power and visibility in their calls to the clean up the city. John Putman, for example, argues that Seattle's pivot toward progressive-era reform originated with white women furious about the Tenderloin's condition, the city's corruption, and officials' open support of commercial sex work. Their sentiment, Putman explains, aligned with the interests of business elites, who viewed the Tenderloin as threatening to Seattle's "well-crafted image" as a modern hub of trade and commerce.[25] The Tenderloin had in fact begun to attract negative attention in the national press; one journal described the district as replete with "all kinds of open gambling games" and "other forms of vice . . . carrying on without interference."[26] Granted the right to vote in 1910, Seattle women spearheaded a campaign to recall the mayor, Hiram Gill, whose open-town policy had mobilized a broad coalition of voters. The recall effort proved successful, and Gill's replacement, George Dilling, began to crack down on vice and prostitution. He reorganized city departments, starting with the Seattle police, whose chief was charged with corruption and bribery just after the election. Dilling also beefed up the city's building regulations and empowered the fire department to conduct inspections and demand upgrades, starting with lodging houses south of Yesler.

But reform came from many different corners of the city and involved a more diverse cast of characters. While middle-class white women were quite visible during this period, in part because they helped oust the city's mayor, other groups also played a role in pushing Seattle into a new era. Unlike middle-class white women, for whom prostitution, gambling, and crime remained abstract concerns, Japanese residents lived in the Tenderloin and operated nearly all of the lodging houses and hotels south of Yesler. Japanese leaders had grown concerned about the state of the neighborhood and, in particular, the participation of their fellow countrymen in the district's underground economy. As the city began to adopt stricter building regulations and target lodging houses south of Yesler, many Japanese residents welcomed these actions, viewing them as an opportunity to clean up their district and implement their own program of reform.

Japanese participation in the housing business had started with their role as labor contractors. When the Japanese first started migrating to Seattle in the 1890s, they opened lodging houses in and around the Tenderloin that catered exclusively to Japanese laborers and those newly arrived from Japan. The businesses consisted of "cheap sleeping quarters, using the basements of buildings," such as the Fujii Hotel on Jackson Street, which charged fifteen cents for "the usual bunk racks."[27] Chojiro Fujii, the hotel's owner, would become a leader of Seattle's Japanese community; he also ran an employment agency on Washington Street.[28] The Great Northern Hotel, located on the corner of Second Avenue South and Jackson Street, also maintained connections with Japanese employment firms.[29] Places like the Fujii and the Great Northern figured centrally in maintaining the system of flexible labor that formed the foundation of the region's economy. As seasonal industries slowed their operations in the winter, Japanese laborers would return to Seattle and find temporary accommodations in Japanese-run lodging houses and hotels.

As the Tenderloin economy grew, some Japanese hoteliers turned their attention to prostitution. The south end had long been home to commercial sex work, with the lodging house often doubling as a brothel. And Japanese residents became well integrated into this industry as brothel owners, sex workers, and customers. Clustered along King and Jackson Streets, Japanese-owned brothels employed both Japanese and non-Japanese women. Tenderloin inhabitant Kunizo Maeno remembered visiting "a corner . . . where there were a mixture of Japanese and Irish girls."[30] Another early Japanese resident recalled "many women . . . engaged in prostitution."[31] Among the infamous establishments of the time was the Tokio, a three-story frame building which housed a saloon on the ground floor and seventy-three rooms on the top two floors above. Japanese women who engaged in commercial sex work were, as historian and activist Yuji Ichioka has argued, "among the pioneers of Japanese immigrant society."[32] Along with employment agencies, brothels formed the foundation of Seattle's first Japanese district and laid the groundwork for future Japanese involvement in the hotel industry.

As these businesses grew more visible, though, so too did their reputation as hotbeds of crime, vice, and other illicit activity. In 1905, Japanese proprietors ran forty-two lodging houses south of Yesler Way; by 1909, the number reached seventy-two.[33] Newspaper articles pushed sensational tales of knife fights, brawls, and dead bodies turning up in dark rooms.[34] In 1904 police busted a West Coast burglary ring that "had regular headquarters in a room in a Japanese lodging house in the lower part of the city."[35] Stories of Japanese smugglers moving drugs and people through a vast network of alleys and

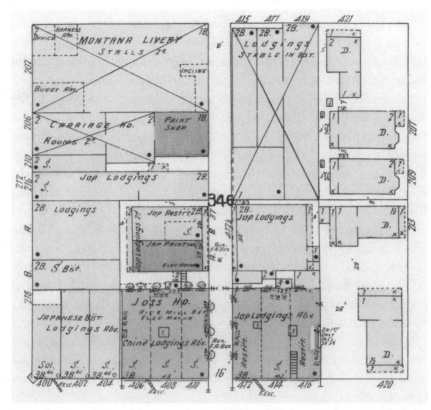

This detail from a 1905 map shows part of the block bounded by South Main and Washington Streets and Fourth and Fifth Avenues South. It illustrates the high density of the district as well as the racial narrative told by the mapmaker, who singles out Japanese businesses and marks them as "Jap" spaces. *Sanborn Fire Insurance Map from Seattle, King County, Washington*, 1904–5.

inside passageways scandalized the public. "Celestials smuggled across the border and found in Japanese lodging houses," screamed one newspaper headline. "The Chinese were taken direct from the sloop to the lodging house and have not been seen on the streets."[36] Health department raids of Japanese hotels further confirmed their unsavory image. Reporting on the arrest of a Japanese hotel proprietor for overcrowding, a local newspaper declared that "almost all cases of contagious maladies when traced to their source are found to come directly . . . from such surroundings." The message was clear: Japanese hotels were now "breeding places" for all of the city's worst problems, a danger to public safety and a threat officials should "purge."[37]

The unwholesome reputation of Seattle's Japanese district deeply troubled local Japanese leaders, as well as government officials in Japan. Historian Eiichiro Azuma notes that the Japanese government kept close tabs on its communities around the world, particularly in the United States. Japan had ascended to global power following its victory against Russia in the Russo-Japanese War of 1904–5, which inaugurated a period of Japanese imperial expansion across Asia and the Pacific world. The government viewed its overseas citizenry as representatives of a modern, civilized Japanese empire and monitored their status through a variety of channels, including a network of Japanese associations that had spread throughout the West Coast.[38] Of particular concern were the Japanese laborers who had arrived the decade prior and who lived and worked in Seattle's south end. Many Japanese officials believed that the workers' unkempt appearance, disorderly neighborhoods, and unsavory forms of sociability—such as gambling, sex work, and fraternization with Chinese people—fueled nativist claims against the Japanese and, more importantly, endangered Japan's standing internationally.[39]

In 1908, the Japanese government dispatched a representative, Secretary Masanao Hanihara, to investigate the activities of all Japanese communities along the West Coast. As early as the 1890s, the Japanese consul in Vancouver, BC, had reported on the prostitution and gambling that pervaded Seattle's Japanese district. Hanihara had already visited Seattle in 1906 and described the Japanese standard of living as "low and unhealthy." Two years later, he was disappointed to find that little had changed. In a report back to the Japanese government, he summed up the district in one word: "disgusting." Laborers and small business operators crowded together in "one disorderly section of the city, forming a sort of irregular and indecent Japanese town next to the lower class Chinese." Other offenses included "shabby houses," "dubious looking posters," and "paper lanterns hung shamelessly at doors." The neighborhood's layout also disturbed Hanihara. The "backs of houses lead to obscure roads," he reported, "where at night obscene sights and words are frequently glimpsed." Overall, he concluded, the district was "indeed far from a community of civilized people."[40]

Until that point, local Japanese leaders could do little to change the district. Some had even profited handsomely from the Tenderloin's economy of commercial sex, gambling, and entertainment. But changes were afoot that created an opportunity and an impetus for reform.

In the early 1900s backlash against the Japanese presence along the West Coast reached a fever pitch, mirroring anti-Asian movements against Chinese laborers three decades prior. As the United States government considered a similar exclusion law, Japan intervened. Concerned that its citizens overseas were being subjected to the same treatment as the Chinese, Japan entered into a series of diplomatic negotiations from 1907 to 1908 known as the Gentlemen's Agreement. Japan agreed to stop issuing passports to laborers bound for the United States in exchange for the city of San Francisco allowing Japanese students to attend public schools, from which they had been banned. While the agreement resembled previous anti-Chinese exclusion laws, there was one key difference. Eager to appease Japan, now a global power, President Theodore Roosevelt agreed to allow Japanese women to reunite with their husbands in the United States.[41] As the migration of Japanese male laborers declined, in their place rose a Japanese middle class populated by married couples and families with children.

With the arrival of women and families, Japanese leaders began to think seriously about changing the conditions of their neighborhood. And here, the city's plan for the Tenderloin created an opening for them. As part of his promise to clean up the city, Dilling began to target Tenderloin lodging houses, going block by block to order upgrades and vacate residents. On February 10, 1912, the fire department declared the entire block from 73 to 85 Yesler Way "unsafe to human life" and ordered all buildings vacated.[42] Over the next three days, inspectors temporarily closed the Seattle Hotel on Jackson Street and permanently shut down a basement lodging house on First Avenue South and Main Street because of the "insufficiency of exits, the arrangement of the rooms and passageways, the lack of ventilation, the condition of the wooden floors, and the lack of light."[43] Two days after that, inspectors targeted the 400 block of Yesler Way, vacating the basements, while allowing the top floors to remain open if owners installed fire escapes and replaced wooden floors with concrete.[44] By the end of 1912, fire and building inspectors had vacated or ordered significant upgrades to twenty-four buildings in Seattle's south end.

Japanese leaders accepted these actions, in part because they weren't targeted. The initial inspections and mandatory upgrades involved the property owners, not the lessees or business owners operating within the buildings. At the time, Japanese community members did not own many of the buildings and so viewed the closures, upgrades, and improved safety

measures as a welcome development. They even began to actively participate in the city's crackdown on the Tenderloin. The Japanese Association of
North America, together with the Japanese consul in Seattle, supplied US
federal immigration authorities with the names of brothel owners, gamblers, and Japanese women working (or thought to be working) as prostitutes.[45] Though it's unclear if the immigration officials ever responded, these
actions on the part of Seattle's Japanese leadership reflected a desire to rid
the community of those they considered troublesome, which aligned with
the city's own agenda within the Tenderloin.

The city's reform of the south end involved more than just upgrading
existing buildings. Authorities opened up land just east of the Tenderloin
through regrade projects, which stimulated new hotel construction. The new
"first-class" hotels caught the eye of local Japanese elites, many of them
former labor contractors whose businesses foundered after the Gentlemen's
Agreement cut off the flow of transpacific labor. They pivoted to other commercial pursuits, investing in real estate and using their influence to build
a new and modern Japantown, leaving the raucous world of the Tenderloin
behind. Though located only a few blocks from the Tenderloin, the new Japantown would function almost as if it were a world away, catering to families
and "respectable" people. Here, as well, Japanese leaders found their interests in sync with those of the city.

FIRST-CLASS HOTELS AND THE NEW JAPANTOWN

From 1906 to 1912, Seattle pursued a series of regrade projects that recon-
figured city streets to make way for urban expansion. Historian Matthew
Klingle points out that the regrade also functioned as de facto slum clearance, expelling poor and vulnerable residents from commercially valuable
land.[46] The 1907 regrade of Jackson Street targeted a portion of the Tenderloin, which stood in the way of industrial expansion to the south. Reshaping
this area rid the city of the Tenderloin's many "shacks and flimsy wooden
structures"; it also created opportunities for real estate investment.[47] Businesspeople quickly bought up property in the regrade district, valuable
because of its proximity to the new railroad terminal on Fourth Avenue
South and King Street. Japanese investors also eyed the area. In 1906 a group
of Japanese elites, including Charles Tetsuo Takahashi and Matajiro Tsu-
kuno, joined two white investors to form the Cascade Investment Company

with $50,000 capital.[48] Between 1906 and 1910 Cascade purchased seven parcels of property in the regrade area, six blocks east of the old Japanese district. By 1910, the Cascade Investment Company had shelled out over $250,000 to build the foundations of the new Japantown, which included hotels and other buildings for Japanese commercial and social life.[49]

Unlike the drinking, gambling, and commercial sex that pervaded the old district, the new Japantown showcased reputable forms of sociability and entertainment. The Nippon Kan Theater epitomized this move toward middle-class respectability. In 1906 the Cascade Investment Company bought two lots on the corner of Washington and Maynard, and in 1909 it financed construction of the Nippon Kan, a three-story brick building that would serve as a social and cultural "cornerstone" of the emerging Japanese middle class.[50] A large stage and auditorium on the first floor hosted performances and activities: classical drama and dance, poetry readings, Japanese film, judo demonstrations. "Nippon Kan Hall was where the Japanese all gathered for entertainment," remembers Japantown resident Shigeko Uno. "It was really a lot of fun, clean fun, where we could meet our friends, and also be entertained by them."[51] The theater provided a much-needed space for Japanese cultural practice; it also stood in stark contrast to the brothels and gambling houses Japanese leaders had attempted to shut down.

In addition to investing in property, Japanese businesspeople leased hotels in the regrade district. The newly constructed buildings resembled uptown hotels like the Diller, rising four to six stories tall and featuring modern amenities like elevators and telephones. The Northern Pacific (NP), on Sixth Avenue South between Main and Jackson Streets, was one of Japantown's original "first-class" hotels. P. J. Murphy, a white businessman, financed construction of the NP Hotel in 1914 and recruited Niroku Shitamae, a Japanese man from Hiroshima, to run it. Shitamae had arrived to the United States in 1907; according to his daughter, Yukiko Fujii, he "wanted to work with whites as much as possible," so he took odd jobs at department stores and restaurants until he connected with Murphy.[52] Shitamae appointed his brother, Shihei, comanager and together the two operated the NP until the outbreak of World War II.

The NP Hotel's design immediately distinguished it from the other structures south of Yesler Way. A brick building measuring 120 feet long by 60 feet wide, the NP occupied one whole city lot and stood six stories high, making it one of the largest buildings in the area. It boasted "fireproof" construction, with a sprinkler system and tin casing around the exterior. While older hotels, built before the strict fire codes, had often added fire escapes leading out of existing guest rooms, the architect of the NP designed each floor around a hallway with windows and fire escapes on each end. Unlike the smaller lodging houses that rarely possessed even a manager's office, the NP featured an expansive lobby and reception area with a marble foyer and powder room. For fifty cents a night, guests could stay in a room equipped with a bed and sheets, a sink, a closet, and a clothes press. Each floor contained twenty-six rooms, two public bathrooms, and a private suite with its own toilet facilities.[53] Amenities included an elevator, a telephone, and chauffeur service to take guests to and from the pier.

By 1920, Japanese businessmen operated half a dozen first-class hotels resembling the NP within Japantown, including the Astor, the Panama, the US, and the Puget Sound, one of the largest Japanese hotels on the West Coast. Together, these structures formed the foundation of the new, modern Japanese district. The hoteliers deliberately adopted the term "first-class" to describe their new businesses. In their eyes, though, "first-class" did not mean only white guests, as it did at the Diller Hotel and other uptown establishments; they expanded the definition to include Japanese professionals, Japanese families, and whites of all economic classes. Yukiko Fujii, daughter of NP operator Niroku Shitamae, remembers her father's hotel as a "first-class place" that housed "mainly whites" as well as members of the Japanese "intelligentsia."[54] The 1920 census corroborates her memory, in part, listing the residents as white workers and Japanese professionals and their families. The Astor, the Puget Sound, and the Panama all housed similar residents during this period.[55]

Overseeing the creation of this new, respectable hotel business was the Japanese Hotel Operators Association (JHOA). Formed in February 1910 with Chojiro Fujii, the labor contractor turned hotelier, as its first president, the JHOA worked under the Japanese Association of North America, sending a representative to present at the association's monthly meetings. During its early years the JHOA had a range of functions, many of them social and economic. Members paid dues according to the size of their hotel and attended approximately three meetings per year. Members discussed issues such as regulating hotel prices and advertising opportunities; they also hosted New Year's parties and planned banquets and celebrations for visiting Japanese dignitaries. JHOA leadership also stayed informed on changes in municipal policy and translated all new ordinances and building codes into Japanese.

The JHOA attempted to establish the new "first-class" hotels as hubs of transpacific trade and travel. As Shelley Lee has shown, Seattle's commercial relations with Japan figured centrally in the city's early-twentieth-century image as an urban metropolis, enabling boosters, businessmen, and local politicians to claim a cosmopolitan identity as "gateway to the Orient."[56] The 1910s marked a high point in this "cordial friendship," with goods to and from Japan increasingly passing through Seattle ports.[57] In one of its first actions as an organization, the JHOA entered negotiations with Nippon Yusen Kaisha (NYK), a global shipping company that provided passenger and commercial service between Seattle and Yokohama.[58] The NYK appointed JHOA hotels as official ticket dealers, with some even operating as travel agencies, arranging transportation and preparing immigration paperwork for those voyaging across the Pacific.[59]

Like its parent organization, the JHOA also had another purpose: to ensure that Japanese hoteliers under its watch adhered to the law. And this is what made the JHOA most valuable to the city as it began to ramp up enforcement of building codes and the policing of south-end residents. The JHOA maintained a "100 percent law-abiding policy." They accepted only members who adhered to city laws and would not violate the "good reputation and trust of our organization." In the early 1920s, a prostitution scandal in Portland prompted a stern warning from the Seattle JHOA, reiterating its policy to "drop from its membership roll those law-breakers who refuse to abide by [warnings]" and "clear out law-breakers by joining with police if necessary."[60] In a sense, the JHOA implemented the city's reformist agenda, doing the work of policing its own members and businesses and enforcing municipal codes.

The city accepted, even welcomed, the creation of a new Japantown south of Yesler, as it aligned with the city's priorities of cleaning up the Tenderloin and building a more modern south-end cityscape. Japanese participation in the hotel business was useful to the city both economically and socially, particularly when the JHOA and other Japanese leaders began to police their own residents and enforce municipal codes and laws. But building a new Japantown and operating first-class hotels south of Yesler was only the beginning for Japanese leaders. What they envisioned was a more ambitious plan: to open hotels all over the city and in the process elevate their role as cocreators in a new, modern Seattle, as they had done in the south end. They would soon find out, however, that the city did not see things the same way.

BEYOND JAPANTOWN

In the early morning hours of February 9, 1919, a fire broke out on the second floor of the Russell House, a three-story frame building formerly known as the Tokio. Nobody really knew how it started. The fire department chalked it up to "carelessness," a cigarette butt thrown into the trash or someone smoking in bed. Lodgers suspected arson. The night clerk, an elderly Japanese man, had patrolled the building thirty minutes before the fire and, finding "everything alright," retired to his room. The flames burned slowly at first, creating a plume of smoke that wafted down the hallway and seeped under doorways. Many failed to wake up, which the police attributed to "much use of alcohol" earlier that evening. The small fire soon transformed into a conflagration that threatened to engulf the entire block. Flames spread up the stairs to the third floor and into the adjoining building before someone finally rang the fire gong, rousing residents from their beds. Trapped in their rooms, lodgers began to throw themselves out windows and onto the alley down below. Two people burned to death in the hallway as they tried to escape. The fire department arrived three minutes later at a grisly scene, with the ground "strewn with bodies of the dead and injured." After containing the fire, they entered the building and began to collect the remains of the dead. Among the six deceased were two "colored soldiers," a white miner, and a Filipino man. Four later died in the hospital.[61]

The owner of the business, a Japanese man named I. Hirota, had adhered to fire codes—so strictly, in fact, that inspectors could not find one violation. But the fire department perceived a danger that went beyond the Russell House, or even Japantown, where the blaze occurred. After completing an investigation and presenting their findings to the mayor, fire officials initiated a citywide sweep of hotels and lodging houses that overwhelmingly targeted the Japanese. The Russell House stood as only one of hundreds of Japanese housing establishments spread throughout the city, a potential hazard on every city block from Dearborn to Denny. Inspectors started with buildings near the Russell House but soon widened their radius, venturing far beyond Japantown to the central business district, Belltown, and Capitol Hill, doling out fines and ordering upgrades to nearly one hundred hotels and lodging houses operated by Japanese people. The buildings ranged from small frame lodgings like the Russell House to six-story brick structures lining the waterfront. "Flophouses" and "first-class" hotels alike came under scrutiny as potential threats to the public. By the end of 1919, seventy-eight Japanese hotel operators had paid out nearly $1,000 in total penalties for violations of city fire laws.[62]

As the Russell House fire and ensuing inspections make clear, Japanese people had spread well outside of the south end by 1919. Japanese hotel operators attained an astounding degree of geographic mobility during the 1910s, but the notion of a geographically contained Japantown has persisted in both scholarly literature and public memory. While Yesler Way remained the primary boundary that split the city into two distinct territories, Japanese hotel operators complicated this divide, expanding into the central business district, the waterfront, Capitol Hill, and other neighborhoods. By 1920, Japanese residents operated 279 hotels in Seattle, nearly half of which stood beyond the borders of Japantown.[63] Once confined to lodging houses in the Tenderloin, the Japanese now operated nearly one quarter of the hotels in Seattle, including such first-class establishments as the St. Charles and the Diller Hotel.

Two major factors influenced this shift in the housing business. The first was the growth of Seattle's defense-related economy in the context of World War I. The shipbuilding industry, in particular, expanded dramatically during this time, as did related industries such as foundries, boilermaking, lumber, and dock work. Tens of thousands of people arrived in Seattle in the mid-1910s to fill the thirty-five thousand jobs that had opened up in the city's booming war economy, sparking a severe housing shortage not seen since the days of the gold rush.[64] The JHOA sensed an opportunity to "develop the hotel industry" in Seattle.[65] In 1916, the organization created a business club with the explicit purpose of recruiting new members and opening more hotels.[66]

At the same time, the hotel business in Seattle had become an increasingly undesirable occupation for whites. The building codes and heightened enforcement passed in the wake of the 1911 mayoral recall created growing financial burdens on property owners, who now had to foot the bill for safety and building improvements. While much of the initial attention had

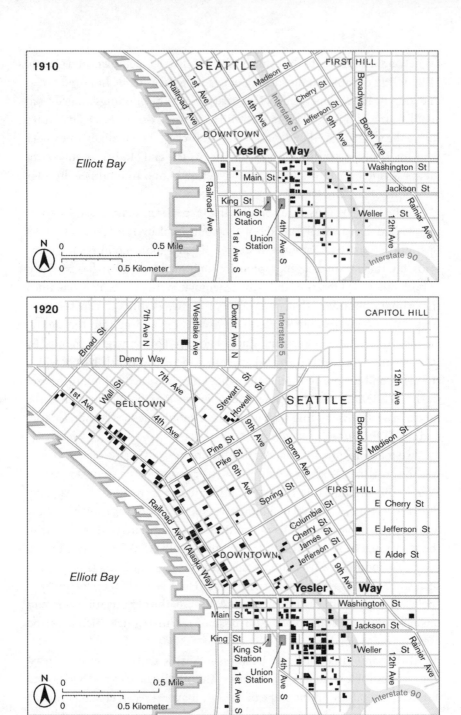

From 1910 (top) to 1920 (bottom), Japanese-operated hotels in Seattle increased in both number and geographic spread. By 1920, nearly half were located north of Yesler Way.

been focused on the Tenderloin, municipal agencies began assessing buildings all over the city and putting property owners on notice for required upgrades. After initiating a flurry of unsuccessful lawsuits and legal actions against the city, alleging that the new regulations put them under unreasonable financial strain, property owners changed tactics and began to require their lessees to foot the bill for improvements.[67] Owners of the Yukon Investment Company building, for example, responded to a list of thirteen city-mandated upgrades by declaring, "We have nothing to do with the making of any repairs or alterations whatever which may be required upon the buildings," directing officials "to these lessees regarding any work which may be required."[68] Other owners inserted clauses into their written contracts holding lessees accountable for any repairs ordered by the city.[69] With few legal regulations around leasing and what property owners could and could not require, lessees were forced to pay or find others to take over their leases.

White hotel operators left the business in large numbers during this period, seeking other jobs or opportunities. This left a void in the industry that Japanese residents were eager to fill. From 1910 to 1920, over one hundred hotel leases changed hands from white to Japanese management, bringing the total number of Japanese hotels in Seattle to 279.[70] By 1920, Japanese operators ran nearly as many hotels in the northern district as they did south of Yesler Way, reflecting a stark transformation in the hotel business and the racial geography of Seattle. Some evidence exists that white hotel operators deliberately targeted the Japanese to take over unfavorable leases. In a 1921 letter between the city's building and fire departments, an official described one such situation at the Congress Hotel, which faced thirteen city-mandated building improvements. According to the official, the hotel operator "has been negotiating for a re-lease of [their] hotel to some Japanese for hotel purposes, and that the lease will make it incumbent on the lessee to make the alterations called for by the city."[71] The scenario's appearance in official communication, with no response or pushback, suggests that it was not an uncommon one.

Japanese hotel operators had their own reasons for pursuing this business, despite its risks. Many of the Japanese hotel operators north of Yesler Way were not from the Japanese elite or wealthy classes—former labor contractors or businessmen, like those who tended to own and operate Japantown's first-class hotels. Those who moved north were mostly families or married couples who had few other options for a stable life, as employment discrimination kept nearly all Japanese people out of professional or well-paying jobs in the city. Operating hotels offered a way to make a good living without the physical demands or poor conditions of hauling lumber, building railroads, or other jobs in manual labor. Among the urban businesses open to Japanese management, hotels had the lowest upfront costs because the leases often included furnishings and bedding.[72] Hotel management was also particularly attractive to married couples, who could share the work rather than pay outside employees to clean or manage the office. It also gave families a place of residence, as all but the wealthiest hotel operators lived in their hotels. Still, running a hotel required hard work and grueling hours; some referred to it as a twenty-four-hour-a-day job. "I did everything from chambermaid work to being a porter, clerk, bellboy, and telephone operator," recalled a Japanese hotel operator, "[and] I continued a very irregular life until midnight every day, getting up, going to sleep, and getting up again."[73]

In family-run hotels, many children worked to help their parents. Frank Yamasaki's parents operated a hotel in Belltown, a fifty-six-room structure on First Avenue and Cedar that served mostly white male workers. With his father busy on another job, Frank and his mother negotiated the lease and set up the business, just the two of them. When his father joined them later on, Frank was still the one who dealt with the customers. "I more or less had to run it," he recalled, "because my parents couldn't speak English."[74] Dorothy Sato remembered cleaning the long staircase in her parents' hotel, "to help my mother and father."[75] Victor Ikeda was not expected to help as much around the hotel, noting that "my sisters and mother did a lot of that."[76] Gendered expectations around labor shaped boys' and girls' experiences quite differently in the hotel business, as they did for men and women. Victor's mother, in fact, ran the hotel by herself in addition to taking care of the children, while his father worked elsewhere, a common arrangement for many married couples in the business.

Moving north required compromises that Japanese hotel operators did not have to make in the south end. In the north, many property owners required their Japanese lessees to sign lease agreements that contained racial clauses restricting occupancy to whites only. In the lease agreement with K. Tarumoto, for example, owners of the Cascade Hotel building on Howell Street in Belltown declared their property a "white man's hotel" and limited hotel residency to "persons of the Caucasian race and not of any other race."[77] Others required Japanese hotel operators to employ a white

Family outside of the Benton Hotel, located at 1420 Sixth Avenue in the central business district, c. 1940. Japanese hotels were often run by families like this one. Courtesy of the Okano Family Collection, Densho.

desk clerk or manager to interact with the white guests, so, as the Hillcrest Hotel building's owners put it, "only a person of the Caucasian or white race shall be known to the public as operating and conducting business at said leased premises."[78] The owners of the Columbia Hotel building in the central business district imposed the most extreme restrictions in this regard. In the lease agreement, the owners forbade their lessee, S. Ishikawa, from residing on or even stepping foot onto the premises, with exceptions allowed if the white manager quit "unexpectedly" or if Ishikawa was entering the building in a menial capacity to "fire the boiler, clean the halls, remove the garbage and send out the laundry."[79] As these lease agreements made clear, Japanese hotel operators' movement into the north did not mean they were welcome in any way, nor that racial restrictions had loosened. Japanese hotel operators were accepted only for their economic services and to perform the crucial labor of housing the city's workforce, which whites were no longer willing to do.

Property owners were not the only ones to view Japanese hotel operators with suspicion. The arrival of Japanese hotels in white neighborhoods also put city authorities on edge. The change disturbed what had been a foundational division of territory between north and south, white and nonwhite. It was in this context that the fire department began to assert control, embarking on a campaign of harassment and surveillance targeting Japanese hotels as hazardous spaces threatening the white public. The department was aided by the heightened power Dilling granted it following the purge and reform of the city government. In 1911, Dilling approved an ordinance creating a new fire prevention team and giving them more power than any other municipal agency, including the police, to access buildings. Under the law, fire officials could enter buildings "at any and all times," monitor interior environments, and order a range of punitive measures, including arrests.[80] Further, they could do so at will, with no need for a warrant or legal justification. All that mattered was their own individual assessment of fire risk, and even then, records show that their actions were rarely questioned by the city.

The fire department's campaign of harassment started after the Russell House fire of 1919. Before this, there's no real evidence that fire officials singled out the Japanese. While Japanese hoteliers do appear in fire records before this time, they don't show up in a systematic way that suggests profiling or targeting. The fire at the Russell House appears to have alerted fire officials to the possibility of using fire and safety codes to police racial boundaries and extract fines and fees from Japanese hotel operators. In the fire's aftermath officials began targeting Japanese hotels all over the city, in a trend that persisted through the next decade. The fire department issued fifty-eight total fire code violations in 1920; of those, fifty-one involved Japanese hotels. The pattern continued the next year, with Japanese hotel operators receiving fifty-two out of the sixty-seven total fire code violations issued in the entire city.[81] Although it is true that Japanese operators ran a large number of the city's hotels, they did not account for the majority.

In the rare cases that fire inspectors cited white hotel operators, the latter often received less harsh penalties than their Japanese counterparts. In late November and early December 1923, fire inspectors visited two hotels just weeks apart: the White Star Hotel, operated by K. Watanabe, and the Loma Hotel, operated by F. Jacobson. Both hotels appeared in the violation book for the same offense: red safety lights not burning and rubbish left in the hallways. The fire inspectors let Jacobson off with a warning, while Watanabe received a twenty-dollar fine.[82] The same disparity occurred in 1925: obstructions in hallways resulted in a five-dollar fine for J. Munson of the New Vendome Hotel, and a ten-dollar fine for F. Katagi of the New England Hotel.[83] Disproportionate fines and penalties amounted to a kind of racial tax for Japanese hotel operators. A revenue-generating opportunity for the city, it echoed earlier forms of discriminatory taxation such as the Foreign Miners' Tax of 1850, levied against Chinese miners by the state of California during the gold rush.[84] Beyond financial costs, the impromptu inspections created undue stress and anxiety for Japanese operators and their families, who knew quite well the power of the fire department to curtail or even end their business operations and livelihoods. Harumi Guiberson, daughter of a Japanese hotelier in Seattle, recalled that her father feared the fire department, adding that the whole family "held their breath" during inspections.[85]

In many ways, the harassment of Japanese hotel operators resembled other forms of anti-Asian policing taking place in cities across North America. In the late nineteenth century, Chinese laundries had faced similar discriminatory treatment. Historians Nayan Shah and Mary Lui have shown that authorities targeted these businesses because they operated in many different areas of the city; in San Francisco, for instance, nine out of ten Chinese laundries were located outside of Chinatown. This mobility sparked fears around race mixing and the presence of Chinese laundry workers in white neighborhoods. In the popular press, cultural narratives portrayed Chinese laundries as fronts for criminal operations and as vectors of disease.[86] City officials, motivated by the potential exposure of white families and neighborhoods to these nefarious influences, targeted Chinese laundries with inspection and even closure under the guise of protecting the white public. As discussed in chapter 1, a similar phenomenon occurred in Seattle during the 1880s, when Chinese laundries began to operate above Yesler Way. In 1885, a group of white residents submitted a petition calling for greater regulation of the laundry business and limiting licenses to "Americans only."[87] In response, the city passed a new law that required all laundry operators to obtain a health inspection certificate in order to continue running their business, or to open a new one. Records show that this law disproportionately burdened Chinese operators and led to the closure of nearly every Chinese laundry in the northern district.[88]

Fire had clear parallels with disease: both could spread uncontrollably through neighborhoods and put white residents at risk. This is why the fire department was less concerned about Japanese hotels operating in the Tenderloin. There, hotels were already located in a bounded area, serving urban residents whom the city largely considered expendable. Once Japanese hoteliers began moving across the line and into the northern districts, they were no longer restricted to the world of the Tenderloin and were present instead among respectable whites, as opposed to the poor or transient whites of the south end. As Japanese hotels expanded geographically, they became a greater threat to the city. Though the Russell House fire originated in a Japantown hotel, inspectors did not respond by targeting buildings of the same location or size. The went after hotels under Japanese management. They connected one isolated fire with the broader problem of Japanese mobility and disruptions of the racial order.

The policing and harassment of Japanese hotels by the Seattle fire department took shape within a growing local, regional, and national debate about the future of Japanese people in US society. Heightened anti-Japanese sentiment in the city and an economic depression following World War I both contributed to increasing hostility against Seattle's Japanese community. Seattle historian Marie Wong notes that the House Committee on Immigration and Naturalization held local hearings in cities along the Pacific Coast in 1920 to discuss the "problem" of Japanese immigration and, in particular, the role of Japanese business activity in urban areas. Each city was required to provide a census of Japanese businesses and to discuss the economic impact on white businesses in the same industries.[89] Anti-Japanese leagues and actions cropped up across the American West, including in Seattle, which saw a revival of the anti-Japanese movement, this one directed more at small business operators and families than the laborers of years past. In 1919, the local Anti-Japanese League submitted a petition to Seattle's city council demanding that hotel licenses be restricted to "only citizens of the United States."[90]

For Japanese leaders, the fire department's campaign painfully clarified the limits of their own reform project. They had pursued the hotel business as a way of cultivating a new image and shaping a respectable, family-oriented Japanese social and commercial life. A central aspect of this reform movement involved greater interaction with whites through the establishment of "first-class" hotels in Japantown and the movement of Japanese families into the northern districts. But these actions did not confer respectability, as leaders had hoped. City authorities did not welcome their presence in white neighborhoods, viewing them instead as a problem to be managed and a danger to be contained. Further, Japanese people's geographic mobility rendered them even more vulnerable to racial violence and hostility. "We were often insulted by whites calling us Jap," remembered a Japanese hotel operator; the hotelier hired a white clerk "to keep our faces out of public view as much as possible."[91] In another instance, when a Japanese couple took over management of an uptown hotel, one of the white residents declared, "I decided to stay for a few days though I felt inferior for doing it, as if I were living in the slums."[92]

Japanese participation in the hotel business failed to bring them into a position of equality with whites, but it did give them advantages over Asians who lacked access to the same opportunities. Despite their efforts to move into northern districts, the real power of Japanese businesspeople remained in the racialized economy south of Yesler Way, where they continued to serve seasonal workers and other migrants who passed through the city. As Filipino laborers began to arrive in the 1920s, they encountered a world dominated by Japanese businesses, managers, and foremen. The relationship between these two groups would grow increasingly complex as the Great Depression put new and urgent pressures on all south-end residents.

CHAPTER 5

Labor, Intimacy, and the Depression

BEN RINONOS ARRIVED IN SEATTLE IN JUNE OF 1928, AFTER A long steamship journey across the Pacific Ocean. Originally from La Union, a northern province in the Ilocos region of the Philippines where his parents operated a small farm, Rinonos had decided to come to the United States to continue his education. Rinonos did not travel alone; his cramped quarters in steerage were shared with a group of friends, all young, single men from his hometown looking to earn a wage or attend school in the Pacific Northwest. Upon arrival in Seattle, Rinonos remembers, "we took a chance to get a taxi and then tell the taxi man to bring us to Chinatown in front of a hotel . . . so that's what we did." With his cash supply dwindling, he headed out to find a job. He applied for work at a nearby employment agency, which dispatched him to a labor camp on the outskirts of the city, where he changed railroad ties for about a month before returning to Seattle. Back in his hotel, Rinonos heard about calls for workers in the Alaska salmon canneries, and he again applied for a job, this time a three-month stint up north in Petersburg. As the salmon runs died down and the cannery slowed its operation, Rinonos found work picking hops in Yakima, where he remained until late fall. After the harvest, he returned to Seattle to wait out the winter.[1]

Anacleto Corpuz, also from a farming background in La Union, followed a similar pattern of migration and residency. Corpuz came over in 1928 as a twenty-one-year-old, eager to start his new life in Seattle, pursuing a college education and career as a teacher. A friend who already resided in the city met Corpuz at the docks and took him "directly to Chinatown." Without enough money for his own room, Corpuz shared a bed with his friend in the Welcome Annex Hotel south of Yesler Way. When the call came out for cannery jobs, Corpuz joined the thousands of other Filipinos heading up to Alaska and then on to Yakima to work in the hop fields. As winter approached, Corpuz returned to the district south of Yesler Way, whiling away the rainy days and cold nights in the cabarets, theaters, and dance halls before heading out again in the spring. After a few years, he met a Japanese farmer in Seattle who was looking for workers to help harvest his strawberry crop on Bainbridge Island. Corpuz hopped on a ferry to Winslow, where he picked berries for the next two months alongside other Filipino men as well as Indigenous women who had migrated down from British Columbia for the season.[2]

In many ways, Rinonos's and Corpuz's stories of arrival and seasonal migration around the region echo the experiences of those who came before them. The temporary jobs in canning and agriculture that took them up and down the Northwest Coast; Seattle's role as a center of employment and temporary housing; their residency in south-end hotels during the off months; and their integration into the racially mixed world of migratory labor—all of this shows a city fully built to accommodate a mobile labor force, the result of decades of previous migrations that brought thousands of laborers through Seattle to fill the same kinds of jobs Rinonos and Corpuz found themselves slotted into. But in just a few short years, much of this world would be gone.

Rinonos and Corpuz arrived in Seattle during the decline of the extractive and seasonal industries that had dominated the broader regional economy. Historian Carlos Schwantes argues that the Great Depression dealt the extractive industries across the Pacific Northwest a "severe blow."[3] Lumber jobs plummeted during the early 1930s; construction projects stalled, which brought down the demand for lumber and other wood products.[4] Farming had also declined in the region, leaving only pockets of agricultural activity around Puget Sound.[5] Salmon canning remained a reliable source of work, but it only lasted a few months and offered very little opportunity; the industry was dominated at the managerial level by Japanese foremen and employment agents. This left Filipino laborers like Rinonos and Corpuz with few options in their search for jobs, forcing them to travel ever greater distances to secure work and leaving them in a highly precarious financial position, made worse by the economic crisis of the Great Depression and the vicious anti-Filipino racism and violence that pervaded the West Coast.

Among the diminishing opportunities, agriculture and salmon canning relied the most on Filipino labor. The Immigration Act of 1924, which established immigration quotas based on country of origin, had largely cut off the global labor supply into the United States. Filipinos remained exempt from immigration restrictions because of their status as US nationals, a category created as the result of US colonization of the Philippines following the Spanish-American War and Philippine-American War, which together lasted from 1898 to 1902.[6] Filipinos were not citizens, but carried US passports and could enter into the United States (until the mid-1930s), making them desirable as low-wage labor in an era of restricted migration from both Asia and Europe. Beginning in the 1920s, therefore, the Filipino population in the Pacific Northwest boomed, increasing from approximately one thousand in 1920 to nearly 3,500 just ten years later.[7]

Their employment in these two seasonal industries put them into frequent contact with the Japanese, as business owners and managers, and Indigenous peoples, as fellow migrant laborers. A complex set of social relations developed among the three groups during the declining years of the resource-based economy. As colonized peoples, Filipinos shared more in common with Indigenous laborers than they did the Japanese, who had ascended to a relatively powerful position, running the small businesses that catered to and employed migrant workers, transients, and other racialized populations residing in and around Seattle. Japanese elites, in particular, viewed themselves as representatives of a powerful Japanese empire, racially superior to other Asians.[8] Filipino laborers encountered Japanese residents most often as bosses, landlords, and employers. For Filipino workers, the deepest bonds and feelings of solidarity emerged with Indigenous laborers, many of them Coast Salish women, who worked in the same jobs and traversed the same kinds of migratory circuits. And yet even the Japanese experienced a kind of precarity, which became all too clear as the United States barreled toward war with Japan.

Filipino migration to the United States did not commence in the 1920s. Its long history stretched back to the age of European imperial expansion. Filipinos began crossing the Pacific as early as the sixteenth century as part of the Manila galleon trade.[9] They worked as laborers and sailors aboard galleons, Spanish ships that passed between the two Spanish colonies of the Philippines and Mexico carrying valuable goods from China. The goods—spices, porcelain, silk—were transported by land across Central America and eventually sold in Europe.[10] The 1521 colonization of the Philippines gave Spain a location from which to transport these goods, bypassing the Portuguese-controlled route across the Indian Ocean and Cape of Good Hope and establishing an alternative passage to Europe. The Filipino crew-members, many of them impressed to serve aboard the galleons and treated brutally, settled in Mexico or jumped ship and headed north to Louisiana, where they intermarried with local populations and established mixed communities across the region.[11]

Subsequent waves of Filipino migration linked more directly with twentieth-century US imperialism. The United States declared war with Spain in 1898, eager to secure a greater presence in Asia. US businessmen and politicians, fearing that years of domestic overproduction would create instability, sought new overseas markets for US goods; the prospect of capturing Chinese markets continued to fuel their expansionist desires.[12] As a Spanish colony within Asia, the Philippines occupied a strategic position for the United States. This era of US expansionism was further bolstered by a heightened sense of white racial superiority, a Manifest Destiny ideology that depicted the Philippines as uncivilized and in need of US "uplift."[13] Following the defeat of Spain in August 1898, the United States acquired the Philippines, along with other Spanish colonies, against the wishes of the Filipino people, who desired their own sovereign nation. When it became clear that the United States would not leave but intended to replace the Spanish as colonial occupiers, Filipinos declared a war of independence against the US. The war officially lasted until 1902, although it unofficially continued in some areas of the Philippines for years after.[14]

The US colonization of the Philippines created the structural conditions for mass emigration abroad. In many areas across the Philippines, US-led commercialization of agriculture severely disrupted land tenure and traditional farming practices, creating a pool of laborers looking for work overseas.[15] According to scholar Rick Baldoz, "By the mid-1920s, it did not take much inducement to find a large base of potential passengers eager to travel abroad in search of economic opportunities."[16] US businesses, meanwhile, eagerly recruited Filipino labor. Hawaiian sugar planters began to import workers from the Philippines in the early twentieth century, after the 1907–8 Gentlemen's Agreement cut off Japanese labor migration to the United States and created a renewed demand for low-wage labor. Mass Filipino migration to the mainland United States began in the 1920s as immigration laws curtailed the flow of labor from many areas around the globe. Categorized as US nationals and thus exempt from immigration restrictions, Filipinos began to replace Japanese and Chinese workers in the agricultural fields of California's Central Valley and the salmon canneries of Alaska.

While the number of Filipinos passing through Pacific Coast port cities increased dramatically through the 1920s, Seattle emerged as a particularly critical hub of Filipino migration. Historian Dorothy Fujita-Rony argues that Seattle functioned as a "colonial metropole," the main center or capital city of an imperial power.[17] Transpacific trade networks and US military presence in the region drew thousands of Filipinos to the Pacific Northwest in search of employment and education. Seattle offered the shortest shipping routes to Asia, and several transpacific steamship companies based in the Pacific Northwest marketed their passenger services to Filipinos heading to the United States. In addition, the University of Washington, a public university located in Seattle, actively recruited students from the Philippines to boost the region's influence in and connections to Asia. Filipinos viewed the possibility of schooling in the United States as an extension of their own American colonial education in the Philippines. Many Filipinos thus came to the Pacific Northwest specifically to pursue educational opportunities, either formally through the Pensionado Act of 1903—which created a federal program to bring Filipino students to the United States for higher education, with the goal of training the next generation of colonial administrators in the Philippines—or, later, through more informal channels and networks.[18]

Most Filipino migrants found it difficult, if not impossible, to continue their schooling in the United States, however, because of structural barriers preventing them from earning a steady wage. Many wanted to attend high school or college in Seattle, but they were turned away from higher-paying jobs that could cover tuition and living expenses. Fred Floresca, who had already attended university for one year in the Philippines, came to Seattle to pursue his college degree in 1927. What he found was "an entirely different environment here where going to school was a problem and [you] have to have a tangible income to support yourself in school."[19] Toribio Martin arrived in Seattle in 1926 as a seventeen-year-old looking to finish high school. He worked summers in the Alaska salmon canneries and picked fruit in California each fall, and still did not earn enough to support himself. Martin tried to attend Broadway High School for a year, even working nights as a dishwasher, but ended up dropping out because he "was tired of it."[20] These stories reveal the wide gulf between what Filipino migrants expected of their life in the United States and their lived experience in a racially hostile society. As one man put it, "Here . . . you cannot win."[21]

Finding steady employment proved one of the steepest struggles Filipinos faced in the Pacific Northwest. Rampant discrimination in hiring shut Filipinos out of skilled or permanent employment, leaving them solely with low-wage, temporary work. The timing of their arrival also coincided with the onset of the Great Depression, making even temporary jobs difficult to obtain. The salmon-canning industry in Alaska offered some of the only guaranteed jobs for Filipino laborers during the summer months, as it had for Chinese and Japanese workers before them. Yet Japanese workers had come to occupy positions of authority in the cannery system as managers, contractors, and foreman, leaving Filipinos little room for upward mobility and higher wages.[22] As a result, Filipinos were forced to travel much greater distances to secure employment than previous generations of Northwest migrant workers. It was common for Filipinos to follow a route from the lodging houses of Seattle to the salmon canneries of Alaska, the farms of central California, then back to Seattle, all in one season. For many, these long journeys, often traversed by railroad or car, brought not a sense of excitement but feelings of suffocation and relentless monotony.[23]

Constantly on the move during summer and fall, Filipino workers returned to Seattle in the off seasons and found limited options for housing and recreation in a deeply segregated city. Though Seattle's urban landscape had been divided by race as well as gender from its origins in the 1850s, the 1920s witnessed a new era characterized by more explicit forms of segregation, such as restrictive covenants placing entire neighborhoods out of reach for nonwhite Seattleites.[24] Moving into northern, all-white neighborhoods, as Japanese families and business operators had done during the previous decade, was not an option for Filipino workers, who were largely confined to the area south of Yesler. Mariano Angeles remembers wandering the city, searching for a room to rent, and ending up in the central business district, where hotel and restaurant managers refused to serve him. "I have to go and look for my own room," he recalled, "but . . . where I like to go they don't like."[25] Other newcomers relied on friends and relatives already living in Seattle for help navigating the city's racial geographies. Romero Alin recalls being guided to a hotel south of Yesler Way by "an old timer that . . . give us idea where to live."[26] The picture looked a bit different for non-working-class Filipinos, whose resources and more stable employment options gave them access to different Seattle neighborhoods. But even Filipino elites found their lives severely constrained by the system of racial segregation that, by 1930, had become deeply entrenched throughout the region.

SOCIAL BOUNDARIES SOUTH OF YESLER

Filipino workers in Seattle relied almost exclusively on Japanese businesses to provide housing, employment, leisure, and other necessities of life. Japanese entrepreneurs had attained a degree of power within the racialized economy south of Yesler, running many of the businesses that catered to Filipinos, African Americans, poor whites, and others shut out of the segregated northern neighborhoods. By 1930, Japanese people operated the bulk of the hotels south of Yesler Way, as well as the majority of laundries, markets, restaurants, and bathhouses. Hotels played a particularly vital role in the lives of Filipinos and other itinerant laborers, providing short-term and seasonal accommodations as they moved into and out of the city. Hotels also functioned as community centers for Filipino workers—places where they could find out about employment opportunities, store belongings during the summer months, and receive mail.[27] As the seasonal economy declined in the late 1930s and 1940s, hotels became permanent residences for many Filipinos and others who could no longer find jobs, or who had aged out of the workforce.

Japanese business operators, meanwhile, depended upon Filipino patronage to keep their businesses afloat. Japanese residents had carved out a place for themselves in the seasonal economy of the Pacific Northwest, but their position remained precarious. The 1920s witnessed widespread hostility in the United States toward Japanese people, who became targets of restrictive laws. In 1921, Washington joined nearly a dozen other states in passing an alien land law, which prohibited "aliens ineligible to citizenship" from owning property or holding long-term leases. The race-neutral language of Washington's law, borrowed from California's 1913 legislation, obfuscated its deeply racialized intent: to dispossess Japanese farmers and protect and consolidate white control over agricultural land and profits. Japanese farmers across Washington resisted the alien land law, challenging it in court and devising strategies to circumvent the restrictions.[28] In the end, though, many ended up losing their farms.[29] While the alien land law had less of an immediate impact in the city, the legislation marked a chilling new phase in the anti-Japanese movement, now aimed at controlling Japanese people's autonomy and economic independence in both the urban and rural contexts.

The 1924 immigration act, which established quotas based on country of origin, dealt a further blow to the hopes of Japanese migrants for permanent settlement in the Pacific Northwest. The legislation cut off all transpacific migration from Japan, effectively nullifying the 1907–8 Gentlemen's Agreement that had allowed the continued entry of Japanese married women and men from the nonlaboring classes. Historian Yuji Ichioka argues that Japanese people "interpreted the law as a culminating act of rejection by the United States."[30] That rejection threatened the growth and economic future of Japanese society in the United States; it also stung because it placed them on par with Chinese people, whose late-nineteenth-century exclusion Japanese elites had attributed to their inferiority and "uncivilized" conduct.[31] The 1924 immigration law revealed and hardened the racialized boundaries of acceptance into US society, and the Japanese found themselves on the wrong side.

The 1924 legislation had other consequences as well. By threatening the economic livelihood of Japanese entrepreneurs—operators of hotels, restaurants, employment agencies, import-export companies, and other businesses reliant on the transpacific circulation of people and goods—the law undermined the foundation of the Japanese middle class. The arrival of Japanese women and children during the 1910s had enabled Japanese men to leave the transient working class and invest in businesses that revolved around a family workforce. "It was obvious that the Japanese community had no future," notes historian Katsutoshi Kurokawa, "unless it would find a new market in addition to decreasing Japanese customers."[32] Without a steady clientele, the businesses risked failure, bringing financial ruin to the families who operated them.

Facing economic and political precarity, Japanese business owners turned to Filipino workers and consumers as a critical source of income. As Filipinos arrived to the Pacific Northwest in large numbers in the 1920s, Japanese entrepreneurs shifted their business practices to attract them. Among businesses south of Yesler, the hotel industry saw some of the sharpest increases in Filipino patronage. By 1930, Japanese residents managed a dozen hotels that catered almost exclusively to Filipino workers. The Midway Hotel was the most infamous of these establishments. In 1920, police had conducted a highly publicized raid of the Midway and neighboring hotels to combat illicit gambling and prostitution.[33] In the late 1920s, the self-proclaimed "hotel king" Tokio Ota acquired the lease to the Midway and opened it as a Filipino hotel. Ota's rise as Japanese hotel magnate had occurred in dramatic, though not atypical, fashion. He arrived as a laborer in 1890, destined for a railroad work camp in Montana. On the road to the worksite, Ota slipped beyond the watchful eye of the contractor and made his way back to Seattle, where he wandered around, penniless and lost, until a Japanese man hired him to wash dishes at his restaurant. He saved up enough money to return to Japan and marry, bringing his new wife with him back to Seattle. Together they opened a lodging house south of Yesler, then a larger hotel near the waterfront. As exclusion laws transformed the urban working-class population, Ota sensed a business opportunity. He purchased a lease to the Midway and began going down to the docks each morning to greet newly arriving Filipino passengers. As his daughter, May Ota Higa, remembers, her father "made a killing very early on" from this Filipino traffic—enough to move the family, then numbering at eight children, into a detached home on the outskirts of Japantown, and hire a Filipino manager to oversee daily hotel operations.[34]

By the 1930s, Japanese business operators and Filipino customers had entered into an interdependent relationship shaped by exclusion and urban racial segregation. Other Japanese hotel operators in addition to Ota saw the opportunity and began to replace their existing customers with Filipino migrants. The Great Northern Hotel, for example, had once headquartered the Japanese-American Employment Office, offering accommodations to Japanese laborers attached to the contracting business.[35] By 1930, the Great

Northern was still under Japanese management, but instead served mostly Filipinos who worked in the farms, railroads, and canneries of the Pacific Northwest. While no longer directly tied to the contracting business, the Great Northern nonetheless profited indirectly from the regional circulation of migratory laborers. The Russell House, site of the infamous 1919 fire, also shifted from its former racially mixed customer base, which had included white, Black, and Japanese residents, to a predominately Filipino clientele. Other hotels popular with Filipino workers included the Welcome Annex, Paris, Sankai, Alps, Mukilteo, and Elk.[36] The Japanese relied on Filipinos as a steady source of income during a period of restricted immigration, while Filipinos relied on the Japanese for housing in a racially stratified city.

But not everyone welcomed Filipino customers with open arms. Though over a dozen Japanese hotels catered to predominately Filipino workers, others remained closed to them. The Bush Hotel, for example, came under repeated fire in the mid-1930s from the United Front Committee, an organization dedicated to combating housing and employment discrimination, for refusing to serve Black and Filipino customers.[37] Located just across the street from the Welcome Annex Hotel, the Bush Hotel (spelled Busch at the time) was built in 1915; real estate investor William Chappell financed the nearly half-million-dollar construction. The finished building boasted a lavish dining room and lobby, deemed "splendid" by the *Seattle Daily Times*, which covered the hotel's opening day in a full-page spread.[38] Chappell was the single largest property owner south of Yesler Way; he leased many of his properties to Japanese business operators.[39] K. Shibayama, along with his wife and three children, began operating the Bush Hotel in the late 1920s. The 1930 census reveals a racially diverse mix of Japanese, Chinese, and white residents at the hotel, but Filipinos and African Americans are noticeably absent from the roster.[40] A 1934 petition filed by the United Front Committee alleging discriminatory housing practices at the Bush, among other hotels, confirms that the census enumeration was not a fluke.[41]

The parallel stories of the Midway and Bush hotels reveal a differential system of housing that emerged south of Yesler Way during this period of Filipino migration. Hotels that opened their doors to Filipinos were typically located in poorly maintained buildings that had attracted negative attention in the past. The Paris Hotel, for example, had been the target of a highly publicized police raid for gambling, illicit sex, and other violations of city code.[42] Changes in immigration law had transformed the working-class population south of Yesler, but the racial geographies enforced by Japanese entrepreneurs remained somewhat intact. While the Japanese middle classes capitalized on the influx of Filipino migrants and their need for seasonal accommodations, they attempted to maintain boundaries separating themselves from the laboring populations.

The social distance between Japanese entrepreneurs and their families and the Filipino laborers who patronized their businesses is apparent in how each group referred to their shared neighborhood. Though physically the same territory, it was called Nihonmachi or Japantown by Japanese residents, while Filipinos called it Chinatown. A Chinatown did exist in Seattle, located around the intersection of Sixth Avenue South and King Street, but the bulk of the hotels catering to Filipino workers were not located there; rather, they stood in the heart of Japantown, next to such community institutions as the Nippon Kan Theater and the Higo Ten-Cent Store on Jackson Street.[43] It's possible that for Filipinos, "Chinatown" was more familiar as a social space, given their lengthy migrations to California and around the American West, where Chinatowns and Chinese business owners more often catered to the agricultural and seasonal workforce than the Japanese.[44] But the two groups' differing conceptions of territory speak powerfully to the social barriers that existed even within multiracial and multiethnic neighborhoods like the one south of Yesler.

Indeed, sharing the same space with Filipinos made some Japanese entrepreneurs work even harder to uphold social boundaries. Higa remembered her father forbidding his daughters from visiting "Papa's hotels." She explains his thinking: "The Filipino men didn't have women, and Dad was afraid they would want us, and so having six girls, he didn't want any of us down there."[45] Higa candidly captures what scholars Arlene De Vera and Eiichiro Azuma have shown in their work: that Japanese elites and community leaders strongly prohibited intermarriage between Japanese women and Filipino men. Scandals erupted in places such as Stockton and the California Delta region in response to relationships between Japanese women and Filipino men, leading to boycotts and even violence.[46] Azuma notes that many Japanese leaders considered Filipinos racially inferior and felt a sexual relationship between a Japanese woman and Filipino man would result in the "'contamination' of their 'pure' bloodline."[47] Intermarriage also threatened the project of middle-class respectability that undergirded Japanese claims of acceptance into white society. Actively policing social boundaries between Japanese women and Filipino men became particularly crucial in places like Seattle, where the Japanese not only occupied the same physical territory as the Filipinos but relied on them as customers and thus had a financial incentive to maintain good relations. This social taboo was understood among Filipinos as well. "One thing too about the Japanese, they were not allowed to intermarry," Seattle resident Jose Acena recalled. "They were pretty strict."[48] Yet despite the proscriptions of Japanese male leaders, people continued to pursue social and sexual relations on their own terms. Even as Acena described the social taboo against interracial relationships, he also remembered a handful of Japanese/Filipino couples who formed during the prewar era, some of them marrying.[49] Others undoubtedly engaged in social and sexual encounters that have not made it into official archives or historical memory.[50]

ENCOUNTERS OUTSIDE THE CITY

Social relations between Filipino laborers and Japanese business operators were shaped by the structural forms of racial segregation and exclusion that forced them to share the same neighborhoods south of Yesler. Their geographic intimacy did not necessarily foster alliances or shared understandings, especially given rising expressions of nationalism in the 1930s among overseas Japanese communities, including Seattle's. More often, Japanese business owners attempted to uphold racial and gender divisions and separate themselves from their Filipino patrons.

Outside the city, though, a new set of relationships formed in the strawberry fields of Bainbridge Island, among Filipino and Indigenous workers and Japanese farmers. Bainbridge, located just a short ferry ride from Seattle, offers an interesting look at how racial and economic hierarchies are upheld and/or transformed in the absence of white people. Japanese residents owned many of the farms on Bainbridge, an area where they had been successful in circumventing the restrictions of the alien land laws. On the surface, this allowed for more harmonious relationships between Japanese farm operators and their Filipino and Indigenous workers, in part because the Japanese occupied a firmer position within the political economy of the island. But the apparent "family-like" atmosphere of the farms belied an entrenched class hierarchy that relied on the same forms of racialized labor and exploitation. Filipino laborers did not ally with their Japanese employers, but rather found solidarity in the shared life experiences of their fellow Indigenous workers. The interracial marriages and mixed communities that formed between Filipinos and Indigenous workers show the importance of thinking beyond our contemporary categories of race in understanding identities and social relations of the past.

In the late 1920s, Japanese farmers on Bainbridge began recruiting Filipino workers based in Seattle. The Japanese had established a significant farming presence on Bainbridge Island; many were former Port Blakely sawmill laborers who had managed to save enough money to purchase small plots of land. Zenhichi Harui and Zenmatsu Seko, brothers who arrived in Seattle in 1908, worked at the Port Blakely mill for several months before opening their own farm on Bainbridge. They soon developed a profitable business selling their strawberries to the Olympic Hotel in Seattle, which allowed them to invest in more land and expand operations. The brothers cleared the second plot of land themselves, spending several years cutting down trees and removing stumps with dynamite. They then built greenhouses to cultivate winter vegetables and year-round produce, supplementing their seasonal income from the strawberry trade. This farm, known as Bainbridge Gardens, became one of the more successful businesses on the island.[51] Other Japanese farmers maintained more modest operations, selling their fruit and produce at stands or local markets.

Japanese farmers on Bainbridge had long struggled to procure enough workers for the harvest season. During the 1910s and early 1920s, they relied predominately on the labor of women and children from around the island, as well as their own families. Frank Kitamoto, whose parents operated a strawberry farm, recalled that "the Japanese went into agriculture, and . . . they were always looking for people to work on their farms or to run their farms. I mean, even in those days, I don't think you had very many people other than the kids on Bainbridge who'd be willing to pick."[52] As Filipino migration increased during the latter half of the 1920s, the Japanese turned to them as a source of labor, particularly during the Depression when many farmers struggled to "make ends meet."[53] Japanese farmers started traveling to Seattle before harvest season to hire Filipino pickers and farmhands. They typically paid around ten cents an hour, sometimes more or less, and provided very basic room and board. Toribio Madayag, who worked on a handful of Bainbridge strawberry farms in the 1930s, described an encounter with a Japanese farmer: "One Japanese I met there in Seattle was from here in this island, and then he was hiring and you know how much he told me he'll pay? He told me he'll pay nine cents an hour. . . . 'If you work I'll pay you nine cents.' So, I worked."[54] Filipinos soon became the dominant labor force employed by Japanese farmers.

The Bainbridge strawberry harvest appealed to Filipino workers for several reasons. It took place after the salmon-canning season, allowing them to supplement cannery wages with steady agricultural work. Easily accessible from Seattle, Bainbridge did not require expensive or time-consuming forms of travel. The farms' proximity to Seattle also meant Japanese recruiters could come directly to Filipino workers, offering guaranteed jobs and greater room to negotiate. The strawberry harvest lasted only two months, but some Japanese farmers kept Filipino workers through the winter and spring, as farm hands or as managers and foremen. Eventually a handful of workers even leased their own farms from Japanese landowners and began to grow berries as well. Doreen Rapada, who grew up on Bainbridge, recalled that her father labored in seasonal jobs on the railroads and in the Alaska salmon canneries before finding work on the Bainbridge strawberry farms. Soon, he "decided that he wasn't gonna go back to Alaska again so he and Tom Almojuela leased a property, the Furukawa land, and they did some strawberry farming there."[55] As Rapada noted, the possibility of a more stable livelihood attracted many Filipinos to the island, as opposed to regions where their opportunities for economic mobility were far fewer.

While the work on Bainbridge Island offered more potential material benefits, Filipinos still occupied a more marginal position than their Japanese employers. Some Japanese farmers on Bainbridge had managed to maintain control over their land following the 1921 alien land law. Bainbridge Gardens owner Zenhichi Harui placed his farm in the name of an American-born relative; Frank Kitamoto's grandparents, Japanese farmers who sold their land to their American-born son and his wife, did the same.[56] Transferring title to a US citizen, either Japanese or white, was a common strategy Japanese farmers pursued to circumvent the alien land law and retain legal ownership of property. Other strategies included creating corporations or using a white intermediary to purchase the land on their behalf. Pressure from anti-Asian groups, white farmers, and politicians meanwhile mounted against these practices in Washington and California, resulting in further restrictions on land ownership.[57]

As the owner of a business and the land it occupied, a Japanese farmer on the island could more easily determine what took place on their property—as opposed to the urban context, where Japanese hotel operators were mostly lessees and had to deal more frequently with municipal regulation and harassment. Tellingly, Japanese farmers reproduced for Filipino employees many of the same poor living and working conditions they themselves had endured as laborers. Filipinos who worked for Japanese farmers on the island recall residing in rough shacks or cabins on the outskirts of farm properties. While accommodations varied, these small wooden structures were often hastily built and contained the barest of essentials—a small stove, a cluster of metal cots. Workers at the Kitamoto farm lived together in one small house just outside the farm property, while Bainbridge Gardens placed its workers in "separate houses . . . back in the woods."[58] Farmers and their families situated these temporary quarters some distance from their own homes and referred to them as the "Filipino house" or "Filipino camp," reflecting the position of Filipinos as both workers and outsiders.[59]

Japanese farmers' more secure socioeconomic position allowed them to have a looser, more intimate set of social relations with their Filipino workers. Some Japanese farmers invited Filipino workers into their homes for meals with the family. While not universal, sharing dinners or meals together was not uncommon. Junkoh Harui, whose father owned Bainbridge Gardens, recalled, "[The Filipino workers] used to eat at our home because they had no facilities to cook. And it was part of the bargain, is that, you get a meal."[60] Other Japanese farmers allowed their children to fish or spend leisure time with Filipino workers. Frank Kitamoto remembered outings with Felix Narte, the foreman on his family's farm: "When I was a kid . . . I'd row the boat while Felix took his fishing net out there and would throw his net to catch shiners . . . and I remember him taking me out to catch *tako*, octopus, and my eyes getting really big watching those suckers suck on his boots."[61] Frank's sister, Lilly Kodama, similarly described the relationship between their mother and Felix as "like family . . . like brother and sister." As a child, Doreen Rapada, whose Squamish mother and Filipino father met on the island, referred to the Japanese farmers' wives as "mama."[62] This picture of Japanese-Filipino relations differs strikingly from its counterpart in Seattle, where Japanese elites, hoteliers, and business operators vigorously policed social boundaries, particularly when it came to gender.

The inclusion of Filipino workers in the domestic space, however, reflected a more hardened social order than what existed in the urban areas. On Bainbridge the Japanese clearly occupied a superior position, as business owners, employers, and permanent residents of the island. This entrenched socioeconomic hierarchy meant Filipinos posed less of a threat to the Japanese on Bainbridge Island than in Seattle, where relations between the two groups remained more fluid and access to physical territory was both more constrained and more equally shared. For Japanese farmers, treating the Filipinos "like family" helped define exactly where those social boundaries rested, and what kinds of relationships were authorized and not authorized. Unlike in the hotels south of Yesler Way, where Japanese girls and young women were warned to stay away from Filipino workers, social relations between Filipino men and Japanese women on the strawberry farms required less overt policing.

It's important to note that the familial atmosphere described by the Japanese farmers and their children did not necessarily reflect Filipino perspectives—particularly the views of Filipino migrant laborers, as opposed to Filipino foremen or other permanent workers. According to Toribio Madayag, who picked strawberries on Bainbridge Island for several seasons, the relations between Japanese farmers and their Filipino workforce were far more complex than the memories of some Japanese farming families capture. As he recalled, many workers did have decent relations with their Japanese employers—but this did not mean the environment was harmonious and conflict-free. At times, Filipino workers grew vocal about their status as a marginalized labor force and engaged in campaigns to improve their conditions and hold their employers accountable. In 1936, for example, Filipino workers on Bainbridge organized a strike for higher pay, demanding their Japanese employers provide a wage increase from seventeen to twenty-five cents an hour. Madayag, then steward of the Cannery Workers' and Farm Laborers' Union Local 18257, led the "sitting down strike," which lasted several days. Gathered in their bunkhouses, the workers refused to leave until the farmers agreed to their terms. The strikers ultimately succeeded, forcing their employers to agree to a pay raise.[63]

Yuriko Kitamoto and Elaulio Aquino on the Kitamoto family strawberry farm, c. late 1930s. Aquino and his cousin, Felix Narte, looked after the Kitamoto farm during World War II. Courtesy of the Bainbridge Island Japanese American Community.

Filipino laborers did not interact solely with their Japanese employers on Bainbridge Island. They also encountered Indigenous workers, many of them Coast Salish women who migrated from British Columbia each season for the strawberry harvest. The appearance of Coast Salish farmworkers on Bainbridge was part of a much longer history. As discussed previously, Indigenous peoples along the Northwest Coast had long engaged in seasonal migrations, traveling the marine spaces of Puget Sound and the broader Salish Sea to gather resources, fish, and socialize with extended family. Hop growers had capitalized on this maritime mobility, situating their farms along the rivers of the Sound to access a temporary labor force before the railroad's arrival. Hop picking had allowed Indigenous workers to continue their seasonal migrations and establish autonomous spaces away from the reservations and reserves where they could freely practice their cultural traditions—speaking their native languages, canoe traveling with their families, and socializing on their own terms.

Japanese farmers began to employ Indigenous labor long before the 1930s. Some reports date the arrival of Indigenous strawberry pickers on Bainbridge as early as 1915.[64] Unlike Puget Sound hop growers of the late nineteenth century, who relied on a mix of workers from both sides of the US-Canada border, it appears that Japanese farmers hired predominately First Nations Coast Salish peoples, including many from the Vancouver, BC, region.[65] Methods for recruitment varied by farmer. Some of the larger farms sent representatives up to Vancouver to gather pickers and transport them down to the island.[66] Others, perhaps lacking resources, went only as far as Seattle, to recruit pickers who then traveled to the island by ferry. Nob Koura, whose parents operated a strawberry farm and employed mostly First Nations Coast Salish laborers, recalled that some years they "[picked] 'em up in Seattle" by truck, while other years they simply waited for them to "come down on their own."[67] Estimates of Indigenous workers' numbers varied widely, with some of the children of Japanese farmers recalling "thousands of 'em here on the island."[68] A newspaper report from 1939 counted between nine hundred and one thousand Indigenous pickers on the island that season, with "most of the pickers" coming from Vancouver, BC.[69] Many workers came back year after year. Dorothy (Nahanee) Almojuela, a Squamish woman who met her Filipino husband, Tom Almojuela,

Indigenous laborers picking strawberries, 1943. This photograph was taken on Vashon Island, which resembled Bainbridge Island in its employment of many First Nations Coast Salish workers, particularly women. MOHAI, *Seattle Post-Intelligencer* Collection, PI23856.

while picking strawberries, first came to the island with her grandmother. When preparing to leave for the two-month harvest, she remembered that her grandmother "knew how to pack because each year for years she was coming down to Bainbridge."[70]

It's difficult to know the full details about how this particular employment system started, but recollections by Japanese farmers suggest that labor scarcity in the United States played a big role in their targeted recruitment of First Nations Coast Salish workers. Koura recalls that his parents started contracting First Nations pickers "way back in the '20s," a time when immigration restrictions had cut off the global labor supply into the United States.[71] These restrictions did not apply to Indigenous peoples born or residing in Canada, who had treaty protections granting their free movement across the border.[72] Similarly, when asked why his parents went up to Canada for workers, Yoshimitsu Suyematsu responded that it was the "only place they could find 'em."[73] As colonial subjects of the United States,

Filipino workers were also exempt from immigration restrictions during this period, making them another desirable source of labor, particularly in the seasonal industries, though they were "reclassified" to alien following the Tydings-McDuffie Act of 1934.[74]

The meeting and mixing of Filipino men and Indigenous women on the strawberry fields and at local dances resulted in both romantic relationships and marriages. While earlier generations of Indigenous migrant workers had consisted of families, the Coast Salish workers who came to Bainbridge Island as pickers during the prewar years were overwhelmingly women— young, single women, as well as older women. This had to do, in part, with gendered employment patterns among First Nations workers, particularly those in Vancouver. Historian Andrew Parnaby describes Squamish men's long history of dock work in Vancouver, where they became highly desired as lumber handlers beginning as early as the 1900s. He shows that Squamish employment in this industry accelerated in the 1930s and into the war years. With longshoring offering higher pay and more stable employment than agricultural work, Squamish men presumably did not go as frequently to work in the fields as they had in years past, leaving the agricultural work-force with a higher proportion of women.[75]

Dorothy Almojuela's story offers insight into the experiences of Squa-mish women who migrated to Bainbridge Island during this time. A member of the Squamish nation, Dorothy was born in North Vancouver in 1918. Her father worked as a longshoreman in Vancouver, as did her paternal grand-father, whose parents were from Hawaii. She attended a Catholic missionary school until eighth grade, when she began caring full-time for her ailing mother, who was sick with Parkinson's disease. Growing up, Dorothy spent considerable time with her grandmother, a widow who supported her chil-dren and grandchildren through a variety of work, for employers including salmon canneries and strawberry farms. It was through her grandmother— or Ta'a, as Dorothy called her—that Dorothy first heard about the oppor-tunities on Bainbridge Island. "My grandmother goes away every year, and every year we ask her, 'Where do you go?'" Dorothy recalled. "She says, 'I go to Boston.' She calls the United States 'Boston.'"[76] When Dorothy was in her early twenties and her siblings became old enough to care for their mother, she began looking for paid work. She hired on first at the salmon cannery for several weeks, working a night shift, and then went to Bain-bridge Island with Ta'a.

Dorothy and her grandmother traveled with a group of mostly older women by boat to Seattle, stopping through Victoria on the way. She described being hassled by customs officers in Victoria when she wandered off from the group, with one sharply demanding her ticket and treating her with suspicion. In Seattle, they met up with relatives, who took them around sightseeing; then they boarded a smaller ferry to Winslow and took a truck to the Furukawa strawberry farm. She recalled being struck by the rurality of Bainbridge: "I thought, where on earth is he taking us? Where's the city? Because I come from a city, Vancouver, North Vancouver." At the farm she and her grandmother lived in an "old shack" with a tin stove and a wooden bed stuffed with straw. Soon, they began picking. Dorothy had caught a glimpse of her future husband, Tom Almojuela, at the ferry terminal, declaring him "the handsomest man I ever saw." Tom leased his own small strawberry farm nearby, and when he asked for help with picking, she jumped at the chance. They ate lunch together and picked together; when it was time for Dorothy to go back home, they decided to marry, going to Seattle for a ceremony at a Catholic church and then returning for a party back on Bainbridge. "All the boys had fixed up a platform for dancing, and they had put fir trees with little decorations," she said. "And I felt like Cinderella coming to a kingdom . . . and so we danced the evening away."[77]

While their story is fully their own, Dorothy and Tom's union was also made possible through the layered complexities of capitalism, colonialism, and gendered patterns of migration that brought them together in the fields. On Bainbridge Island, while women comprised the bulk of the Indigenous agricultural workforce, Filipino pickers were heavily male, which reflected the broader demographic profile of Filipinos in the region. Scholars have examined the relationships that formed between Filipino men and white women, arguing that these interracial encounters, and the reactions they provoked among white men, fueled racial violence that swept the Pacific Coast during the late 1920s and early 1930s.[78] Just as white women pursued interracial relationships, so too did Indigenous women encountering Filipino men in the fields and canneries of the Northwest. Dorothy and Tom were one of many Indigenous/Filipino unions that formed as a result of the Bainbridge strawberry harvests. Dorothy estimated some eight to ten couples married that summer alone. Many of them met at dances held "almost every night" during strawberry picking season.[79] The dances attracted workers from all over the island and took place "around in the barn or anyplace, in the street or anyplace as long as somebody gonna play music."[80] This interracial sociability and leisure also occurred in the Alaska salmon cannery towns where Indigenous women worked or resided. As Filipino elder Magno Rudio recollected, "After Filipinos get off work in the evening, they invite the Indian girls to dances."[81]

The entry of the United States into World War II marked a time of transition and divergent paths for the residents of Bainbridge. The migration of Squamish and other First Nations women intensified during the war, as labor shortages opened up more opportunities for young women like Dorothy to join the workforce. Filipino men also found wartime employment in the shipyards at Bremerton and Winslow, allowing them to save up money and purchase farms and homes of their own. In 1940, Filipinos gained the right to own property following community leader Pio DeCano's successful challenge to Washington's alien land law, which had been amended three years earlier to include Filipinos among the restricted groups.[82]

Japanese farmers on Bainbridge experienced the war years very differently. In the aftermath of Pearl Harbor and Executive Order 9066, which granted the military broad powers to remove any person, citizen and noncitizen alike, from designated areas along the West Coast, Japanese farmers were forced to leave the island and banished to concentration camps in the interior of the country. Bainbridge Island Japanese Americans were among the very first to be removed from the West Coast and sent to Manzanar, leaving their strawberry farms in the hands of sympathetic neighbors or else simply abandoned in the rush to leave. Some Filipinos on the island cared for the farms and properties of their former Japanese employers, including Felix Narte, who had worked for the Kitamoto family. Only about half of the Bainbridge Island Japanese residents returned after the war.[83]

World War II painfully clarified the precarious position Japanese farmers and hoteliers occupied within Pacific Northwest society. The hierarchies they had tried so hard to maintain remained tenuous at best, quickly swept away in the aftermath of Pearl Harbor and the vanquishing act of removal that followed. Toribio Madayag put it best when he summed up his first impressions of Japanese residents on Bainbridge Island: "When I come here [to Bainbridge], these Hayashida people here they are one of the richest people, Japanese here, and they don't even, they only *torogotog* car. You know what's *torogotog* car? Junk . . . it could barely run."[84] As Madayag conveyed, the mass removal of Japanese Americans reflected an economic transformation that had been years in the making. The Japanese had long played a crucial role within the urban and regional economy, as intermediaries who served and employed the itinerant, racialized workforce of the Pacific Northwest. As the resource-based economy declined, the Japanese were no longer useful and became disposable once again, their fates ultimately linked with the workforce they had relied upon and, at times, treated with distain. All would find themselves soon fighting against municipal slum clearance projects that targeted their neighborhoods for demolition, clearing out the unsightly and unnecessary to make way for a new workforce and a new city.

CHAPTER 6

Demolition on
the Eve of War

DURING THE LATE 1930s AND EARLY 1940s, THE CITY OF SEATTLE
initiated several large-scale clearance projects targeting the slums, shantytowns, and other informal spaces that had sprouted up during the Great
Depression. Though in the past city authorities had considered these spaces
a kind of necessary evil—socially problematic, but vital to the regional
economy—by the late 1930s this was no longer the case. War in Europe,
which broke out in 1939, stimulated Seattle's manufacturing sector, creating
a sharp demand for ships and airplanes. Even before the United States
entered World War II, the Boeing Airplane Company had emerged as one
of the region's largest employers.[1] Founded in the early twentieth century
by former lumber operators and headquartered in Seattle, Boeing experienced particularly rapid growth during wartime, employing nearly ten
thousand people by mid-1941.[2] The rise of Boeing and expansion of the
existing shipbuilding industries marked a profound and lasting shift away
from a resource-based economy and more firmly toward manufacturing.[3]
No longer as dependent on the seasonal, extractive industries and their
mobile workforce, city leaders began to demolish the troublesome areas
migrant workers occupied in order to prepare for a new kind of urban
workforce: skilled, educated, and stationary.

Though the city pursued several clearance projects at this time, including the demolition of Hooverville, a shantytown that had sprouted up near the waterfront during the Great Depression, Profanity Hill was the only neighborhood that officials replaced with new housing. There, the Seattle Housing Authority (SHA) used New Deal funds to construct a new public housing project called Yesler Terrace. Outwardly, Yesler Terrace appeared to be a welcome development for Profanity Hill residents, many of whom were restricted from housing elsewhere in the city; the community encompassed single male migrants and laborers, the poor and unemployed, sex workers, interracial couples, and a large community of Japanese families. But it soon became clear that the SHA was using this program to clear out most of the population. The vast majority of Profanity Hill residents were unable to gain access to the new Yesler Terrace housing due to restrictive eligibility criteria, which limited tenants to legally married US citizens. While the SHA did not maintain an overt policy of discrimination, these tenancy restrictions created racial and gender segregation that heavily favored white families and resulted in the mass displacement of everyone else from Profanity Hill.

The local motivations for building Yesler Terrace have not been critically examined. Often celebrated in local memory as a positive contribution to the city and evidence of Seattle's open-mindedness about race, Yesler Terrace started first and foremost as a slum clearance project that targeted undesirable people, and the spaces they inhabited, as roadblocks to urban progress.[4] In that way, Yesler Terrace was not exceptional; it repeated a familiar historical pattern that stretched back to Seattle's founding in 1853, prioritizing white families at the expense of all others. Yesler Terrace differed only in that by the late 1930s and early 1940s, the racialized migrants, single men, and Japanese families who had once played a vital role in sustaining the urban and regional economy were no longer a necessary presence within the city.

EQUIVALENT ELIMINATION

The demolition of Profanity Hill and construction of Yesler Terrace took place during the 1930s as the federal government dramatically increased its involvement in the housing sector. The Depression had exposed the failures of private industry to provide adequate shelter for the nation's poor and working classes. With new home construction plummeting as unemployment rose to record heights, the federal government initiated a series of policies related to nonmarket housing developments. The first of these appeared in 1933, when a housing division was formed under the Public Works Administration (PWA) to oversee the construction and maintenance of public housing facilities. Though the PWA provided well-designed homes for thousands of working-class people, it remained a temporary measure, tied to emergency legislation passed during President Franklin Delano Roosevelt's first one hundred days in office. Catherine Bauer, president of the Labor Housing Conference and a leader in the US public-housing movement, introduced a permanent public housing bill to Congress in 1935. New York senator Robert Wagner refashioned it into the Federal Housing Act, also known as the Wagner-Steagall Act, which President Roosevelt signed into law in 1937.[5]

The final version of the Wagner-Steagall Act differed considerably from Bauer's original bill. It introduced an "equivalent elimination" clause that linked public housing construction to slum clearance. For each unit of public housing built, the law now required the destruction of "slum housing" in equal number. Though Bauer and other public housing advocates had spent years pushing for comprehensive federal housing legislation, many were reportedly "distressed" by the outcome, viewing the final bill as anything but a victory.[6] Bauer had long opposed slum clearance, calling it a "reactionary measure" that diverted critical funds from public housing projects and financially rewarded exploitative landlords.[7] In addition, the final bill ensured that public housing would be concentrated in already impoverished areas, a concession to the real estate industry, which objected to the prospect of competition over undeveloped land on the outskirts of the city. Slum clearance remained politically popular, however, and Bauer and other housing activists reluctantly supported the final version, viewing it as "the best they were likely to get."[8]

Equivalent elimination shaped the entire project of public housing on the local level. The Wagner-Steagall Act required local agencies to complete a lengthy and comprehensive application that, if successful, resulted in the release of millions of dollars in low-interest loans that would subsidize their projects. The application process included studies surveying housing conditions in the sponsoring cities and towns, state legislation enabling the formation of local housing authorities, and an extensive written application submitted to the United States Housing Authority (USHA) for approval.

Equivalent elimination oriented each of these steps around slum clearance. Housing studies not only measured the need for public housing, but also identified potential sites for demolition, while legislation gave equal weight to slum clearance and public housing construction. Local agencies had to make the case for slum clearance as much as for public housing in their written applications; an argument for public housing also became an argument for slum clearance. Equivalent elimination made it impossible for any local agency to avoid incorporating slum clearance into its plans for public housing.

In Seattle, the idea for Yesler Terrace originated in 1937 with Jesse Epstein, an attorney who worked for the University of Washington's Bureau of Government Research, connecting local towns around Washington State with New Deal programs. Through his work, Epstein read about the housing law and began to set up meetings with local politicians to discuss the best way to access federal funds. Up to that point, Seattle had not developed any municipal housing programs, leaving most of the work to private agencies and charities. But the Depression had hit the city hard, resulting in homelessness, poverty, and deteriorating housing conditions that were among the worst in the nation.[9] In this context, Epstein managed to convince a skeptical city council and eventually state government to move forward with the appropriate legislation. In 1939, the City of Seattle formally established the Seattle Housing Authority (SHA) and appointed Epstein as its first chairman.

As the Wagner-Steagall Act necessitated, these efforts made slum clearance as much a priority as public housing. The law passed by the Washington State legislature in 1939 enabled "housing authorities to undertake slum clearance and projects to provide dwelling accommodations for persons of low income."[10] The cooperation agreement signed between the SHA and the City of Seattle in 1939 similarly emphasized slum clearance, while the SHA devoted more than half of its USHA application to a discussion of the existing site and plans for demolition.[11] Though commended in recent discussion as an exception to the national trend, the SHA mirrored every other local housing authority formed under the Wagner-Steagall Act in its prioritization of slum clearance.

The language of the law, though, remained vague about what exactly constituted a slum. The law itself stated that any structure could be considered slum property and thus be subject to clearance if "detrimental to safety, health, or morals," a phrase repeated in the cooperation agreement signed between the SHA and City of Seattle.[12] Lacking an objective definition, slum clearance became much more than just a measurement of physical or structural deficiencies. It enabled local agencies to target any area based on social factors or moral judgments about the inhabitants. In Seattle, the SHA quickly came to a consensus about Profanity Hill as the clearance site, calling the decision "unanimous" among its members.[13] Selecting the site proved straightforward; the SHA's remaining challenge involved conveying what was essentially a shared, unspoken understanding of the city's social geography to the federal officials reading the application and making a determination based on its contents. Though the Wagner-Steagall Act gave local agencies free rein in choosing the demolition sites, it also demanded an accounting of the process in objective, formulaic terms. The SHA turned to mapping to make the case for Profanity Hill as an expendable slum area—the one neighborhood above all others most deserving of demolition. Mapping technology helped the SHA justify its selection of Profanity Hill in the seemingly objective language of the visual.

PROFANITY HILL

In 1939, Profanity Hill stood as a kind of border zone clustered around Yesler Way, a major thoroughfare that continued to function as a division between white, residential neighborhoods to the north and multiracial, transient areas to the south. This division shaped the geography of Profanity Hill somewhat, with the northern blocks housing more families and the southern blocks more single people.[14] As a whole, though, the Profanity Hill neighborhood remained socially stigmatized and widely disparaged around the city as a slum.

This had not always been the case. In the 1870s and 1880s, Profanity Hill had been called Yesler Hill. It was home to the city's elite classes, including its namesake, Henry Yesler, and his wife Sarah Yesler, settlers whose wealth derived from timber and land sales. The hillside location offered the Yeslers and other prominent Seattle residents beautiful views of the Puget Sound at a safe distance from the laborers, migrants, and seamen who lived and worked at the mill and along the waterfront. In the late nineteenth and early twentieth centuries, this physical distance had narrowed as tens of thousands of people streamed into Seattle, lured by the prospect of gold in Alaska. The city grew and expanded to accommodate this population boom, and the elites fled Yesler Hill for land tracts farther away on the outskirts of the city, selling their Victorian mansions to buyers who subdivided the properties and leased the cramped apartments. During the 1920s, Yesler Hill had emerged as a center of commercial sex after a widespread crackdown on prostitution near the waterfront; the area then acquired the nickname Profanity Hill.[15]

Though considered an unsightly slum area by some, Profanity Hill was vital to those who could not find housing elsewhere in the city. By the late 1930s, Seattle's housing market was highly segregated, with whole neighborhoods sealed off to nonwhite residents. Historian Quintard Taylor has shown that Black and Asian Seattleites faced severe restrictions in housing, particularly through the use of racial covenants, clauses written into the deeds of homes prohibiting sale to nonwhite people.[16] Asians had an additional burden in the form of the alien land law, which prohibited "aliens ineligible to citizenship" from owning property. These policies and practices made it very difficult for nonwhite people to purchase or lease homes and live where they wanted to. As one of the few neighborhoods in Seattle with no housing restrictions, Profanity Hill became an important destination for marginalized groups. Located just a few blocks east of Japantown up a steep hill, Profanity Hill offered more space than the cramped hotel rooms and crowded street corners of the waterfront and other south-end areas. By 1939, Profanity Hill housed one of the highest concentrations of nonwhite residents in Seattle. Though 96 percent of the city's overall population, whites accounted for fewer than half the residents of the neighborhood.

The 1940 census opens a window into the neighborhood on the eve of its demolition.[17] Before 2012, when the census was made publicly accessible for the first time, the only demographic information about Profanity Hill came from the SHA's real property survey, a local collection of data on the city's entire housing stock and residential population.[18] Though the real property survey contained a wealth of information about Seattle's built environment, it provided only summaries of the demographic data, which left large gaps in publicly available knowledge about who actually lived on Profanity Hill. The census, while far from perfect—particularly in a neighborhood with a high transient population—offers more details about residents' identities and social lives. Further, the census count took place in April of 1940, two months after SHA officials notified residents of the impending evictions, compared with the real property survey, which relied on data gathered during the fall of 1939. The timing of the census is important because it shows a neighborhood less white and more Japanese than the real property survey, thus giving a more accurate picture of those most affected by slum clearance.[19] Residents with fewer problems relocating most likely moved first, leaving the neighborhood with a higher concentration of Japanese families and others who struggled against a segregated and exclusionary rental market.

According to the census, people of Japanese ancestry constituted the largest group on Profanity Hill: 429 out of the 971 total residents displaced by Yesler Terrace's construction. That population consisted almost exclusively of nuclear families, mostly Japanese parents and their American-born children. In terms of actual numbers, the group included 160 married adults, 226 children (187 under age eighteen, and 39 adult children living with parents), 32 single men, and 11 single women.[20] The concentration of families on Profanity Hill, as well as their generational divisions, reflected broader shifts in national policy that shaped Japanese life and society starting in the early twentieth century. Though the earlier wave of Japanese migration to the Pacific Northwest had been heavily male, this gender imbalance changed with the 1907–8 Gentlemen's Agreement, which cut off the flow of Japanese laborers into the United States. At the insistence of the Japanese government, the Gentlemen's Agreement contained a loophole that allowed Japanese men living in the United States to bring their wives and children over from Japan. From 1908 to 1924, Japanese society in the Pacific Northwest transformed from mostly male to a more even mix of men, women, and children, generating a sharp class hierarchy between male laborers and middle-class families. Many of these families began moving to the Profanity Hill neighborhood to distance themselves from the Japanese laboring classes and occupy homes with more space for small farms and gardens.

Seattle's Japanese population had diminished since its peak in the 1920s. Though still the city's largest nonwhite group, the number of Japanese people in Seattle had dropped by approximately 20 percent during the late 1920s and 1930s, from approximately 8,500 to 7,000, due largely to exclusionary laws passed in the '20s. In the 1922 *Ozawa v. United States* case, the Supreme Court reaffirmed the status of Japanese immigrants as nonwhite people, legally barred from naturalizing as US citizens. Two years later, Congress passed the Immigration Act of 1924, which introduced quotas based on country of origin and effectively cut off all migration from Japan.[21] The cumulative impact of these exclusion laws, along with the economic devastation wrought by the Depression, directly curtailed the growth of Japanese society and generated a wave of reverse migration back to Japan, as many no longer saw a future for themselves in the United States.[22]

As Japanese residents relocated to Profanity Hill, they brought with them small businesses and spaces of cultural and religious practice, creating a hub of Japanese social and commercial activity outside of the older and more established Japantown. Profanity Hill's Japantown included a laundry, a fish market, a butcher, three grocery stores, two gardening businesses, a shoe repair shop, two gas stations, two hotels, two lodging houses, and a Buddhist church.[23] The Seattle Buddhist Church played a particularly important role in prewar Japanese community life. The history of the church stretched back to 1901, when a group of Japanese men came together and founded what they called the Buddhist Mission.[24] Without a permanent site, they moved from place to place, meeting in noodle shops, restaurants, and the basements of hotels until 1908, when they raised enough money to purchase property on Main Street in the heart of Profanity Hill. By 1940, the church served over 1,300 members and functioned as both a religious site and a community center, hosting weddings, funerals, theatrical performances, and festivals.[25] It also anchored what was then a center of Japanese religious activity; three other religious organizations began offering services in the nearby area. By 1940, the Japanese Congregational Church, the Japanese Baptist Church, and the Tenrikyo Washington Church all operated within blocks of the Buddhist Church.[26] Although the three nearby churches escaped demolition, the construction of Yesler Terrace dramatically altered the character of their religious communities.

Second to Japanese families, Profanity Hill's most populous demographic (232 out of 650 adult residents) consisted of single men who listed their occupation on the census as laborers. Though predominately US-born white and Black men, the group also included Filipino men, Chinese men, Japanese men, Indigenous Alaskan men, and European men from over a dozen countries, most notably Finland and Sweden.[27] The concentration of single men on Profanity Hill had to do both with the regional economy around agriculture and natural resource extraction, requiring a seasonal and highly mobile workforce, and the particular factors that confined these

A funeral at the Seattle Buddhist Church, 1920s. Japanese church members gather in front of the Buddhist Church, a building the SHA regarded as slum property and demolished in 1940. Courtesy of David Perley, Densho.

workers to one area of the city. From Seattle's late nineteenth-century emergence as a hub of regional and transnational labor migrations—a stopping-over place for seasonal workers and migrants passing through the city on their way to the hinterlands' labor camps and canneries—laborers had resided in hotels and lodging houses along and below Yesler Way, pushed to the southern part of the city by the same forces of racial and gender exclusion that reserved the northern district for white families. During the 1930s, as the economy shifted away from resource extraction and seasonal jobs became scarcer, many of these men moved to Profanity Hill in search of an affordable and more permanent place to live.

The census also recorded twenty-five Black families and three Black-white interracial families on Profanity Hill. Nearly all of the Black married couples and families with children were new to Profanity Hill at the time of the census; about half had previously lived in different areas of Seattle, while the others came from elsewhere around the state and country. These families joined a small Black population in Seattle that had formed in the mid-nineteenth century and numbered about 3,800 in 1940. As with Japanese residents, class and gender figured centrally in the communities' geographic organization: middle-class and elite Black families occupied Madison Valley to the east, and working-class single men and women lived south of Yesler toward the waterfront, though by the end of World War II these two communities would blend together and form the Central District.[28] Profanity Hill reflected the beginnings of this convergence, with a wide range of income and marital status recorded among Black residents.

In addition to the three Black-white families, nine other interracial families from a variety of backgrounds lived on Profanity Hill: Filipino and white, Filipino and Indigenous, Chinese and white, Japanese and Indigenous.[29] One of these families consisted of Fred Egawa, Grace Celestine-Egawa, and their three children. Fred was Japanese American from Hawaii; he had run away from an unhappy home life at the age of twelve and headed to San Francisco, where he found odd jobs working in restaurants and selling newspapers. He became an amateur boxer, a career that brought him to Seattle; there, he met Grace, a member of the Lummi Nation who had moved to the city following her graduation from the Chemawa boarding school in Oregon. After they married, Fred and Grace settled down on Profanity Hill, renting one half of a duplex alongside the Akutsu family, whose best-known member was Jim Akutsu, leader of the draft resistance movement in camp and inspiration behind John Okada's classic novel *No-No Boy*.[30] It was there that the Egawas had their three children, Marie, Fred Jr., and James. Fred worked a number of jobs over the years—in the Alaska salmon canneries, in a sawmill, and then as a janitor in an office building downtown—while Grace worked inside the home, raising their three children.[31]

The Egawa family experienced two major disruptions during this time. The first occurred in 1940 with their displacement from the Profanity Hill neighborhood. The second happened in 1942, when the family was removed from Seattle and confined to Minidoka following Executive Order 9066. Though not Japanese herself, Grace chose to go with her husband and children and was one of the handful of non-Japanese Americans who were incarcerated during the war. In 1943, when leaving camp became possible for the first time through resettlement programs, Grace returned to the Lummi Reservation with the children.[32] According to her son James, Grace couldn't bear to see her children growing up in Minidoka. James testified about his parents' story during Seattle's redress hearings in 1981. He made a point to mention his mother, bringing her experience into the official record and connecting Indigenous and Japanese Americans' shared histories of forced displacement in the Pacific Northwest.[33]

Profanity Hill residents did not live their lives in isolation from one another. They interacted on the streets, in hallways, and in a variety of commercial spaces throughout the neighborhood. The 900 block of Yesler Way, for example, contained three Japanese businesses (a laundry, a grocery store, and a fish market), one Chinese restaurant, and the Black Elks Club, a Black nightclub and jazz venue.[34] Not limited to commercial activity, the block was also home to individuals and families, including over forty long-term tenants of the Broadway Hotel. The hotel population reflected the broader demographics of the neighborhood: its residents were about half married and half single, only a handful were children, and the majority were Black or Japanese.[35] Washington Street lay one block south of Yesler Way and also featured a mix of commercial and residential spaces. A row of brothels lined Washington Street's 700 to 900 blocks; they operated alongside lodging houses that provided short- and long-term accommodations to Black, white, Japanese, and Filipino men. Gene Akutsu, Jim Akutsu's brother, remembers playing as a child near the brothels along Washington Street. "I thought they were nice ladies," he recalls. "They'd ask me to go pick up some bread or newspaper or milk for them, I'd go out to get it at a grocery, which was about a block away, and in return they'll give me a nickel or dime."[36]

Profanity Hill represented a very different kind of social landscape than the housing project that would replace it. Unlike Yesler Terrace, which would house a group of mostly white families hand-selected by the city, Profanity Hill's community emerged more organically and reflected an integrated world created and sustained by Seattle's most marginalized inhabitants. This is the same community the SHA would dismiss both publicly and privately as an expendable slum, laying the groundwork for its demolition and the mass displacement of its residents.

MAPPING THE SLUMS

In preparing its application to the federal government, the SHA relied on mapping to show that Profanity Hill was the best possible target for clearance under equivalent elimination. Mapping proved a valuable technology for the SHA; it allowed the agency to make arguments about the neighborhood that were laden with moral and racial assumptions about the inhabitants, while doing so in ways that appeared objective and scientific. The agency's maps, which appeared more than any other source in the written application, perfectly encapsulated the equivalent elimination mandate, highlighting aspects of the site that made it ideal for both slum clearance and public housing. Ten detailed maps of Profanity Hill, plus a handful of smaller maps, showed the site as it related to other parts of the city. The site maps each represented a different feature of the neighborhood, from topography to transportation to zoning. Each map contributed to the SHA's case. The topographic map, for example, highlighted the site's location on the face of a long, steep hill, emphasizing the visibility of the current slum area as well as the future housing project. The transportation map depicted various train and streetcar lines converging near Profanity Hill. It illustrated that future Yesler Terrace residents could utilize public transportation with ease, while suggesting that the transportation hub itself would become more upscale with the slum's removal.

While all the maps focused on the suitability of the site's location, only one made a direct argument about Profanity Hill as a slum. The neighborhood map coded each piece of property—inside and outside the targeted area—according to a variety of criteria. These included "residential areas except slums," "slum areas," "areas inhabited primarily by Japanese," "business and commercial areas," "industrial areas," "parks, playgrounds, etc.," and "churches and institutional buildings." Simplified, the criteria measured use, condition, and inhabitants, denoted with a specific color, mark, or combination of both. Though meant to offer an objective assessment of the neighborhood, a close reading of the neighborhood map shows two major inconsistencies in the SHA's visual logic: one related to building use and the other to building inhabitants. The two inconsistencies highlight the subjective nature of the mapping process itself, which revealed very little about the actual neighborhood it purported to depict.[37]

When representing building use, the SHA employed a color-coded system: yellow for residential, green for parks, pink for churches, blue for commercial, and purple for industrial. The system had one exception. The SHA reserved brown for slum areas, which meant that any structure colored brown could not be depicted as anything other than a slum—not a church, commercial area, or residence. In this way, the map presented slums as physical structures without uses. Perhaps unsurprisingly, the SHA categorized nearly the entire demolition zone as a slum area, obliterating the diverse ways in which Profanity Hill residents actually used the buildings. The Japanese Buddhist Church received a slum designation, as did the

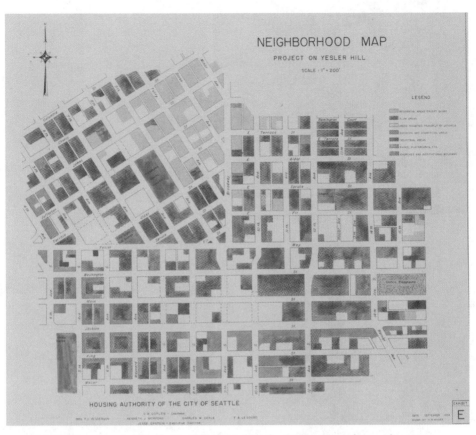

Neighborhood map of Profanity Hill created by the SHA as part of its application to the federal government, 1939. The SHA used colors to categorize the various buildings: yellow for residential, brown for slum areas, blue for business and commercial, purple for industries, green for parks, and pink for churches and institutional buildings. It also used vertical dash marks to indicate areas inhabited primarily by Japanese. The map figured centrally in the SHA's argument that Profanity Hill was an expendable slum area. Washington State Archives, Puget Sound Branch.

commercial strip on Yesler Way dotted with at least twelve small businesses, a hotel, and a nightclub. The SHA applied the slum label to justify their selection of the site, creating an official cartography that supported the goal of clearance. Whole city blocks of commercial, cultural, and social life disappeared as slums on the map, an erasure that would soon materialize in the physical demolition of the area.

The SHA's depiction of Profanity Hill residents likewise revealed more about its own agenda than about the residents themselves. The SHA created a separate category for areas of Japanese inhabitants, the only group of people marked anywhere on the map. By singling out the Japanese and not others, the map gives the impression of a homogenous Japanese district both inside and outside the boundaries of the proposed site. In addition, the map shows almost complete overlap between slum areas and areas inhabited by Japanese residents. While no contextual notes appear on the map itself, the SHA hints at its reasoning in the written portion of the application. When asked to describe the residents of the existing demolition site and plans for their relocation, the SHA lists the Japanese as one of the groups living on Profanity Hill, stating that "they are tending to move from the site and this trend will be expedited to their advantage."[38] In other words, the clearance would simply accelerate a process already underway, helping Japanese inhabitants in their efforts to leave the area. The SHA failed to mention the structural barriers that prevented Japanese people from moving into other neighborhoods, just as their declining numbers in Seattle reflected hardship and not prosperity. But the Japanese presence on the map performed an important symbolic function. It enabled the SHA to claim Profanity Hill as a slum while also obscuring the violence of clearance. The assertion that Japanese people inhabited slum areas but would eventually move away on their own made Profanity Hill appear to be both an ideal demolition choice and one that caused little harm. The visual representation of the Japanese thus figured centrally in the SHA's argument about clearance, while their actual expulsion from the site ensured the success of the Yesler Terrace project. The appearance of the Japanese on the map prefigured their removal from the neighborhood.

Communicating with the public about Yesler Terrace required a different set of arguments than those used with the federal government. The SHA submitted its application in October 1939 and by December received word of its approval by the USHA, which also guaranteed three million dollars in loans to subsidize the project. With funding secured, the SHA embarked on a publicity campaign to raise awareness about Yesler Terrace. Though it had fulfilled all of the legal and financial requirements under the Wagner-Steagall Act, the SHA could not move forward without support from the local public, whose opposition could stall or even sink the project. Powerful Seattleites did not need convincing that Profanity Hill was a slum; they were familiar with the social geography of Seattle and already viewed Profanity Hill as a troublesome, unsightly district that had become an embarrassment to the city. Seattle's elites were much less certain, though, about the question of public housing. Unlike cities such as New York, which had experimented with public housing under the PWA, Seattle had never pursued federally subsidized housing programs for the poor. With no way of knowing how the public would react, the SHA framed Yesler Terrace primarily in terms of slum clearance. Jesse Epstein, in particular, sold the idea of public housing as a way to rid the city of Profanity Hill, appealing to elites, reformers, business leaders, and politicians who would not have otherwise welcomed such a project. As the SHA stated in its USHA application, "From the standpoint of popular as well as civic cooperation, no better choice could possibly have been made."[39]

The SHA turned to photography to make its case to the public. It circulated images of Profanity Hill's buildings in various states of dilapidation, frequently pairing them with descriptions or sketches of the new housing project. A photo collage printed in the first annual report of the SHA exemplified this public messaging. The collage contained eight photographs of Profanity Hill, each showing a different building type found in the neighborhood: a small shack, a three-story Victorian home, a larger apartment building. Peeling paint, broken windows, overgrown brush, decaying fences, and haphazard construction conjured an image of Profanity Hill as broken beyond repair, while the lack of structural uniformity lent an appearance of chaos and disarray. On the other side of the page, a sketch of a future Yesler Terrace building depicted a modern, spacious community center surrounded by grass, trees, and well-manicured shrubs. Unlike the diversity of building types found in Profanity Hill, the new community center and structures surrounding it presented a sleek, uniform façade. To emphasize the contrast, the SHA included a written caption explaining, "These structures are typical of those demolished to make way for Yesler Terrace," adding, "Their elimination not only ends a colorful phase of

Seattle's history, but also signifies a forward step in our community's progress."[40] Relegated firmly to the past, these structures had no place in the modern city, their demolition a necessary and even inevitable step in Seattle's advancement. The caption also made an overt appeal to its audience through the use of the phrase "our community." Clearly, "our community" did not include the residents of Profanity Hill, so glaringly absent from the photographs, but rather the elites and businesspeople whose support the SHA desperately needed to move forward with the project.

The absence of people in the SHA's photo collage contrasted with its neighborhood map depicting Profanity Hill as a homogenous Japanese district. In fact, people never appeared in any of the official photographs of Profanity Hill created for public consumption—just empty, abandoned buildings. This difference underscores how each image's audience shaped what the SHA did and did not say about the project. In communicating in private with the federal government, the SHA revealed truths about Yesler Terrace that it could not openly acknowledge otherwise—namely, that the success of the project depended on the destruction of an existing neighborhood inhabited largely by Japanese individuals and families. Meanwhile, residents' visual absence from the SHA collage was possible precisely because the collage's public audience knew who lived on Profanity Hill and already viewed those residents as expendable. The SHA built public support for Yesler Terrace by masking a social reality that everyone knew to be true. In this sense, the public photographs and the private neighborhood map shared the symbolic work of erasure. Though differing in audience and content, both visual projects functioned to conceal the harm slum clearance necessarily entailed.

The SHA supplemented its circulation of official photographs and sketches with radio addresses and public talks about Yesler Terrace. Like the photographs, these speeches, delivered mostly by Epstein, emphasized the benefits of both slum clearance and public housing. In a 1939 radio address, he discussed the selection of Profanity Hill as the demolition site. "No district in the city," he argued, "more badly needs rehabilitating than this more than forty-acre smudge on the map of Seattle." With the construction of Yesler Terrace, he continued, "we know that a center of low health and morality standards, of high crime and death rates, will cease to exist; we know that the most unsightly urban area in the state will be transformed."[41] Epstein did not shy away from discussing what he viewed as the root cause

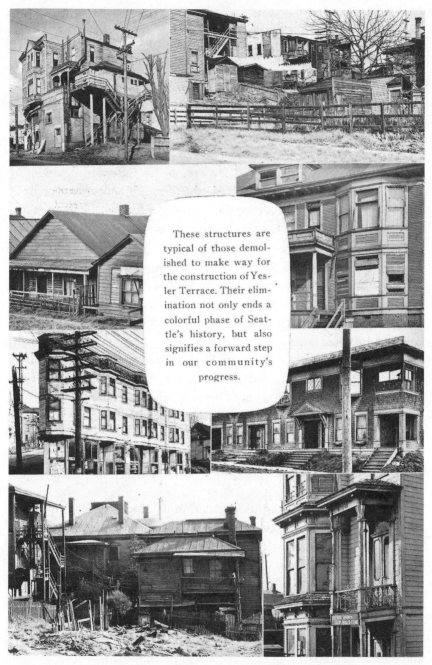

These structures are typical of those demolished to make way for the construction of Yesler Terrace. Their elimination not only ends a colorful phase of Seattle's history, but also signifies a forward step in our community's progress.

Photographs of Profanity Hill as shown in the SHA's first annual report, 1940. Seattle Municipal Archives.

of the housing crisis in the United States: private industry and its inability to provide quality accommodations at affordable prices. But he was able to make these arguments because he positioned the clearance of Profanity Hill as part of the solution, fixating on the dilapidated state of the neighborhood and its possibilities for renewal as major selling points.

The SHA's message appears to have resonated with business leaders and politicians, who did not mount any serious challenges to Yesler Terrace. The project never faced any kind of large-scale public opposition by anyone in the business or real estate industry, two sectors that had fought strongly against the passage of the national housing law. Though tempting to read this lack of opposition as generosity or altruism on the part of Seattle elites, in fact the Yesler Terrace project was part of a larger citywide effort to clear out impoverished urban areas in the post-Depression era. As the economy recovered and the Boeing Airplane Company emerged as a major regional employer, Seattle officials demolished the shantytowns, encampments, and other informal spaces that had sprouted up during the Great Depression to make way for the wartime economy and skilled workforce Boeing had already started to attract. Just months after the clearance of Profanity Hill, city officials burned down Seattle's Hooverville, a nine-acre shantytown on the outskirts of the downtown commercial district.[42] And while the construction of Yesler Terrace could be seen as an effort to alleviate poverty by improving housing conditions for the poor and unemployed, the project's stringent tenancy requirements, which limited access to legally married US citizens with steady jobs, excluded the immigrants, seasonal laborers, single mothers, and others who inhabited places like Hooverville and Profanity Hill. Slum clearance made Yesler Terrace politically possible, and the SHA did what it could to sell the project in exactly those terms.

The SHA received help promoting Yesler Terrace through its relationship with the *Seattle Post-Intelligencer* (the *P-I*), one of Seattle's two main daily newspapers at the time. A husband-and-wife team, publisher Clarence John Boettiger and editor Anna Roosevelt Boettiger, had been hired by *P-I* owner William Randolph Hearst in 1936 and given full control over the newspaper's content. Anna was the daughter of President Franklin Roosevelt. Given Yesler Terrace's origins as a New Deal program, the *P-I* took an interest in the project from the beginning. Irene Burns Miller, a social worker hired by the SHA to oversee the relocation of Profanity Hill residents, recalls in her memoirs close ties between John Boettiger and the SHA leadership.[43] In one case, Ellis Ash, the SHA's assistant director, told Miller that "Boettiger has promised to send a photographer and feature writer next week" in order to generate publicity.[44] At times, the coverage of Yesler Terrace that appeared in the *P-I* closely mirrored the language the SHA used to describe the project. In October of 1939, the newspaper published an article on the proposed Yesler Terrace design, praising its "modern" features and "attractive landscaping, with trees, lawns, and shrubs where barrenness now prevails."[45] To emphasize its point, the article presented a sketch of the new site alongside two photographs of empty, dilapidated Profanity Hill structures. The *P-I*'s coverage made it all the more difficult for the residents of Profanity Hill, most of them renters with little power and few resources, to publicly express any opposition or dissent. They had little control over how their neighborhood was presented to the public.

The SHA's public messaging did not always go as planned, however. In February 1940, the SHA arranged for a *P-I* reporter to shadow its employee, David Young, as he informed residents for the first time about their impending evictions. Though the SHA presumably hoped for a positive spin, the article captured the pain and anger this news caused among the inhabitants of Profanity Hill. The reporter featured the response of Hilda Lundquist, a woman who had lived with her husband in their home for eighteen years: "We don't want a better home," she declared. "We wouldn't be happy anywhere else." The author also profiled Profanity Hill residents Mr. and Mrs. Nogaki, a Japanese couple with ten children, and Esther Blomskog, who told Young she was planning on consulting an attorney. These homes, the reporter concluded, "are hallowed with memories and made precious by the dramas of joy and sorrow enacted there." While the article presented Profanity Hill as part of a fading past, calling the homes "queer old gingerbread houses," it simultaneously offered a more complex and sympathetic view of the neighborhood than the one directly promoted by the SHA.[46]

Expressions of dissent also emerged in private meetings and negotiations. As word spread about the coming evictions, Japanese leaders discovered that the Buddhist Church was located within the demolition zone. The news came as an "awful blow" to the leadership as well as to the church's 1,300 members, many of whom wondered "if the long years it took to finance and build the church in the first place had been in vain."[47] The English-language Japanese press did not present an editorial opinion about the evictions, only flatly reporting on the developments as they happened. The church's leadership, however, sprang into action, hiring an attorney, Mervyn Williams, to explore their legal options. The SHA countered with an offer of $10,000 for the property, which Williams encouraged the church leaders to accept. If they refused, he reasoned, the city would take it anyway through eminent domain, and they would be left with much less. Realizing they could not successfully fight the SHA, leaders handed over the church, which city bulldozers reduced to rubble that winter.[48]

A COMMUNITY DISPLACED

In the fall of 1940, a crisis erupted at SHA headquarters about the issue of racial segregation. Though the SHA had already initiated the eviction process, it remained deliberately vague about who exactly would be chosen to occupy the new housing project. Miller remembers confronting "many erroneous rumors" about Yesler Terrace that summer; yet even she had little information to share with the residents, telling those who asked that "definite decisions regarding tenant selection had not yet been determined."[49] In the absence of any official communication about the matter, word soon spread that the housing authority planned Yesler Terrace as a segregated facility, culminating in a series of articles in the *Northwest Enterprise*, Seattle's local Black newspaper, demanding a public response from the SHA.[50] In addition, lawyers for the NAACP and Urban League wrote to Epstein directly, expressing strong objections to any kind of segregation based on race.[51]

For Epstein, and others involved with the Yesler Terrace project, the charges of racial segregation cut particularly deep. Epstein envisioned Yesler Terrace as a kind of social experiment, to prove that Black and white residents could live together without conflict; if successful, it could serve as a model for future racially integrated housing projects. In part, the SHA's silence about race emerged out of real concerns about how the white public would react to this controversial strategy, one of the few of its kind in the United States. Epstein also worried about interference from local officials if these plans became public. But the agency's lack of clarity about both tenant selection and its broader stance on integration backfired, compelling Epstein to address the issue. In a public meeting with an estimated 1,500 attendees, most of whom were African American, Epstein emphatically stated that the SHA would not enforce any form of discrimination in tenant selection, a point he reiterated several days later in an open letter published by the *Northwest Enterprise*.[52] Seemingly satisfied with his response, Black leaders and organizations threw their support behind Epstein and the Yesler Terrace project, and the controversy soon died down.

Behind these public declarations, however, a more complicated story unfolded. It seems Epstein was less than forthcoming in his statement that the SHA would not discriminate against African Americans. In correspondence with the federal government, Epstein claimed, "Since they represent 95.9% of the population, the city's white group will essentially represent total occupancy."[53] Instead of selecting a tenant population more in keeping with the demographics of the actual site, where whites constituted a minority group, Epstein apparently planned to transform Profanity Hill into a mostly white community with a handful of Black and other nonwhite families scattered throughout. Though the claim could be seen as a tactical move on his part—telling the government what it wanted to hear to avoid controversy or interference—Epstein also pushed for quotas in private, basing the tenant selection process on a predetermined number of slots for Black residents. Miller recalls the existence of a "secret quota system" enforced by the SHA "to avoid creating a ghetto."[54] The residency rates for Yesler Terrace's first two years in operation reflect this tightly controlled selection process: white families occupied 342 units, Black families occupied 12.[55]

While African Americans appeared as only a token presence in this vision of the modern city, Asian Americans did not figure much at all. To those involved in the SHA, race relations meant those between Black people and white people, a framework that left little room for Japanese residents, despite their dominant presence on Profanity Hill. Though SHA leaders did not devote much attention to the question of Asian American integration, they did not have to. The US citizenship requirement for all Yesler Terrace tenants rendered the vast majority of Asian Americans ineligible anyway. Of the nearly one hundred Japanese families living within the demolition zone, only two would have qualified for Yesler Terrace, both of them American-born married couples with children. Further, though US citizens of Japanese ancestry actually outnumbered non-US citizens on Profanity Hill, most of these citizens were children and thus the alien status of their parents effectively extended to them, nullifying their rights and protections.[56] The citizenship clause enforced by the SHA additionally excluded the majority of the city's Chinese and Filipino populations, also considered racially ineligible for citizenship. As with the Japanese, this alien status extended to their American-born children, as well as spouses who were US citizens. Though Yesler Terrace did not maintain an explicit prohibition on interracial families, the SHA's requirement that residents be US citizens rendered ineligible the Japanese, Chinese, and Filipinos in mixed marriages.

Though the SHA focused more on the question of African American access to Yesler Terrace, a handful of Asian American families did make it through the tenant selection process. In its first year, the SHA recorded four Japanese American families and five Chinese American families living in Yesler Terrace. The appearance of these nine Asian American families could be viewed as a step toward true integration. Given the full history of the Profanity Hill site and the displacement of over one hundred Japanese families who did not make it into Yesler Terrace, however, the picture looks much different. The SHA did not need a secret quota system or other informal mechanisms to limit Asian American residency, as it did with African Americans. The citizenship restriction already performed the work of exclusion, ensuring Asian Americans would not constitute more than a small minority within Yesler Terrace.

When looking at who actually benefited from this housing program, Yesler Terrace appears not as an exception to the national trend but very much in line with what was happening around the country. Urban historian Lawrence Vale has pointed out that the Housing Act of 1937, like other New Deal programs, largely targeted working-class white families temporarily down on their luck, giving them a pathway to socioeconomic mobility and, eventually, home ownership.[57] In other words, the program was less about need than it was about shoring up the white nuclear family, weakened in an era of economic catastrophe. Though Yesler Terrace differed from most of its contemporaries in its inclusion of a handful of nonwhite families, the city itself remained deeply segregated by race. Without also transforming the real estate industry and opening up housing throughout the city to nonwhites, Yesler Terrace would continue to function differently for its Black residents, whose paths would not lead to a middle-class life and home in the suburbs. Unlike whites, for whom Yesler Terrace served as a temporary resting place and springboard into the middle class, Black residents encountered structural barriers and widespread resistance in their attempts to access new areas of the city and achieve socioeconomic mobility. The construction of Yesler Terrace and its restrictive tenancy requirements actually exacerbated the problem of racial segregation because it demolished one of the few areas in the city with housing open to nonwhites. Yesler Terrace as a social experiment both revealed and reinscribed the limits of citizenship for African Americans and Asian Americans in Seattle.

Single people and cohabitating couples also lost out in the Yesler Terrace project. The SHA allowed entry only to legally married couples, which disqualified over two hundred single male laborers from a variety of racial backgrounds who lived on Profanity Hill.[58] Though these workers played a critical role in building Seattle and sustaining the area's seasonal and extractive industries, their presence often signaled an area's undesirable character—one of transiency, high crime, and general delinquency. "It was an area of many single people," explained Epstein when asked to describe Profanity Hill, as if to convey the obviousness of both their displacement from the area and their exclusion from Yesler Terrace.[59] The marriage requirements also affected single women, female-headed households, and those in family arrangements that did not include a male breadwinner. According to the 1940 census, seventy-eight single, divorced, or widowed women lived on Profanity Hill at the time of demolition.[60] While these populations may have been in the most need of subsidized, high-quality accommodations, their deviation from the norm barred them from public housing, blocking the avenue for social inclusion and economic mobility it offered.

Yesler Terrace's physical layout quite deliberately revolved around this nuclear family structure. Early in the process, Epstein had decided to eschew standardized government plans and instead recruit a team of prominent local architects to design the new housing facility and its extensive grounds. The architects drew inspiration from European social housing, as well as from the Farm Security Administration's resettlement program, to develop a garden city–style enclave in the heart of Seattle. Instead of the institutional towers that would come to characterize public housing elsewhere in the United States, Yesler Terrace featured two-story row houses with plenty of trees and surrounding green spaces. Though the floor plans and sizes of the dwellings varied, each was built for a married couple or nuclear family and offered a kitchen with an oven and stove, a living room, a bathroom, and separate bedrooms. The site also made available a community center and field with recreational equipment, amenities the SHA described as "basic to the adequate development and safeguarding of family life."[61] To ensure that the tenants were properly caring for their new homes, the SHA employed a team of social workers who periodically inspected the housekeeping efforts.[62] This surveillance of families, borne mostly by the women tenants, highlighted the reformist dimension of the Yesler Terrace project: quality, affordable housing was provided only to those who showed their ability to conform to the SHA's standards of middle-class respectability.

In that sense, the Acor family represented the ideal tenants. In 1940, the *P-I* shadowed the Acors as they applied for housing in Yesler Terrace, and the paper published their story as a series of photographs. Part of a promotional campaign pushed by the SHA, the photos were meant to soothe potential concerns and in general make the white public more comfortable with the project. In a before-and-after pairing, the first photograph depicts the Acors—husband, wife, and two children—in their dark, cramped apartment. Mr. Acor is helping Mrs. Acor hang laundry while the children look on from the bed. While the photograph itself is staged to show their tight quarters, it nonetheless conveys an image of respectable family life. All the people in the photograph are well dressed, their apartment appears reasonably tidy, and Mrs. Acor persists in her domestic duties despite the less-than-ideal conditions. The second photograph depicts the Acor family in the living room of a Yesler Terrace unit, furnished with an armchair, dining set, sofa, side table, and two lamps. The room is bright and spacious, flanked by a wall of large windows. No longer crowded together, Mrs. Acor sits near the couch with one child while Mr. Acor lounges in the armchair, smiling and holding the second child in his lap.

The *P-I* images conveyed two strong visual messages to elicit support for the Yesler Terrace project. First, the photographs presented the Acors as a family deserving of the public good, whose unfortunate conditions had to do not with their own personal failings, but with circumstances beyond their control. Yesler Terrace would provide financial assistance and a proper social environment to help them along their rightful path to the middle class. Second, this visual pairing invited the viewer to imagine what would happen if the Acors remained in their dingy apartment instead of moving to Yesler Terrace. What would become of the children? How much longer would Mrs. Acor be able to maintain proper domestic routines? The SHA assumed that the largely white middle-class readership of the *P-I* identified with the Acors,

Acor family in crowded apartment, c. 1940. MOHAI, *Seattle Post-Intelligencer* Collection, PI23744.

especially given the recent experience of economic instability from the Depression that had left many families vulnerable to financial ruin. The familiar images of domesticity further helped the reader connect with the Acors and Yesler Terrace. The SHA generated support by presenting a white family as the universal ideal, normalizing whiteness not only through policies, practices, and design, but also through images that drew on, and helped shape, prevailing prejudices and fears among white audiences.

The record is vague about how many Profanity Hill residents actually found a place in the Yesler Terrace housing project. Out of roughly 1,000 residents within the demolition site, approximately 750 would have been automatically disqualified through various tenancy restrictions. Fuzzier still is what happened to the neighborhood's residents, mostly renters, after the evictions forced them from their homes. In a report to the housing authority, Miller, who headed Profanity Hill's relocation assistance program, offered some insight: "Some of the white families," she wrote, "moved to the country where the children would have better opportunities for

Acor family in Yesler Terrace model apartment, c. 1940. MOHAI, *Seattle Post-Intelligencer* Collection, PI23745.

health and recreation." Those from racial minority groups "stayed near the southern fringe of the project where there were few restrictions," just as the houses of prostitution "moved to a more segregated district on the edge of Chinatown." Miller recalls that Filipino men married to white women faced great difficulties, calling their search for housing a "headache all its own" because few landlords "were willing to accept them as tenants."[63] Race and gender continued to shape the experiences and opportunities of those displaced by Yesler Terrace: the evictions prompted some to move to neighborhoods with newer housing and more space, while others ended up in more crowded and segregated conditions than they had left behind.

EXCLUDED FROM SEATTLE

The evictions the SHA enforced in 1940 foreshadowed a much larger displacement of Seattle residents. On December 7, 1941, just months after the SHA opened its doors to Yesler Terrace tenants, Japan bombed Pearl Harbor.

Scrap metal donation, 1940s. Japanese Americans were the largest group forcibly displaced by the construction of Yesler Terrace, a model community of predominately white families (pictured here). The message on the sign ("Yesler Terrace: Scrap to Slap the Japs") is particularly striking given the absence of the Japanese at that time, not only from the site on which Yesler Terrace was built but also from the city as a whole. MOHAI, *Seattle Post-Intelligencer* Collection, PI28169.

That evening, FBI agents swarmed the south end, rounding up Japanese leaders and prominent community members identified in the preceding months as threats to national security. Though the government never charged these men with a crime, nor uncovered any evidence of wrongdoing, they endured the war years detained in a labyrinth of immigration facilities, prisons, and enemy alien internment camps.[64] In addition, the US Treasury Department froze the assets of all non-US citizens, leaving the remaining Japanese American community with no leadership and few resources. Four months after this initial roundup, a time remembered by Japanese Americans as one of intense anxiety and uncertainty, government signs began appearing around Seattle ordering all persons of Japanese ancestry to depart the city. They had less than one week to prepare. By the end of May 1942, not a single Japanese person remained in Seattle. Nearly ten thousand city residents, the majority US citizens, were gone seemingly overnight.

The arrests of prominent Japanese "aliens" in the wake of the 1941 Pearl Harbor bombing decimated the leadership of the Buddhist Church. After church leaders had lost their fight against the SHA in 1940, they started the arduous process of rebuilding. They selected a site not far from the original church, just outside the boundaries of Yesler Terrace on the 1400 block of South Main Street. After months of fundraising, they hired Allen K. Arai, a Harvard-trained Japanese American architect from Seattle, to design the new church building. On October 5, 1941, with major construction largely completed, church leaders organized a dedication ceremony attended by over one thousand community members as well as Buddhist ministers from San Francisco, Tacoma, Yakima, and White River valley. Preceded by a "colorful street parade," the ceremony involved the enshrinement of a Buddha statue at the main altar of the church accompanied by classical Japanese music and song.[65] The celebratory mood would not last. One of the first Japanese people arrested after the December attack on Pearl Harbor was Chusaburo Ito, president of the church's board of directors. One by one, trustees, board members, and ministers disappeared, leaving the church's welfare first to the small group who escaped arrest and, eventually, to William Hughes, a white man appointed as guardian of the property in the weeks before the mass exclusion orders came down. During the war, the church suffered extensive damage and its contents were pillaged. Among the items stolen were the belongings many departing Japanese Americans had stored in the church for safekeeping.[66]

On the surface, the demolition of Profanity Hill and the mass expulsion of Japanese Americans from Seattle have little in common. One appears as the unfortunate consequence of a housing project for the poor, and the other as a racially motivated response to war and nationalist fervor. When viewed through the lens of erasure, though, the two acts of displacement look uncomfortably similar. Yesler Terrace required the destruction of a largely Japanese American community, the project's success enabled by decades of laws and policies marginalizing the Japanese in Seattle and the broader United States. In that sense, the well-intentioned whites at the SHA's helm shared with the xenophobes and anti-Asian racists a vision of a world devoid of the Japanese and quite effectively turned that vision into a reality.

Though the Japanese bore the brunt of the demolition of Profanity Hill, they were not alone. The Yesler Terrace project also involved the displacement and erasure of single Black men and women, migrant laborers, sex workers, female-headed households, and Asian-Indigenous mixed families. The modern city envisioned and enacted by the SHA did not include them, either. Though these groups had played a key role in building Seattle and sustaining the regional economy, the city swept them away as it prepared for their replacements: a new manufacturing workforce and a community of white families. The clearance of Profanity Hill and the exclusionary policies implemented at Yesler Terrace were a chilling sign of things to come for Black workers, who began arriving to Seattle in growing numbers during and after World War II, drawn by the Pacific Northwest's booming employment in shipbuilding, airplane construction, and other related industries.[67] As their numbers rose, increasing almost 450 percent from 1940 to 1950, so too did anti-Black hostility. Black workers would find themselves shut out of the highest-paying jobs and restricted from many of the same neighborhoods as the previous generations of workers, excluded as well from the vision of postwar prosperity they themselves were helping to build.[68]

Displacement and Exclusion, Past and Present

"WE ARE NOT A WELCOMING CITY IN THE WAY THAT SEATTLE HAS historically been," former mayor Mike McGinn declared in a 2018 article on the city's skyrocketing cost of living.[1] That year marked something of a Seattle milestone; home prices had shown double-digit increases for the fourth straight year. By April, the median Seattle home price had surged to over $800,000, shattering records and confirming what many residents had long suspected: that their city was changing, and not always for the better.[2] As local and national news outlets rushed to cover the story of Seattle's dizzying post-2008 rise, quotes like McGinn's became commonplace. Long-term Seattleites, politicians, and newcomers alike lamented a city that had strayed from its roots as a welcoming place with a modest, low-key culture. The infusion of corporate power and concentrated wealth threatened to transform Seattle into another San Francisco or New York, a gilded enclave for the rich and privileged.

No place seemed to embody the city's transformation more than the University Village shopping mall. Located in northern Seattle on the outskirts of the University of Washington campus, U Village (as it became known) had opened in 1956 as the city's first residential shopping mall. Unlike Northgate and other malls that would open during the era, U Village featured locally owned stores, such as the Rhodes Department Store and

Malmo Nurseries, that catered to people in the surrounding neighborhoods. After U Village fell on hard times in the 1980s, a new company
bought the struggling mall and rebranded it as an upscale shopping destination. The mall's glitzification accelerated dramatically in the 2010s, mirroring Seattle's broader economic and cultural shifts. The 2018 opening of
a University Village Tesla showroom served as a final nail in the coffin for
many longtime residents, who viewed the arrival of this luxury electric car
manufacturer as an apt metaphor for the fate of the city as a whole. A slew
of blog posts and newspaper articles reminisced about the old mall and the
humbler, kinder Seattle that was slipping further away.[3]

But the notion that there once existed a better version of Seattle ignores
much of the city's actual history, which isn't as rosy as some would like to
believe. The University Village mall provides a stark example. Before it was
U Village, the land on which the mall now sits was once underwater, a
marsh created by the natural ebb and flow of Union Bay and the larger Lake
Washington watershed. The lakes, marshes, rivers, streams, and inlets that
shaped Seattle's distinctive topography made up the homelands of the
Duwamish, the Indigenous peoples of Seattle, who navigated the waters by
canoe and inhabited the surrounding lands for thousands of years. This
particular marsh, known in Lushootseed as *slu?wił* or "perforation for a
canoe," intersected with several freshwater channels, providing a crucial
connection point between Lake Washington and other parts of Duwamish
territory. slu?wił also served as a site for fishing and resource gathering.[4] In
1916, the City of Seattle embarked on a massive engineering project to link
the city's freshwater lakes with Puget Sound and create an industrial water-
way for commercial traffic. The project lowered the water level of Lake
Washington by several feet, which destroyed slu?wił, among other Indigenous sites, and further displaced the Duwamish from their homelands
and waters.[5]

The University of Washington took over the newly available slice of
property and leased it to the city for use as a landfill beginning in the mid-
1920s. Nicknamed the Montlake Fill, the site frequently caught fire, spewed
toxic fumes and dust, and attracted swarms of rats and flies.[6] Around this
time, two Japanese families arrived in the area and opened up produce
farms just a short walking distance away from the Montlake Fill, on the
precise location of what would become the University Village mall. Widespread anti-Japanese hostility, discriminatory laws, and prohibitions on

property ownership had driven many Japanese from the farming business. But these families occupied what the city and real estate industry then considered worthless land, so they encountered little resistance as they built homes, raised children, and worked every day of the year to provide fresh vegetables to local markets around Seattle.[7] Their hard-earned livelihoods quickly unraveled in the aftermath of Japan's attack on Pearl Harbor and the entry of the United States into World War II.[8] As renters, the families had little protection or recourse when President Roosevelt ordered that all persons of Japanese ancestry be removed and confined to inland concentration camps in 1942. What they couldn't sell or store in the frantic days before their removal, the landlords confiscated for themselves.[9]

After the war, investors began to eye this newly desirable land as an ideal location for a shopping mall. During the postwar period, the northern areas of Seattle had transformed from rural farmlands into a sprawling residential district for white families. The U Village company owners envisioned the mall as an explicitly suburban retail space and a gateway to the segregated, exclusionary neighborhoods of North Seattle.[10] The mall's construction went hand in hand with postwar white suburban development, raising property values and offering an insulated retail environment to match the area's insulated racial environment. The longer history of the U Village mall thus reveals its creation not as an open, accessible retail space for down-on-their-luck Seattle families, but as an engine of segregation and white wealth accumulation built upon colonized lands and racialized displacement.

As the story of University Village makes clear, we cannot understand Seattle's present without radically reconceptualizing the city's urban past. This book has sought to reframe the early history of Seattle as a history of displacement, focusing on the laborers who built the city and then were excluded and displaced as they tried to create stable lives for themselves. In doing this, I hope to shed light not only on the early period of Seattle history but also what came after, when the economy shifted and Black workers, many from the South, arrived in growing numbers, as they did in cities up and down the West Coast during World War II.[11] Seattle's transformation into a full-fledged manufacturing economy changed the workforce of the city—from migratory and seasonal laborers to factory workers and others whose jobs did not require constant movement. What didn't change, though, was the embedded structure of race, and the vision of Seattle as a city for white families who could live where they wanted and enjoy all of the fruits of postwar economic expansion. For them, Seattle was indeed the "welcoming" place described by McGinn. But Black workers did not find a welcoming city. Their Seattle was an exclusionary city, one that accepted them for their labor but not their full inclusion in urban society.

The nostalgia that infuses current thinking about Seattle's past not only erases the exclusionary roots of the city's founding but also ignores how these forces continued, and continue, to structure racial inequalities. Our current moment of heightened inequality and rampant gentrification underscores the dire need for critical historical analyses that refuse to romanticize the past. It's through the routes of the past that we can begin to reimagine our present and chart new paths toward more equitable futures.

NOTES

INTRODUCTION

1   Frank Shigeo Kubo, "As I Recall," Frank Kubo Collection, Densho Digital Repository.

2   Kubo, "As I Recall."

3   Cronon, *Nature's Metropolis*.

4   Studies are too numerous to list comprehensively, but key titles include Pacyga, *Polish Immigrants and Industrial Chicago*; Pacyga, *Slaughterhouse*; Fisher, *Urban Green*; Peiss, *Cheap Amusements*; and Brody, *Workers in Industrial America*.

5   See Trotter, *Workers on Arrival*; Nicolaides, *My Blue Heaven*; and Vargas, *Proletarians of the North*.

6   The exception here is the work on Filipino migration in the Pacific Northwest and California. Scholars such as Dorothy Fujita-Rony, Linda España-Maram, and Dawn Mabalon have identified the wide circuits of migration that Filipino laborers traversed in order to find jobs. This book builds on their insights and research by extending the idea of the city as a hub of migratory labor to a much earlier period, involving many different groups. Filipino laborers entered into a preexisting geography of labor migration that originated with the founding of Seattle itself. See España-Maram, *Creating Masculinity in Los Angeles's Little Manila*; Fujita-Rony, *American Workers, Colonial Power*; and Mabalon, *Little Manila Is in the Heart*.

7   In some ways, this disconnect between extractive industries / nonurban labor and manufacturing / urban labor is most pronounced in Seattle. Much of the literature on Seattle labor history is devoted to the Seattle General Strike of 1919, which started along the waterfront with dock and shipyard workers and spread throughout the city. As a result, dock and shipyard work dominates the scholarship on the urban working class. There also exists a large scholarship on Pacific Northwest labor history—logging, in particular—but these works remain outside of the urban context and don't really connect with Seattle history. The exception, as mentioned earlier, remains Filipino/a labor history. See

Nelson, *Workers on the Waterfront*; Friedheim, *The Seattle General Strike*; and Magden, *History of Seattle Waterfront Workers*.

8   Urban historian Carl Abbott argues that Seattle's relationship to its regional hinterland explains the city's "more rapid growth" than Portland. Abbott, "Regional City and Network City," 302.

9   This figure comes from sociologist Norman Hayner's work on hotel living in the 1920s. He used data from the Bureau of Labor Statistics to calculate the number of hotel rooms per inhabitant for each major city in the United States, and found that San Francisco and Seattle ranked first and second, with Los Angeles third. As he notes, "These three Pacific Coast cities have approximately three times as many hotel rooms for their populations as New York or Chicago." While not a perfect measurement of transiency, it does give a very good picture of the kind of urban population present in Seattle and other Pacific Coast cities at this time. See Hayner, "Hotel Life and Personality," 785.

10   I first started thinking about Seattle differently, beyond the nation and outside of the east-west linear narrative ingrained in accounts of this period of United States history, when I read James Clifford's "Fort Ross Meditation." In it, he stands on the California coast and contemplates the intersecting temporalities and perspectives that constitute the "historical." See Clifford, *Routes*, esp. 299–348.

11   Many works on Pacific Northwest history center the water and highlight the unique maritime environment of the Salish Sea, including the Puget Sound. My book builds on these works by examining how this maritime environment shaped Seattle's distinctive history as a city, in terms of social history and the formation of its urban economy and geography. See Reid, *The Sea Is My Country*; Wadewitz, *The Nature of Borders*; Carlson, ed., *A Stó:lō Coast Salish Historical Atlas*; Cummings, *The River That Made Seattle*; Wagner, *Once and Future River*; Thrush, "City of the Changers"; and Williams, *Homewaters*.

12   I am using the word as it appears in *Puget Sound Geography* by T. T. Waterman. This version was edited and revised by Vi Hilbert, Jay Miller, and Zalmai Zahir and republished in 2001 by Lushootseed Press. The name refers to a specific place called "the little place where one crosses over," but became used over time as the name for Seattle as a whole. See Waterman, *Puget Sound Geography*, 44 and 62.

13   Historian Thomas Cox examines the early formation of the Pacific Northwest lumber industry around Pacific markets. As he notes, "The cargo mills were often more affected by what transpired in the lands of the Pacific Basin than by what was taking place in other parts of the United States" (x). Cox, *Mills and Markets*.

14   Chang, *Pacific Connections*, 12.

15   As Karuka writes, "There is no 'national' U.S. political economy, only an imperial one, which continues to be maintained, not through the rule of law, contract or competition, but through the renewal of colonial occupation." See Karuka, *Empire's Tracks*, xii.

16   Harmon, "Coast Salish History," 30–49.

17   Raibmon, *Authentic Indians*, 103.

18   Few scholars of Pacific Northwest history have made the connection between Asian and Indigenous peoples in terms of the maritime environment of the Puget Sound. David Williams's book *Homewaters*, for example, has an extended discussion of the mosquito fleet, a group of vessels that offered transportation to the early Puget Sound settler communities. What he doesn't mention, though, is that the Chinese provided most of the labor aboard these early steamships, including the mosquito fleet. An exception to this is Lissa Wadewitz's crucial work on fishing in the Salish Sea. See Wadewitz, *The Nature of Borders*, 122–143; and Williams, *Homewaters*, 75–87.

19   The connections between western imperialism, capitalist expansion, and Asian migration are well covered in the scholarship. See Cheng and Bonacich, *Labor Immigration under Capitalism*, esp. 211–338; Okihiro, *Margins and Mainstreams*, 3–30; Choy, *Empire of Care*, esp. 1–16; Jung, *Coolies and Cane*; and Chang, *Pacific Connections*.

20   Asians were not immigrants, but rather labor migrants who arrived to the United States to fill a specific economic role. Their exclusion and racialization as unassimilable aliens served to validate white settler claims to Indigenous lands and resources, while also maintaining a critical source of low-wage, disposable labor. This racialized exclusion occurred in the arena of immigration restriction (prohibiting Asians from entering the country altogether once they ceased to be useful as a form of labor) as well as in local laws and policies preventing Asian laborers already in the United States from becoming settlers themselves. These included prohibitions on citizenship and property ownership, as well as segregation ordinances and slum clearance measures that sought to preclude the possibility of Asian residency and permanent settlement. See Lake and Reynolds, *Drawing the Global Colour Line*, 1–48; Moreton-Robinson, *The White Possessive*, xi–31; and Day, *Alien Capital*.

21   For a Los Angeles–based urban history that examines the hobo phenomenon and concerns around transiency specifically with white men, see Hernandez, "Hobos in Heaven: Race, Incarceration, and the Rise of Los Angeles, 1880–1910," 410–47.

22   Shah, *Stranger Intimacy*; and Boag, *Same-Sex Affairs*.

23   I use the term "south end" or "southern district" to describe the area south of Yesler Way, which never had a stable name or identity during this period.

Though certain neighborhoods within the district had their own unique characteristics (Japantown/Nihonmachi, Skid Road, Pioneer Square), they were all formed through the same processes of exclusion and marginalization. Today, these neighborhoods are treated almost as separate worlds in terms of their histories. This book acknowledges the unique historical character of these various districts while also highlighting the fluidity of this world, whose residents shared more commonalities and histories of exclusion than currently addressed in the scholarship or public memory.

24 See Rothstein, *The Color of Law*; Jackson, *Crabgrass Frontier*, 190–218; Woods, "The Federal Home Loan Bank Board," 1036–59; and Winling and Michney, "The Roots of Redlining," 42–69. For digital projects featuring maps and analysis, see Nelson et al., "Mapping Inequality"; and Seattle Civil Rights & Labor History Project, "Segregated Seattle."

25 "Ordinances of the Town of Seattle," *Seattle Weekly Gazette*, March 4, 1865. This will be discussed in more detail in chapter 1. The removal ordinance officially expelled all Indigenous people from the town of Seattle, except for the purposes of labor. It remained officially on the books for four years. The Washington Territorial Legislature dissolved the city government in 1867, then approved its reincorporation two years later, at which time town leaders did not reinstate the removal ordinance. Still, the law had formalized existing sentiments about the Duwamish and influenced the opinions of city leaders about the Duwamish people's presence and future within Seattle—conditions that did not go away when the law ceased to exist.

26 This will be discussed in more detail in chapter 1. See Office of the Commissioner of Indian Affairs, *Report of the Commissioner of Indian Affairs for the Year 1865*, 70.

27 Lake and Reynolds, *Drawing the Global Colour Line*, 1–48; and Atkinson, *The Burden of White Supremacy*, 19–48.

28 Stanger-Ross, "Municipal Colonialism in Vancouver," 541–80; Edmonds, *Urbanizing Frontiers*, 113–83; and Mawani, "'The Iniquitous Practice of Women,'" 43–68.

29 Mawani, *Colonial Proximities*, 37.

30 Lee, *Claiming the Oriental Gateway*; and Fujita-Rony, *American Workers, Colonial Power*.

31 Taylor, *The Forging of a Black Community*.

32 See also Thrush, *Native Seattle*; and Dubrow, *Sento at Sixth and Main*.

33 Taylor, *The Forging of a Black Community*, 159–89. This phenomenon occurred in cities along the Pacific coast, which all saw a massive influx of Black workers during World War II.

34 Shah, *Stranger Intimacy*, 6–9. Marissa Fuentes has also compellingly discussed the issue of archival silence and the erasure of enslaved Black women. See Fuentes, *Dispossessed Lives*, esp. 1–20.

35 Though not a work of history, I'm building here on Don Mitchell's study on migratory laborers and their circulation outside of the state, which he calls "subversive mobility." See Mitchell, *The Lie of the Land*, 58–82.

36 Shah, *Stranger Intimacy*.

37 For more on the built environment as an archive, see Hayden, *The Power of Place*.

38 For a history of the SRO hotel and urban social life, see Groth, *Living Downtown*. For a Seattle-specific history of SRO hotels, see Wong, *Building Tradition*.

39 See, for example, "Gambling Dens Fitted Up Says Mayor of City," *Seattle Daily Times*, March 31, 1920; and "Weird Forts South of King Street Intrigue the Mayor," *Seattle Post-Intelligencer*, March 31, 1920.

40 Hayner, "Hotel Life and Personality," 785.

1. THE SAWDUST

1 "Henry Yesler and the Founding of Seattle," 273.

2 Here, I draw on works in geography and urban history that explore how Indigenous dispossession shaped cities in North America, in terms of property, municipal law, segregation, and other arenas. These works refute the notion that Indigenous dispossession was something that occurred before the city became a city; they instead look at the city as a settler colonial formation, constituted through the ongoing occupation of Indigenous lands. See, for example, Blomley, *Unsettling the City*; Edmonds, *Urbanizing Frontiers*; Mawani, "'The Iniquitous Practice of Women'"; Stanger-Ross, "Municipal Colonialism in Vancouver"; and Thrush, "City of the Changers."

3 Coll Thrush was one of the first historians to highlight the role of Indigenous labor in building Seattle. I expand on his crucial work by including Chinese workers and their role within the urban economy and geography of early Seattle. See Thrush, *Native Seattle*, 47–49.

4 Bagley, *History of Seattle*, 25–27.

5 Gray Whaley offers a detailed and illuminating analysis of the Donation Land Claim Act in Oregon. The act granted land rights to colonists already occupying Indigenous lands, in what Whaley terms "folk imperialism." Furthermore, the primary proponent of the legislation, Representative Samuel Thurston, envisioned the act as a way to prevent African Americans and "Kanakas" (Native Hawaiians), who had worked for the Hudson's Bay Company and remained in

the area, from formally acquiring any of these lands as well. Whaley, *Oregon and the Collapse of Illahee*, 161–89.

6   Robbins, "Extinguishing Indian Land Title in Western Oregon," 11.

7   Denny, *Pioneer Days on Puget Sound*, 16.

8   Prosch, *David S. Maynard and Catherine T. Maynard*, 26.

9   Coll Thrush and Alexandra Harmon have both stressed the fluidity of early Seattle and Puget Sound settler societies. Thrush, *Native Seattle*, 66–78; and Harmon, *Indians in the Making*, 43–72.

10 Miller, *Lushootseed Culture and the Shamanic Odyssey*, 105–10; and Tollefson, "Political Organization of the Duwamish," 135–49.

11 Harmon, "Coast Salish History," 34.

12 Guilmet et al., "The Legacy of Introduced Disease," 1–32; and Harris, *The Resettlement of British Columbia*, 3–30.

13 Quoted in Hill-Tout, *The Salish People*, 22.

14 Denny, *Pioneer Days on Puget Sound*, 13.

15 Leighton, *Life at Puget Sound*, 118.

16 Bagley, *History of Seattle*, 17.

17 Bagley, *History of Seattle*, 20.

18 Waterman, *Puget Sound Geography*, 44.

19 Morgan, *Skid Road*, 30.

20 Finger, "Seattle's First Sawmill," 24–31.

21 Denny, *Pioneer Days on Puget Sound*, 13–14.

22 Letter from Catharine Blaine to her family, August 4, 1854, reprinted in Seiber, ed., *Memoirs of Puget Sound*, 102.

23 Watt, *The Story of Seattle*, 141. As Watt describes, "A bossy little whistle regulated their very lives; they got up by the mill whistle, they ate by the mill whistle, and they set their clocks by the mill whistle."

24 Bancroft and Victor, *History of Washington, Idaho, and Montana*, 24.

25 Bagley, *History of Seattle*, 21.

26 Prosch, *David S. Maynard and Catherine T. Maynard*, 38.

27 Phelps, *Reminiscences of Seattle*, 35.

28 US Federal Census, King County, Washington Territory, 1860.

29 Finger, "Seattle's First Sawmill," 31.

30 "Business of Seattle," *Puget Sound Dispatch*, December 18, 1871.

31 Bass, *Pig-Tail Days in Old Seattle*, 41.

32 Redfield, *Seattle Memories*, 36.

33 "Ordinances of the Town of Seattle," *Seattle Weekly Gazette*, March 4, 1865.

34 *The Statutes at Large*, 1133. For more on fishing, reserved rights, and the fight for Indigenous sovereignty in the Pacific Northwest, see Brown, "Treaty Rights," 1–16; and Wilkinson, *Blood Struggle*, 150–76.

35   Klingle, *Emerald City*, 37.

36   Father Eugène Chirouse, a Catholic missionary on the Tulalip reservation, observed in an 1866 report to the federal government that the Indians living off the reservations were "far better clothed and fed" than those on the reservations. Office of the Commissioner of Indian Affairs, *Office of Indian Affairs Report for the Year 1866*, 394.

37   See Asher, *Beyond the Reservation*. Asher makes a similar argument about the importance of looking "beyond the reservation" to understand Indian-white relations in Washington because of the high proportion of Indigenous peoples who worked in the wage economy and/or chose to live outside of the reservation system. Asher looks at laws passed on the territorial level and disputes over these laws that appeared in the courts.

38   Office of the Commissioner of Indian Affairs, *Report of the Commissioner of Indian Affairs for the Year 1865*, 70.

39   Bonita Lawrence, for example, discussed these gendered dimensions of colonialism. See Lawrence, "Gender, Race, and the Regulation of Native Identity," 3–31.

40   See "The Quarantine," *Puget Sound Dispatch*, June 20, 1872; "The Authorities at Port Townsend," *Puget Sound Dispatch*, June 27, 1872; and "Ordinance No. 30," *Puget Sound Dispatch*, July 4, 1872.

41   "Proceedings of the City Council," *Puget Sound Dispatch*, August 8, 1872.

42   "Ordinance No. 42: In Relation to Indian Women," in *Puget Sound Dispatch*, August 21, 1873.

43   Seltz, "Epidemics, Indians, and Border-Making," 91–114. Seltz writes about how Indian agents, local officials, and others made a connection between Indian mobility across the US-Canada border and the spread of disease. She notes that the 1870s saw growing efforts to control Indian mobility through public health measures.

44   Coll Thrush includes a discussion of the term "sawdust women" in *Native Seattle*, 60. A selection of newspaper articles that use the term include "Sawdust Jack vs. John Thomas," *Seattle Gazette*, March 22, 1864; "The Mud Flat," *Seattle Gazette*, March 29, 1864; and "Siwash Affair de Fisticuffs," *Seattle Gazette*, April 5, 1864.

45   Bass, *Pig-Tail Days in Old Seattle*, 19.

46   Cole and Darling, "History of the Early Period," 119–25.

47   Meares, *Voyages Made*, 3.

48   Lee, *The Making of Asian America*, 45–47.

49   For more on gold rushes and Chinese migration, see Ngai, *The Chinese Question*; and Lake and Reynolds, *Drawing the Global Colour Line*, 13–46.

50   US Federal Census, Columbia Barracks, Clark County, Oregon Territory, 1850.

51 Chin, *Seattle's International District*, 15.

52 Washington Territorial Legislature, *Statutes of the Territory of Washington* (1865), 28. The act was officially titled "An Act to Protect Free White Labor from Competition with Chinese Coolie Labor, and to Discourage the Immigration of the Chinese into This Territory." This "police tax" has been erroneously represented as a "poll tax" in several publications, including Chew, ed., *Reflections of Seattle's Chinese Americans*, 131. In fact, a poll tax was passed during that same legislative session, but it required "white males between 21 and 50" to pay two dollars to vote, not Chinese people. California had passed a similar "police tax" in April 1862.

53 "Tax upon Chinamen," *Washington Statesman*, February 6, 1864. The author of the article goes on to express opposition to removing Black residents from the police tax law: "It is in fact a bill to promote the interests of the white man and to protect white labor; and why a preference or distinction should be made between a black man and a Chinaman we cannot divine."

54 Washington Territorial Legislature, *Statutes of the Territory of Washington* (1868), 46. For more about Indigenous Hawaiian history in the Pacific Northwest, see Barman and Watson, *Leaving Paradise*.

55 Washington Territorial Legislature, *Statutes of the Territory of Washington* (1869), 351.

56 Chang, *Pacific Connections*, 17–53.

57 "A Chinese Wash-house," *Seattle Gazette*, April 5, 1864; and "A Malicious Act," *Puget Sound Weekly*, December 24, 1866.

58 "The Wedding," *Puget Sound Gazette*, March 25, 1867. According to the article, Chen Cheong invited the entire town of Seattle to the wedding; while many people came, no other Chinese people were present.

59 Wong, *Building Tradition*, 32–34; and Lee, *Claiming the Oriental Gateway*, 25–26.

60 For more on Chin Gee Hee, see Chang, *Pacific Connections*, 17–53.

61 Wong, *Building Tradition*, 32–35.

62 *1876 Seattle Business Directory*, 88–90.

63 *Sanborn Fire Insurance Map from Seattle, King County, Washington*, Sanborn Map Company, July 1884, Sanborn Fire Insurance Maps; and advertisement for Wa Chong & Co., *Seattle Post-Intelligencer*, August 8, 1877.

64 US Federal Census, Seattle, King County, Washington Territory, 1880.

65 *Sanborn Fire Insurance Map from Seattle* (1884), Sanborn Fire Insurance Maps.

66 "No Mongolians," *Puget Sound Dispatch*, July 24, 1873.

67 "Letter from San Francisco," *Seattle Post-Intelligencer*, August 6, 1877.

68 Day, *Alien Capital*, 25.

69 Lui, *The Chinatown Trunk Mystery*, 52–80.

70 Prosch, *David S. Maynard and Catherine T. Maynard*, 72.

71 Hunter, *To 'Joy My Freedom*, 74–97.

72 "A Big Fire! A Timely Warning to Seattle," *Seattle Post-Intelligencer*, August 9, 1877.

73 San Francisco had passed a similar law in 1880, requiring a license for all laundries that operated in wood buildings. Though not explicitly stated, the law clearly targeted Chinese laundries in its implementation, as the city approved all of the white applicants and none of the Chinese. Yick Wo, a longtime laundry operator, sued for a writ of habeas corpus after being imprisoned for refusing to pay a fine for operating a laundry in a wooden building. His case was taken to the US Supreme Court, which ruled in his favor in the 1886 case *Yick Wo v. Hopkins*. See "Supreme Court: *Yick Wo v. Hopkins*, May 10, 1886," in Odo, *The Columbia Documentary History*, 76–80.

74 Ordinance 263, "In relation to laundries and wash houses within the fire limits," and Ordinance 223, "Establishing fire limits," in *Ordinances of the City of Seattle*, 643, 641.

75 The 1884 Sanborn map shows eleven Chinese laundries, all located south of Mill Street. *Sanborn Fire Insurance Map from Seattle* (1884), Sanborn Fire Insurance Maps.

76 In a letter, Seattle Fire Chief Gardner Kellogg claims to have "brought suit against five of them" following the passage of the ordinance. Letter from Chief Kellogg to the Seattle City Council, undated, clerk file 991299, Seattle Municipal Archives.

77 In 1894, for example, a group of Chinese businessmen wrote a letter to the city on behalf of the Chinese business operators protesting "the habit and custom of some of the detectives on the police force of the City of Seattle, to enter their residences and places of business, at all hours of the day and night, and without warrant, to search their premises." They invoked the Fourth Amendment, which protects against unreasonable searches and seizures, to plead their case against the police. May 25, 1894, clerk file 992090, Seattle Municipal Archives.

78 Letter from Chief Kellogg.

79 Petition, December 4, 1885, clerk file 991854, Seattle Municipal Archives.

80 Ordinance 710, "An ordinance regulating the establishment and maintenance of public laundries and public wash-houses within the limits of the city of Seattle," February 6, 1886, Seattle Municipal Archives, accessed from the online database of ordinances, September 23, 2020, http://clerk.ci.seattle.wa.us/~public /CBOR1.htm.

81 See clerk files 991422 and 991861, Seattle Municipal Archives.

82 Shah, *Contagious Divides*, 17–76. Shah connects the racialization of people and space in his discussion of the Chinese "health menace" and its containment, which gave rise to a municipal health regime that allowed San Francisco to tout

its status as a modern, forward-looking city. In particular, he discusses the use of local public health ordinances to produce a logic of containment. One such ordinance required five hundred cubic feet of airspace for all adult residents; authorities frequently used this ordinance to harass Chinese lodgers and shut down Chinese lodging houses. While Shah addresses the specific context of San Francisco, his insights apply to Seattle, which passed the same laws and targeted Chinese migrants and business operators in similar ways.

83   US Federal Census, Seattle, 1880.

84   US Federal Census, Seattle, 1880. See also Thrush, *Native Seattle*, 73.

85   See Prosch, *David S. Maynard and Catherine T. Maynard*, 72. For scholarship on Indigenous women and domestic work, see Keliiaa, "Unsettling Domesticity," esp. 1–51.

86   For more on race, migration, and domestic work along the Pacific Coast, see Urban, *Brokering Servitude*.

2. URBAN ROOTS OF PUGET SOUND AGRICULTURE

1   Harrington and Stevenson, eds., *Islands in the Salish Sea*, 9.

2   Miller, *Lushootseed Culture*, 15.

3   Wa Chong to Captain Renton, November 22, 1878, box 38, folder 52, Port Blakely Mill Company Records.

4   Morse, *The Nature of Gold*, 166–90. The National Park Service operates a national historic site in Seattle dedicated to the role of the gold rush in the city's history. The park website's opening text states, "Seattle flourished during and after the Klondike gold rush. Merchants supplied people from around the world passing through this port city on their way to a remarkable adventure in Alaska." "Klondike Gold Rush—Seattle Unit," National Park Service, accessed November 7, 2021, https://www.nps.gov/klse/index.htm.

5   Historian Beth Lew-Williams shows that in Tacoma, for example, the Chinese community was not as segregated as it was in Seattle, with the Chinese more spread out across the waterfront area. Lew-Williams, *The Chinese Must Go*, 99.

6   Some scholars have studied the high participation of Indigenous workers in the hops industry, exploring their complex motivations for pursuing this work. The most notable study, Paige Raibmon's examination of hops as a tourist industry, offers the notion of the "authentic Indian" as a key logic that drove white tourist fascination with the hop fields. She explores how Indigenous hop pickers negotiated their role within an economy that revolved around their commodification. Others have examined the ways that hop picking allowed Indigenous workers to maintain cultural practices by giving them social gathering spaces outside of the highly controlled environment of the reservations. Much less attention has been

paid to the participation of Chinese laborers in the hops industry. Occasionally Chinese hop pickers appear as a small footnote or marginal passage in larger studies on anti-Chinese violence, but no standalone books or articles have been published on the topic. A handful of studies have looked at Chinese and Indigenous labor through a comparative or relational lens, though the books that explore these topics tend to focus on fishing and the canneries. Virtually nothing exists on agriculture. See Raibmon, *Authentic Indians*, 74–115; Parham, "'All Go to the Hop Fields,'" 317–48; and Wadewitz, *The Nature of Borders*, 89–121.

7   Dover, *Tulalip, From My Heart*, 55.

8   Dover, *Tulalip, From My Heart*, 14.

9   Meeker, *Pioneer Reminiscences*, 60.

10   Bagley, *History of Seattle*, 101.

11   This testimony was taken from a petition filed by the Puget Sound tribes in the US Court of Claims for restitution of treaty violations. Though the petition was filed in 1926, the printed version did not appear until 1933. Duwamish Indians et al., *Consolidated Petition No. F-275*, 675.

12   Duwamish Indians et al., *Consolidated Petition No. F-275*, 163.

13   Meeker, *Ox-Team Days*, 155.

14   Dover, *Tulalip, From My Heart*, 52.

15   Meeker, *Hop Culture*, 8.

16   James Hunter Shotwell, letter to Margharete Ross, September 23, 1891, box 1, folder 7, Margharete Ross Shotwell Papers, University of Washington Libraries, Special Collections Division.

17   Burke, *A History of the Port of Seattle*, 8.

18   Friday, *Organizing Asian American Labor*, 20.

19   "Hop Pickers Wanted," *Daily Pacific Tribune*, August 27, 1877.

20   See Harmon, *Indians in the Making*, 72–102; and Asher, *Beyond the Reservation*.

21   Friday, *Organizing Asian American Labor*, 89.

22   Friday, *Organizing Asian American Labor*, 27–47.

23   Muszynski, *Cheap Wage Labour*, 6.

24   "Indians in Town," *Seattle Post-Intelligencer*, September 30, 1879.

25   Bull, "Indian Hop Pickers," 546.

26   Bull, "Indian Hop Pickers," 546.

27   "Indians in Town."

28   Bull, "Indian Hop Pickers," 546.

29   "Local," *Seattle Post-Intelligencer*, September 30, 1882.

30   *Sanborn Fire Insurance Map from Seattle, King County, Washington*, Sanborn Map Company, July 1884, Sanborn Fire Insurance Maps.

31   Bull, "Indian Hop Pickers," 546.

32   "News Items," *Youth's Companion*, 110.

33 Canada Department of Indian Affairs, *Dominion of Canada*, 80.

34 "Puyallup Correspondence," *Tacoma Daily Ledger*, September 6, 1883.

35 The Puyallup River served as a major conduit into the valley. In 1883, a local observer counted "87 canoes containing Indians" that passed up the Puyallup River during hop season. Growers often did what they could to ensure the workers' safe transit; according to a government engineer, local residents removed several blockages in the Puyallup River "to permit the passage of canoes." See "Local News," *Tacoma Daily Ledger*, September 2, 1883; and United States Army Corps of Engineers, *Annual Report of the Chief of Engineers*, vol. 3, 2419.

36 Meeker, *Hop Culture*, 88–89; and Tomlan, *Tinged with Gold*, 120–40.

37 Meeker, *Hop Culture*, 20.

38 Meeker, *Hop Culture*, 20.

39 "Puyallup Correspondence."

40 *1876 Seattle Business Directory*, 88–90.

41 Wong, *Building Tradition*, 32–35.

42 Advertisement for Wa Chong Company, 1879, University of Washington Libraries, Special Collections.

43 "The Difficulty at Squak," *Seattle Post-Intelligencer*, September 10, 1885. The article lists the contracting firm as "Quong Chong," though I could find no further evidence of this company in city directories or census data. It's possible the newspaper made an error and meant the Wa Chong Company, but the primary source may have been correct.

44 "Hop Picking Items," *Seattle Post-Intelligencer*, September 12, 1879.

45 "Hop Pickers Wanted," *Daily Pacific Tribune*, August 27, 1877.

46 "Hop Pickers Wanted."

47 "Puyallup Hop Growth," *Seattle Post-Intelligencer*, September 11, 1877.

48 US Federal Census, Puyallup and Puyallup Valley, Pierce County, Washington Territory, 1870.

49 US Federal Census, Puyallup, Pierce County, Washington Territory, 1880. The census lists fifty Chinese people living in Puyallup in 1880.

50 "Puyallup Tribe: The Story of Our People," Puyallup Tribe, accessed September 27, 2021, http://www.puyallup-tribe.com/ourtribe/.

51 Reddick and Collins, "Medicine Creek to Fox Island," 374–97.

52 Tomlan, *Tinged with Gold*, 126; and Frank S. Bell, letter to family, September 23, 1899, Frank S. Bell Collection.

53 Ezra Meeker, financial records, 1893, Ezra Meeker Manuscript Collection.

54 "From Puyallup," *Seattle Post-Intelligencer*, September 17, 1877.

55 Parham, "'All Go to the Hop Fields,'" 181.

56 Raibmon, *Authentic Indians*, 103–10.

57 "From the Puyallup," *Seattle Post-Intelligencer*, September 20, 1877.

58 Raibmon, *Authentic Indians*, 98–115.

59 "From the Puyallup."

60 Bell, letter to family, September 23, 1899, box 1, folder 7, Frank S. Bell Collection.

61 "Puyallup Correspondence," *Tacoma Daily Ledger*, September 6, 1883.

62 "From Puyallup"; and "From the Puyallup."

63 "Puyallup Correspondence."

64 Eells, *Ten Years of Missionary Work*, 73.

65 Office of the Commissioner of Indian Affairs, *Report of the Commissioner of Indian Affairs for the Year 1865*, 67.

66 Child, "The Boarding School as Metaphor," 37–57.

67 Office of the Commissioner of Indian Affairs, *Report of the Commissioner of Indian Affairs for the Year 1867*, 34.

68 Letter from Charles H. Ayer, 1886, Charles H. Ayer Manuscript Collection.

69 "A New Hop Country," 384.

70 E. Meeker & Co., "Prospectus of the Puyallup Hop Company," May 21, 1891, box 17, folder 2B, Ezra Meeker Manuscript Collection.

71 Meeker, *The Busy Life*, 227; and Tomlan, *Tinged with Gold*, 75.

72 Meeker's mansion still stands today and is preserved and maintained by the Ezra Meeker Historical Society. For more information, including photos, see http://www.meekermansion.org/ (accessed September 27, 2021).

73 Meeker, *Ox-Team Days*, 156.

74 Testifying in a hearing with the US Senate, Meeker stated: "The harvesting is the principal expense. That costs us about 8.5 cents a pound as against 12.5 in New York and 18 cents in England." United States Senate, *Relations with Canada*, 395.

75 Canada Department of Indian Affairs, *Dominion of Canada*, 82.

76 "Hop Picking," *Tacoma Daily Ledger*, September 2, 1884.

77 "Hop Pickers," *Tacoma Daily Ledger*, August 29, 1884.

78 Armbruster, "Orphan Road," 7–18; and Schwantes, *Railroad Signatures*, 35–122.

79 E. Meeker & Co., hop contracts, 1888–1890, box 17, folder 7, Ezra Meeker Manuscript Collection.

80 US Federal Census, Squak, King County, Washington Territory, 1880.

81 "Hops in Washington Territory," *Seattle Post-Intelligencer*, September 1, 1880; and untitled article, *Seattle Post-Intelligencer*, September 21, 1882.

82 Receipt for hops merchandise, box 1, folder 43, George D. Hill Papers.

83 Lew-Williams, *The Chinese Must Go*, 53–90. Lew-Williams reperiodizes the era of Chinese Exclusion, showing that federal Chinese immigration restriction was a more gradual process than scholars have recognized. She notes that the

continued migration of Chinese people into the US after 1882 was a driving force behind the anti-Chinese movements in the Pacific Northwest.

84 Squire, *Report of the Governor* (1886), 4.

85 US Census Bureau, *Washington Territory Population by Race, 1880*, prepared by Social Explorer, accessed December 8, 2021, https://www.socialexplorer.com /tables/Census1880/R12986404.

86 "The Difficulty at Squak," *Seattle Post-Intelligencer*, September 10, 1885.

87 "War of the Races," *Seattle Post-Intelligencer*, September 9, 1885.

88 "War of the Races."

89 Chang, *Pacific Connections*, 17–53.

90 "The Perry Bayne Trial: The Evidence for the Prosecution Still Being Heard," *Seattle Post-Intelligencer*, October 29, 1885.

91 "Arrest of the Murderers," *Seattle Post-Intelligencer*, September 11, 1885.

92 "The Squak Massacre," *Seattle Post-Intelligencer*, September 11, 1885.

93 An Indian agent was a bureaucratic official appointed to act on behalf of the federal government in dealings with Indigenous people in a designated region. Indian agents fell under the jurisdiction of the secretary of the interior and produced yearly reports on the status of the Indigenous populations in their areas. Agents oversaw Indian affairs at the state or territorial level as well as on individual reservations; they involved themselves in local Indian life to varying degrees, with some asserting their power more than others. In Washington Territory, some missionaries also acted as Indian agents, such as Father Eugène Chirouse, a Catholic priest who worked on the Tulalip Reservation.

94 George Tibbetts to George D. Hill, September 21, 1885, box 1, folder 43, George D. Hill Papers.

95 "The Trial of Perry Bayne," *Seattle Post-Intelligencer*, October 28–November 2, 1885.

96 Saxton, *The Indispensable Enemy*; and Jung, *Coolies and Cane.*

97 "War of the Races."

98 "Trial of Perry Bayne," *Seattle Post-Intelligencer*, October 28, 1885.

99 "Perry Bayne Trial," *Seattle Post-Intelligencer*, October 29, 1885.

100 "Trial of Perry Bayne."

101 "Hop Picking Items."

102 Squire, *Report of the Governor* (1884), 9.

103 Raibmon, *Authentic Indians*, 123–28.

104 Genetin-Pilawa, *Crooked Paths to Allotment*, 112–33.

105 For a more detailed discussion of the anti-Chinese violence that swept the western states, including Washington, during the 1880s, see Lew-Williams, *The Chinese Must Go*, 91–168.

106 Friday, *Organizing Asian American Labor*, 47.

107   "Puyallup: News from the Valley Where the Hop Vine Twineth," *Seattle Post-Intelligencer*, August 30, 1888.

108   "Hop Pickers Wanted," *Seattle Post-Intelligencer*, September 5, 1888.

109   "Work for All: In the Hop Fields of White River," *Seattle Post-Intelligencer*, September 6, 1888.

110   Semple, *Report of the Governor*, 50.

111   US Census Bureau, *Washington Territory Population by Sex, 1880*, prepared by Social Explorer, accessed December 8, 2021, https://www.socialexplorer .com/tables/Census1880/R12986430; and US Census Bureau, *Washington Territory Population by Sex, 1890*, prepared by Social Explorer, accessed December 8, 2021, https://www.socialexplorer.com/tables/Census1890 /R12986432.

112   Armitage, "Tied to Other Lives," 17.

113   "Report of John Lamb, Commissioner of Labor Statistics," 1894 and 1895, Civil Service Commission Annual Reports, box 1, folder 1, Seattle Municipal Archives. In 1895, for example, 2,100 white women were placed into homes as "general housework girls" and 1,599 were sent to the hop fields.

114   Semple, *Report of the Governor*, 51.

115   Letters submitted by Pierce County residents and hop growers, as quoted in Semple, *Report of the Governor*, 52.

116   Semple, *Report of the Governor*, 51.

117   "Hop Pickers Wanted," *Seattle Post-Intelligencer*, September 5, 1888.

118   See "Puyallup," *Seattle Post-Intelligencer*, August 30, 1888; and "Work for All," *Seattle Post-Intelligencer*, September 6, 1888.

119   James Hunter Shotwell, letter to Margharete Ross, September 9, 1891, box 1, folder 7, Margharete Ross Shotwell Papers.

120   "Puyallup Items," *Seattle Post-Intelligencer*, October 13, 1880.

121   "Puyallup Pickings," *Tacoma Daily Ledger*, September 2, 1885.

122   Frank Bell, letter to family, August 12, 1899, Frank Bell Collection.

123   Semple, *Report of the Governor*, 51.

124   This is an example of what scholar Juliana Hu Pegues calls "space-time colonialism," a foundational logic of settler colonialism that rendered Asians as out of place and Indigenous peoples as out of time. She connects the spatial with the temporal in her discussion of Asian and Indigenous entanglements and encounters in Alaska. Hu Pegues, *Space-Time Colonialism*.

125   Meeker, *The Busy Life*, 227.

126   Ezra Meeker, "E. Meeker & Co.'s Monthly Hop Circular," November 1892, Ezra Meeker Manuscript Collection.

127   Meeker, *The Busy Life*, 228.

128   Meeker, *The Busy Life*, 228.

129 Newbill, "Farmers and Wobblies," 80–87; and Jones, "The Hops Capital of the World."

130 Raibmon, *Authentic Indians*, 1–14.

131 Raibmon, *Authentic Indians*, 116–34.

132 So far I have only been able to locate two photographs of Chinese hop pickers in Washington, contrasted with the hundreds of photographs taken of Indigenous pickers.

133 Thrush, "City of the Changers," 89–117.

134 "Indians Burned Out: Exodus of Red Men from West Seattle," *Seattle Daily Times*, March 7, 1893.

3. RACE, RADICALS, AND TIMBER

1 "Employment Sharks Cause Trouble," *Industrial Worker*, March 18, 1909, 1.

2 US Department of Commerce, Thirteenth Census, 1910, 252. This report puts the figure at 63 percent.

3 Geoghegan, "The Migratory Worker," 11.

4 Geoghegan, "The Migratory Worker," 11.

5 "The New Immigration Movement," 7.

6 While not specifically about the IWW, Dana Frank's *Purchasing Power* explores the decline of Seattle's labor movement in the decade following the Great Seattle Strike of 1919.

7 Lumber is one of the most studied industries in the scholarship on Pacific Northwest history, but little of the scholarship discusses race—and, more specifically, whiteness—and how the concerns about labor radicalism in the lumber workforce were also concerns about whiteness. See Erik Loomis, *Empire of Timber: Labor Unions and the Pacific Northwest Forests* (New York: Oxford University Press, 2017); Robert Ficken, *The Forested Land*; Cox, *Mills and Markets*; Tyler, *Rebels of the Woods*; and Rajala, "A Dandy Bunch of Wobblies."

8 Cox, *Mills and Markets*, 71–100; Ficken, *The Forested Land*, 1–77; and Buchanan, "Lumbering and Logging," 34–53.

9 Coman and Gibbs, *Time, Tide and Timber*, 51–73.

10 Coman and Gibbs, *Time, Tide and Timber*, 70.

11 It's important to note as well that Indigenous workers continued to play an important role in the Northwest lumber industry beyond the early period, particularly in logging, but they didn't use Seattle as an employment hub as Indigenous agricultural laborers did. See Susan Roy and Ruth Taylor, "'We Were Real Skookum Women,'" in Williams, *Indigenous Women and Work*, 104–19.

12 Teekalet is mentioned in Wray, *Native Peoples of the Olympic Peninsula*, 53. *Klallam* refers to a language group shared by different bands on the Olympic

Peninsula and across the border in Canada. On the US side, there are three Klallam-speaking nations, including the Port Gamble S'Klallam, the Jamestown S'Klallam, and the Lower Elwha Klallam. The history recounted here focuses on the Port Gamble S'Klallam.

13 Wray, *Native Peoples of the Olympic Peninsula*, 53.

14 As quoted in Wray, *Native Peoples of the Olympic Peninsula*, 55.

15 Wray, *Native Peoples of the Olympic Peninsula*, 55–58.

16 Myron Eells, a missionary on the Skokomish reservation, discussed "Clallam" work and seasonal migration in *Ten Years of Missionary Work*, 72–73. He noted that the "Clallam" engaged in seal hunting off the coast of Washington from January through May and hop picking August and September. They spent the rest of the year working at the sawmills or "taking freight and passengers in their canoes" (72).

17 Jerry Gorsline, "History," Port Gamble S'Klallam Tribe, accessed December 8, 2021, https://www.pgst.nsn.us/land-and-people-and-lifestyle/history.

18 Ficken, *The Forested Land*, 56–117; and Wharf, "Regional Transformation," 326–46.

19 Meany, "The History of the Lumber Industry," 283–84.

20 I did not find any mention of private employment agencies in lumber company records, but they show up in municipal government files, labor hearings, and worker testimony and publications. See *Fifth Annual Report of the Labor Commissioner*, 1898, Civil Service Commission Annual Reports, Seattle Municipal Archives; "Testimony of Hon. Hiram C. Gill" and "Testimony of J. G. Brown," in Commission on Industrial Relations, *Industrial Relations*, 4099–112, 4207–24; various cartoons depicting corrupt employment agents in *Industrial Worker*, including October 27, 1909, and December 26, 1912; and clerk file 47403, April 29, 1912, Seattle Municipal Archives. The final source is a complaint filed by Vincent Sorvilla about "extortionate charges exacted by the office above named, which are more than twice the fees charged by most other offices"; Sorvilla requested that the matter be investigated by the city.

21 J. G. Brown, quoted in Commission on Industrial Relations, *Industrial Relations*, 4214.

22 Geoghegan, "The Migratory Worker," 11.

23 R. L. Polk & Co., *Polk's Seattle City Directory* (1896); and R. L. Polk & Co., *Polk's Seattle City Directory* (1905).

24 Polk's 1901 Seattle directory lists seventeen employment agencies operating in Seattle. This is almost certainly an undercount, as the directory printed only the names of legitimate businesses and not those of unregulated or under-the-table businesses. See R. L. Polk & Co., *Polk's Seattle City Directory* (1901), 1322.

25 *Sixth Annual Report of the Labor Commissioner*, 1899, Civil Service Commission Annual Reports, box 1, folder 2, Seattle Municipal Archives.

26 Dillingham et al., *Immigrants in Industries*, 346.

27 Lee, *Claiming the Oriental Gateway*, 46–75.

28 Chang, *Pacific Connections*, 33–43.

29 Chang, *Pacific Connections*, 34.

30 Wray, *Mitsubishi and the NYK*, 408. Wray notes that the primary motivating factor in NYK's pursuit of a deal with Hill was Seattle's location: "Using Hill's rail network, with which it connected at Seattle, the NYK could quote through-freight rates for trade between Asia and the Midwest as well as the east coast of the United States. Japan's principal export, raw silk, could reach east coast ports one day faster via the Seattle route than it could through San Francisco. This gave the NYK an advantage over the Toyo Kisen Kaisha, which had opened a line to San Francisco in 1898."

31 R. L. Polk & Co., *Polk's Seattle City Directory* (1901), 42.

32 US Federal Census schedules, King County, Seattle, 1890, 1900, and 1910.

33 Kihachi Hirakawa, "Autobiography," Kihachi Hirakawa Papers, 10.

34 Japanese American National Museum, *Japanese American History*, 142–43.

35 In many cases, companies simply replaced Chinese labor contractors with their Japanese counterparts. This occurred at the Port Blakely sawmill, which had a contract with Wa Chong to supply labor in the mill and on the company's steamship fleet. As regional anti-Chinese violence escalated during the mid-1880s, Wa Chong struggled to procure workers, searching as far south as Portland, which proved both costly and time-consuming. The sawmill company eventually replaced Wa Chong with the Furuya Company in Seattle. See Letter from Wa Chong to Port Blakely Mill Company, August 30, 1886, box 38, folder 53, Port Blakely Mill Company Records.

36 Japanese American National Museum, *Japanese American History*, 142–43; and "Seattle Historical Sites: 220 Second Ave," Seattle Department of Neighborhoods, accessed August 8, 2020, https://web6.seattle.gov/DPD/HistoricalSite/QueryResult.aspx?ID=1655591672.

37 Dillingham et al., *Immigrants in Industries*, 289.

38 Hirakawa, "Autobiography," 19.

39 This comes from the records of Port Blakely Mill Company, which show that Japanese laborers suffered a disproportionate number of accidents on the job. In August 1902, for example, the Japanese suffered half of all injuries reported to the company, despite being less than 10 percent of the workforce. Insurance Accident Reports, 1902–1919, box 90A, folder 1, Port Blakely Mill Company Records.

40 Ronald L. Olson, "Pacific National Lumber Company," July 16, 1924, box 1, folder 31, William C. Smith Papers.

41 Ronald L. Olson, "Orientals in the Lumber Industry in the State of Washington," box 1, folder 29, William C. Smith Papers.

42 This statistic comes from Olson, "Orientals in the Lumber Industry." Anecdotal evidence also underscores the importance of sawmill and other lumber work for those newly arrived from Japan. Oral histories with Nisei (second-generation Japanese Americans) point to how widespread this work was among their parents' generation. Sociologist Frank Miyamoto noted that most Japanese migrants first worked in sawmills and railroads when they came to the United States, including his father. See Frank Miyamoto, interview with Stephen Fugita, February 26, 1998, Densho Digital Repository.

43 Dillingham et al., *Immigrants in Industries*, 354.

44 Ronald L. Olson, "Crown Lumber Co., Mukilteo, Wash.," August 12–13, 1924, box 1, folder 30, William C. Smith Papers.

45 For more on European immigration to New York, see Anbinder, *City of Dreams*.

46 Pierce, *Making the White Man's West*, 151–78.

47 Pierce, *Making the White Man's West*, 160.

48 Dahlie, *A Social History*, 17.

49 "The New Immigration Movement," 7.

50 Howe, *The Great Northern Country*, 2.

51 Dahlie, *A Social History*, 17–19.

52 Dillingham et al., *Immigrants in Industries*, 346.

53 For more on Europeans, immigration, and the question of whiteness, see Jacobson, *Whiteness of a Different Color*, esp. 13–136.

54 By contrast, Jews in the Pacific Northwest faced barriers in housing and other arenas before World War II. As documented by the Seattle Civil Rights and Labor History project, racial covenants often included Jews among the restricted groups, which reflected their not-quite-white status compared with Scandinavians. "Seattle's Race and Segregation Story in Maps, 1920–2020," accessed December 22, 2021, http://depts.washington.edu/civilr/segregation_maps.htm.

55 Lundstrom and Teitelbaum, "Nordic Whiteness," 151 (quoted passage); and Painter, *The History of White People*, 201–11.

56 Day, *Alien Capital*, 25–31.

57 Dillingham et al., *Immigrants in Industries*, 346.

58 Interview with Signa Linnea Steel (née Anderson), May 17, 1982, Seattle, WA, Scandinavian Immigrant Experience Collection, Pacific Lutheran University, Tacoma, WA.

59 Runblom and Norman, eds., *From Sweden to America*, 249.

60 Kafū, "An Early Account," 59.

61 Kafū, "An Early Account," 59.

62 Kafū, "An Early Account," 59.

63 Kafū, "An Early Account," 59–60.

64 It's difficult to find in-depth scholarly works on race and racial hierarchy in the lumber workforce. I found the sociological study by Ronald Olson conducted in the 1920s to be the most informative. Olson, "Orientals in the Lumber Industry."

65 Dillingham et al., *Immigrants in Industries*, 355.

66 Dillingham et al., *Immigrants in Industries*, 352.

67 Dillingham et al., *Immigrants in Industries*, 352.

68 Japanese laborers typically did not appear on company payroll records, making it difficult for historians to know much about their identities or experiences within the industry. I had to piece together much of the information for this chapter using sources other than company records. In this way, Japanese lumber workers endured a kind of double marginalization, both within the workforce and then again in the archive.

69 Ronald L. Olson, "Crown Lumber Co., Mukilteo, Wash.," August 12–13, 1924, box 1, folder 30, William C. Smith Papers.

70 Robert L. Olson, "Walville Lumber Co., Walville, WA," 1924, box 1, folder 31, William C. Smith Papers.

71 Dillingham et al., *Immigrants in Industries*, 276–77.

72 Dubofsky, *We Shall Be All*, 67–83.

73 "The Preamble of the IWW," *Industrial Worker*, April 29, 1909, 4.

74 Bird, Georgakas, and Shaffer, eds., *Solidarity Forever*, 99.

75 Foner, *History of the Labor Movement*, 218.

76 *Sanborn Fire Insurance Map from Seattle, King County, Washington*, Sanborn Map Company, 1905, Sanborn Fire Insurance Maps.

77 For an example of this rhetoric, see Gompers and Gutstadt, *Meat vs. Rice*, 14–15.

78 Fletcher, "Race Is About More Than Discrimination," 24.

79 "Silly Race Prejudice," *Industrial Worker*, April 22, 1909, 2.

80 "'Cheap Asiatic Labor,'" *Industrial Worker*, May 20, 1909, 2.

81 "Whites Cheaper than Chinks," *Industrial Worker*, April 1, 1909, 4.

82 "Preamble (in Japanese)," *Industrial Worker*, April 29, 1909, 4; and "An Appeal for Solidarity," *Industrial Worker*, June 15, 1909, 1.

83 "IWW Wins Free Speech Fight," *Industrial Worker*, April 1, 1909, 1.

84 For more on the IWW's free speech movement, see Rabban, "The IWW Free Speech Fights," 1055–1158.

85 James Omura, interview by Arthur Hansen, August 22–25, 1984, in Hansen, *Japanese American World War II Evacuation*, 201.

86   Frank, "Race Relations," 37.

87   Itō, *Issei*, 397.

88   Itō, *Issei*, 155–56.

89   Daisho Miyagawa, letter to Bill Hosokawa, February 26, 1968, Daisho Miyagawa Papers.

90   "National Leader of IWW and His Japanese Bodyguard," *Seattle Daily Times*, September 11, 1917, 3.

91   Interestingly, as Dana Frank argues, Japanese workers had some success organizing within the AFL despite the organization's hostile and exclusionary policies. This is because they were able to organize independently in a way that did not "threaten white workers' entrenched position." Frank also notes that she doesn't know how many Japanese workers joined the IWW. See Frank, "Race Relations," 35.

92   George L. Drake, interview by Elwood R. Maunder, 1958, Forest History Society Oral History Collection.

93   DeWitt Ayres, letter to his family, July 6, 1917, DeWitt Ayres Letters to his Family.

94   Willard E. Hotchkiss, in a memo to the federal government, identified "concerted denial of employment" as the most common method of dealing with subversives and potential agitators. See Hotchkiss, "Labor in the Inland Empire Lumber Territory."

95   Activist and trade unionist Charlotte Todes describes the systematic "blacklisting" of potential radicals through a labor clearinghouse maintained by the Western Operators' Association. According to Todes, the association compiled information about workers obtained through employment agencies and refused to hire those suspected of association with the IWW or any radical or subversive political views. See chapter 5, "Breadlines," in Todes, *Labor and Lumber*, 90–100. The labor clearinghouse is also mentioned in Resner, *Trees and Men*, 122.

96   For firsthand accounts of the Everett massacre, see Smith, *The Everett Massacre*; and Everett Massacre of 1916 Digital Collection, University of Washington Libraries, accessed September 20, 2021, https://content.lib.washington.edu/pnwlaborweb/index.html.

97   Historians remain mixed on the legacy of the IWW strike. Robert Ficken views the 1917 strike as a clear victory for lumber companies, who outsourced the repression of the IWW to the federal government. See Ficken, "The Wobbly Horrors," 341.

98   For a discussion of anti-Asian immigration laws (before 1924), see Lee, *At America's Gates*, 19–74; Peffer, *If They Don't Bring Their Women Here*, 1–11; and Chang, "Enforcing Transnational White Solidarity," 671–96.

99   Avrich, *Sacco and Vanzetti*, 122–36.

100   *IWW Deportation Cases*, 4.

101   *IWW Deportation Cases*, 13.

102   Ogburn, "Causes and Remedies," 11.

103   President's Mediation Commission, *Report of President's Mediation Commission*, 13.

104   Ogburn, "Causes and Remedies," 11–14.

105   *Proceedings, Tenth Session of the Pacific Logging Congress*, 20.

106   Howd, *Industrial Relations*, 43.

107   Elwood R. Maunder, interview with Lowell Thomas Murray Sr., 1957, Forest History Society Oral History Collection.

108   Urban historian Margaret Crawford argues that the twentieth-century company town was often built in response to labor struggle. She writes: "Although acutely aware of the Pullman Strike and other labor upheavals in company towns, many employers also saw company towns as a way of avoiding labor problems. The record of labor organizing, unionization, and strikes during this period reveals labor activity as the specific incentive to many 'new' company town commissions. After 1900, there is a startling correlation between strikes and other labor struggles and the subsequent appearance of new company towns." Crawford, *Building the Workingman's Paradise*, 7.

109   Letter from Snoqualmie General Manager to George S. Long, November 22, 1918, box 126, Weyerhaeuser Timber Company Incoming Correspondence.

110   Letter from Snoqualmie General Manager to George S. Long, November 22, 1918.

111   Hebner, *Memories of a Mill Town*, 61.

112   Dillingham et al., *Immigrants in Industries*, 358.

113   Maunder, interview with Murray, 1957.

114   "Manufacturing Plant of Snoqualmie Falls Lumber Co., Snoqualmie Falls, Washington," *4L Bulletin*, December 1919, 18.

115   President's Mediation Commission, *Report of President's Mediation Commission*, 14.

116   Robert L. Olson, "Crown Lumber Co., Mukilteo, Wash.," 1924, box 1, folder 30, William C. Smith Papers.

117   Robert L. Olson, "Crown Lumber Co., Mukilteo, Wash.," 1924, box 1, folder 30, William C. Smith Papers.

118   US Federal Census, Snohomish County, 1920.

4. JAPANESE HOTELS AND HOUSING REFORM

1   Hendrick, "The 'Recall' in Seattle," 652.

2   Lee, "Contradictions of Cosmopolitanism," 277.

3   Hayner, "Hotel Life and Personality," 785.

4   Lee, "Contradictions of Cosmopolitanism," 277.

5   Klingle, *Emerald City*, 86–118.

6   Berner, *Seattle 1900–1920*, 67.

7   "Portland Man to Be Given a Reception," *Seattle Daily Times*, February 19, 1901.

8   Frank S. Bell, letter to family, September 15, 1901, and November 4, 1901, box 1, folder 8, Frank S. Bell Collection.

9   *Annual Report of the Civil Service Commission and Public Employment Office of the City of Seattle*, 1899, box 1, folder 3, Civil Service Commission, Seattle Municipal Archives.

10   "Seattle: A City of Hotels," *Seattle Daily Times*, February 12, 1905.

11   R. L. Polk & Co., *Polk's Seattle City Directory*, 1896 and 1901.

12   "Seattle: A City of Hotels," *Seattle Daily Times*, February 12, 1905.

13   Frank S. Bell, letter to family, September 15, 1901, and November 4, 1901.

14   Wong, *Building Tradition*, 42–48.

15   Hume, ed., *Prosperous Washington*, 118; "Hotel Rates," 24; and "Historical Sites: Diller Hotel," Seattle Department of Neighborhoods, accessed September 21, 2021, https://web6.seattle.gov/DPD/HistoricalSite/QueryResult.aspx?ID=585308361.

16   US Federal Census, Seattle, King County, 1900.

17   *Sanborn Fire Insurance Map from Seattle, King County, Washington*, 1904–5, Sanborn Map Company, vol. 1: 1904.

18   Legally, hotels and lodging houses differed only in size. In 1910, the city defined a lodging house as "a building or any part thereof used for lodging purposes and having more than five and less than twenty-one sleeping rooms," while a hotel was "a building or any part thereof having more than twenty sleeping rooms designed and used for lodging transient guests." Grant, *Ordinances Relating to Buildings*, 14–15.

19   Itō, *Issei*, 520.

20   Itō, *Issei*, 522.

21   Itō, *Issei*, 766.

22   Putman, *Class and Gender Politics*, 70–114.

23   "Sheriff Mark for Final Grand Jury Criticism," *Seattle Daily Times*, March 6, 1910.

24   "Immoral Women Protected," *Seattle Daily Times*, March 28, 1904.

25   Putman, *Class and Gender Politics*, 99–100.

26   "News Narrative," 34.

27   Itō, *Issei*, 519.

28   "Japanese Fujii Employment Office," *Seattle Daily Times*, September 15, 1901.

29   "Japanese-American Employment Office," *Seattle Daily Times*, July 18, 1901.

30   Itō, *Issei*, 766.

31   Itō, *Issei*, 766.

32   Ichioka, *The Issei*, 28.

33   Dillingham et al., *Immigrants in Industries*, 274.

34   "They Fought among Themselves," *Seattle Daily Times*, August 31, 1900.

35   "Forty Burglaries Committed by Five Men," *Seattle Daily Times*, September 11, 1904.

36   "Ten Chinese May Be Deported: Celestials Smuggled across the Border and Found in Japanese Lodging House," *Seattle Daily Times*, July 18, 1904. See also "Alien Japanese Arrested: Four Men Captured Leaving for San Francisco by Boat," *Seattle Daily Times*, June 18, 1904.

37   "War on Lodging Houses," *Seattle Daily Times*, Feb. 25, 1903.

38   Azuma, *Between Two Empires*, 43–48.

39   Azuma, *Between Two Empires*, 48–49.

40   Masanao Hanihara, Secretary of the Japanese Embassy, letter to Ambassador Kotaro Takahira, November 24, 1908, in Itō, *Issei*, 787–88.

41   Hing, *Making and Remaking Asian America*, 27–30; and Daniels, *Asian America*, 100–154.

42   Yesler Estate Building, file 1100, February 10, 1912, box 46, folder 5, Fire Department Central Files, Seattle Municipal Archives.

43   Lodging House Inspection, file 1369, February 13, 1912, box 46, folder 5, Fire Department Central Files, Seattle Municipal Archives.

44   Lodging House Inspection, file 1369, February, 15, 1912, box 46, folder 5, Fire Department Central Files, Seattle Municipal Archives.

45   D. H. Johnson, interview with Wakabayashi, July 15, 1924, box 1, folder 68, William C. Smith Papers; Waka Yamada, *A Trail of Footprints*, as quoted in Itō, *Issei*, 775; and "Two Reformers First Suggested Taxing Women," *Seattle Daily Times*, May 31, 1911.

46   Klingle, *Emerald City*, 97.

47   "Regrade Work to Make Many Changes," *Seattle Daily Times*, October 31, 1906.

48   "New Corporations," *Seattle Daily Times*, March 2, 1906.

49   "George Stetson: The Buyer," *Seattle Daily Times*, March 5, 1906; "The Past Six Days in the Realty World," *Seattle Daily Times*, April 8, 1906; "Seattle's Crying Need: More Stores and Offices," *Seattle Daily Times*, May 27, 1906; "Realty Men Believe Nominal Considerations Should Be Abolished," *Seattle Daily Times*, June 10, 1906; "Something about Seattle's Numerous New Manufacturing Industries," *Seattle Daily Times*, July 1, 1906; "July Realty Trading Now Exceeds Four Million Dollars," *Seattle Daily Times*, July 22, 1906; "Several Big Transfers Are Announced: Market Assumes a Cheerful Tone," *Seattle Daily Times*, April 7, 1907; "Building Permits," *Seattle Daily Times*, December 13, 1908; and "Notes about Building and Real Estate," *Seattle Daily Times*, August 29, 1909.

50 Frank Miyamoto, interview with Stephen Fugita, March 18, 1998, Seattle, Washington, Densho Digital Repository.

51 Shigeko Sese Uno, interview with Beth Kawahara and Alice Ito, September 18, 1998, Seattle, Washington, Densho Digital Repository.

52 Itō, *Issei*, 533.

53 Building plans for 306 Sixth Avenue South, 1914, Microfilm Library, Department of Planning and Development.

54 Itō, *Issei*, 533.

55 US Federal Census, Ward 2, Seattle, 1920.

56 Lee, *Claiming the Oriental Gateway*, 46–75.

57 "City Center of Growing Trade with Far East," *Seattle Daily Times*, July 17, 1917.

58 Seattle Japanese Hotel and Apartment Owners Association, meeting minutes, November 26, 1913, translated by Naoko Tanabe, Seattle Hotel Operators Domeikai Records.

59 Seattle Japanese Hotel and Apartment Owners Association, meeting minutes, January 24, 1914.

60 Warning Notice of the Japanese Hotel and Apartment Association, undated, in Itō, *Issei*, 535.

61 Fire Marshal Harry W. Bringhurst, report to the mayor and city council, February 10, 1919, box 103, folder 4, Fire Department Central Files, Seattle Municipal Archives.

62 Fire Code violation cards, 1919, box 1, Seattle Fire Marshall Fire Code Violation Cards, 1919–1968, Seattle Municipal Archives.

63 US House of Representatives, *Japanese Immigration*, 1115–118. City officials presented a census of Japanese businesses in Seattle as part of the hearings, including a list of all hotels operated by Japanese immigrants.

64 Berner, *Seattle 1900–1920*, 94–95.

65 Seattle Japanese Hotel and Apartment Owners Association, meeting minutes, April 1, 1916.

66 Seattle Japanese Hotel and Apartment Owners Association, meeting minutes, April 1, 1916, and October 19, 1916.

67 *Schlumpf vs. City of Seattle*, 152 P. 673, 88 Wash. 192. See also letters between the fire chief and the Collins Building owners, who contested several of the orders, box 46, folder 19, Fire Department Central Files, Seattle Municipal Archives.

68 Yukon Investment Company to Chief Stetson, Jan. 23, 1913, box 67, folder 46, Fire Department Central Files, Seattle Municipal Archives.

69 Many examples of such leases exist. By 1920, it was common for building owners to agree to pay only for repairs to the roof and foundation, leaving other upgrades and maintenance to the lessees. See lease agreements, 1916–1921, Leases, vols. 36–41, microfilm, King County Archives.

70 These numbers come from my own analysis of several sources. In 1920, Congress conducted local hearings in cities along the Pacific Coast as part of a larger national push to restrict Japanese immigration. Seattle officials presented a census of all Japanese businesses operating in the city; this included a list of Japanese hotels. Local officials tallied 279 businesses for this government report. I located these hotels in the 1920 federal census and mapped them using a digital mapping program. I then tried to find these same hotels in the 1910 federal census to understand how many were previously operated by whites. I found that 110 hotels had changed hands from white to Japanese management from 1910 to 1920. US House of Representatives, *Japanese Immigration*, 1115–18; US Federal Census, Seattle, 1910; and US Federal Census, Seattle, 1920.

71 Superintendent James E. Blackwell to Arne S. Allen, September 21, 1921, box 4, folder 46, Fire Department Central Files, Seattle Municipal Archives.

72 Lease agreements, 1916–1921, Leases, vols. 36–41, microfilm, King County Archives.

73 Itō, *Issei*, 526.

74 Frank Yamasaki, interview with Lori Hoshino and Stephen Fugita, Lake Forest Park, Washington, August 18, 1997, Densho Digital Repository.

75 Dorothy Sato, interview with Linda Tamura, Hood River, Oregon, October 30, 2013, Densho Digital Repository.

76 Victor Ikeda, interview with Richard Potashin, Las Vegas, Nevada, November 6, 2007, Densho Digital Repository.

77 George A. Smith to K. Tarumoto, Jan. 24, 1918, Leases, vol. 39, King County Archives.

78 S. Kreielsheimer et al. to Thomas C. Abe, Aug. 15, 1918, Leases, vol. 39, King County Archives.

79 Ella Hall to S. Ishikawa, Sept. 1, 1919, Leases, vol. 39, King County Archives.

80 Ordinance 28324, "An Ordinance Limiting Fire Hazard in the City of Seattle," November 14, 1911, Comptroller Files, Seattle Municipal Archives.

81 Fire code violation cards, 1919–29, box 2, Fire Department, Seattle Municipal Archives.

82 Fire code violation cards, 1919–29, box 2, Fire Department, Seattle Municipal Archives.

83 Fire code violation cards, 1919–29, box 2, Fire Department, Seattle Municipal Archives.

84 Kanazawa, "Immigration, Exclusion, and Taxation," 779–805.

85 Harumi Guiberson to author, Sept. 25, 2011.

86 Shah, *Contagious Divides,* 46–76; Lui, *The Chinatown Trunk Mystery,* 52–80; and Molina, *Fit to Be Citizens?*, 15–45.

87 Petition, December 4, 1885, clerk file 991854, Seattle Municipal Archives.

88 See, for example, *Committee Report on Health and Police*, n.d., clerk file 991861; and letter from Hop Lee, n.d., clerk file 99142, both in Seattle Municipal Archives.

89 Wong, *Building Tradition*, 179–82.

90 Petition of the Anti-Japanese League for Legislation to Curb Activities of Asiatics in Seattle, October 24, 1919, comptroller file 75079, Seattle Municipal Archives.

91 Itō, *Issei*, 530.

92 As quoted in Hayner, *Hotel Life*, 36.

5. LABOR, INTIMACY, AND THE GREAT DEPRESSION

1 Ben Rinonos, interview with Teresa Cronin, March 27, 1975, Oral History Transcripts, 1974–1977, Washington State Oral/Aural History Program (hereafter abbreviated as WOHP).

2 Anacleto Corpuz, interview with Teresa Cronin, June 23, 1975, WOHP.

3 Schwantes, *The Pacific Northwest*, 381.

4 Berner, *Seattle 1921–1940*, 178–87.

5 Richard Berner notes that Japanese farmers were responsible for the bulk of Puget Sound agricultural activity during the prewar period. Berner, *Seattle 1921–1940*, 188–89.

6 Ngai, *Impossible Subjects*, 96–126.

7 Numbers come from Schmid and Nobbe, "Socio-Economic Differentials," 549–66.

8 Azuma, *Between Two Empires*, 187–207.

9 Mercene, *Manila Men in the New World*, 1–11.

10 Giraldez, *The Age of Trade*, 145–73.

11 Lee, *The Making of Asian America*, 33; and Cordova, *Filipinos*, 1–7.

12 Jacobson, *Barbarian Virtues*, 15–58; and Brewer, "Selling Empire," 3.

13 Jacobson, *Barbarian Virtues*, 221–60; Kaplan, *The Anarchy of Empire*, esp. 121–45; and Immerwahr, *How to Hide an Empire*, 81.

14 Kramer, *The Blood of Government*, 87–158.

15 Baldoz, *The Third Asiatic Invasion*, 45–69; and Friday, *Organizing Asian American Labor*, 126.

16 Baldoz, *The Third Asiatic Invasion*, 60.

17 Fujita-Rony, *American Workers, Colonial Power*, 19.

18 Fujita-Rony, *American Workers, Colonial Power*, 51–75.

19 Fred Floresca, interview with Carolina Koslosky, May 2, 1975, WOHP.

20 Toribio Martin, interview with Dorothy Cordova, April 1976, WOHP.

21 Leo Aliwanag, interview with Cynthia Mejia, August 19, 1976, WOHP.

22 Friday, *Organizing Asian American Labor*, 125–32.

23 The nightmarish quality of Filipino labor migration and Filipino workers' constant search for employment is vividly captured in Bulosan, *America Is in the Heart*.

24 The best examination of restrictive covenants in Seattle's history can be found online with the Civil Rights and Labor History Project at the University of Washington. The project has compiled a comprehensive database of all Seattle neighborhoods with restrictive covenants; it presents this primary source material along with interpretive essays and oral history interviews. Though restrictive covenants existed before the 1920s, the Supreme Court in 1926 ruled that they could not be challenged legally, enabling their proliferation in cities across the United States. In cities on the West Coast, restrictive covenants often targeted Asians specifically, as well as African Americans and Jews. Seattle Civil Rights and Labor History Project, http://depts.washington.edu/civilr/index.htm.

25 Mariano Angeles, interview with Cynthia Mejia, November 6, 1975, WOHP.

26 Mr. and Mrs. Romero Alin, interview with Dorothy Cordova, May 12, 1976, WOHP.

27 Fujita-Rony, *American Workers, Colonial Power*, 123–25.

28 California's original alien land law, passed in 1913, prohibited "aliens ineligible for citizenship" from owning property or holding long-term leases. Washington State passed a similar law in 1921. These laws contained loopholes that enabled many Japanese farmers to retain control of their land, by means including placing land in the names of their American-born children and forming corporations with white shareholders to purchase the land. In 1920, California moved to close the loopholes by prohibiting short-term leasing of property and the use of stock companies to purchase agricultural land. In 1923, Washington State similarly passed an amendment seeking to limit the practice of purchasing land in Nisei children's names. Japanese immigrants challenged the alien land laws in both states, with varying degrees of success. For general discussions of the alien land laws, see Ichioka, *The Issei*, 226–43; and Daniels, *Asian America*, 100–154. For a study of how California's 1920 revision of the alien land law impacted Japanese agriculture in the state, see Suzuki, "Important or Impotent?" 125–43. For Washington's law, see Nishinoiri, "Japanese Farms in Washington," 15–19 and 61–85.

29 Nishinoiri shows that Japanese farming declined significantly in Washington State from 1921 to 1924, dropping from 11,705 acres to 1,164. Nishinoiri, "Japanese Farms in Washington," 18.

30 Ichioka, *The Issei*, 244.

31 Azuma, *Between Two Empires*, 37.

32 Kurokawa, "The Condition of Japanese Immigrants," 155–66.

33 "Gambling Dens Fitted Up Says Mayor of City," *Seattle Daily Times*, March 31, 1920; and "Police Details Switched after Probe Is Made," *Seattle Daily Times*, April 1, 1920.

34 May Ota Higa, interview with Tom Ikeda, December 17, 2004, Seattle, Washington, Densho Digital Repository. Tokio Ota also opened an adjoining restaurant serving Filipino food; May claims it was the first Filipino restaurant in the city.

35 Advertisement for the Japanese-American Employment Office, *Seattle Daily Times*, July 18, 1901.

36 US Census, Seattle, King County, Washington, 1930.

37 Little information exists on Seattle's United Front Committee beyond a handful of similar petitions filed with the city around the same time. It does appear from these petitions that the committee was associated with the IWW or allied groups. In one, the committee requested "free transportation to unemployed to attend May Day demonstration." Comptroller file 135508, Seattle Municipal Archives.

38 "Dream of Youth Realized: Splendid Seven-Story Busch Hotel Now Opens," *Seattle Daily Times*, October 10, 1915.

39 Wong, *Building Tradition*, 125–45.

40 US Census, District 168, Seattle, King County, Washington, 1930.

41 "Petition of United Front Committee for Equal Rights of Citizens Regardless of Race or Color," February 19, 1934, comptroller file 142889, Seattle Municipal Archives.

42 "Weird Forts Are to Be Inspected," *Seattle Post-Intelligencer*, March 31, 1920; and "Police Details Switched after Probe Is Made," *Seattle Daily Times*, April 1, 1920.

43 In the dozens of oral history interviews I consulted in my research, not once did I come across a Filipino laborer referring to this area as Japantown.

44 See, for example, España-Maram, *Creating Masculinity in Los Angeles's Little Manila*, 51–72.

45 Higa, interview.

46 Azuma, "Racial Struggle," 163–99; and Arlene De Vera, "The Tapia-Saiki Incident: Interethnic Conflict and Filipino Responses to the Anti-Filipino Exclusion Movement," in Matsumoto and Allmendinger, eds., *Over the Edge*, 201–10.

47 Azuma, "Racial Struggle," 171.

48 Jose Acena, interview by Dorothy Cordova, July 28, 1975, WOHP.

49 Acena, interview.

50 Writer Hisaye Yamamoto explores this social taboo in her short story, "Yoneko's Earthquake." She describes the emotional fallout of an affair that takes place on

a Japanese farm between a Japanese woman and a Filipino laborer. See Yama-moto, *Seventeen Syllables and Other Stories*, 46–56.

51 Junkoh Harui, interview with Donna Harui, July 31, 1998, Bainbridge Island, Washington, Bainbridge Island Japanese American Community Collection (hereafter referred to as BIJAC), Densho Digital Repository.

52 Frank Kitamoto, interview with John DeChadenedes, April 14, 2007, Bain-bridge Island, Washington, BIJAC, Densho Digital Repository.

53 Kitamoto, interview with DeChadenedes.

54 Toribio Madayag, interview with Teresa Cronin, July 2, 1975, WOHP.

55 Doreen Rapada, interview with Debra Grindeland, February 17, 2007, Bain-bridge Island, Washington, BIJAC, Densho Digital Repository.

56 Harui, interview with Harui; and Frank Kitamoto, interview with Lori Hoshino, April 13, 1998, Bainbridge Island, Washington, BIJAC, Densho Digital Repository.

57 Cuison, "Rediscovering *Oyama v. California*," 979–1042.

58 Kitamoto, interview with DeChadenedes; and Junkoh Harui, interview with John DeChadenedes, February 3, 2007, Bainbridge Island, Washington, BIJAC, Densho Digital Repository.

59 Kitamoto, interview with DeChadenedes.

60 Harui, interview with DeChadenedes.

61 Harui, interview with DeChadenedes.

62 Lilly Kodama, interview with Joyce Nishimura, February 3, 2007, Bainbridge Island, Washington, BIJAC, Densho Digital Repository; and Rapada, interview.

63 Madayag, interview.

64 Montgomery and McNett, "Historic Property Inventory," 9.

65 "Indians Take Bainbridge Island Strawberry Trail," *Seattle Daily Times,* June 18, 1939.

66 Montgomery and McNett, "Historic Property Inventory," 9.

67 Nob Koura, interview with Frank Kitamoto, March 24, 2007, Bainbridge Island, Washington, BIJAC, Densho Digital Repository.

68 Akio Suyematsu, interview with Debra Grindeland, December 3, 2006, Bain-bridge Island, Washington, BIJAC, Densho Digital Repository.

69 "Indians Take Bainbridge Island Strawberry Trail."

70 Dorothy Almojuela, interview with Hisa Matsudaira, February 17, 2007, Bain-bridge Island, Washington, BIJAC, Densho Digital Repository.

71 Koura, interview.

72 Historian Marian Smith provides a detailed overview of the legal status of Native North Americans in immigration matters during the twentieth century. While the Jay Treaty did grant the rights of free movement across the US-Canada border, there were periods when US immigration authorities did not

uphold these rights and policed Indigenous migration in various ways. Following the Immigration Act of 1924, for example, Native Canadians were classified as aliens and granted only temporary visitor status when entering the United States. Following significant protest by the Indian Defense League of America (formed in 1925 to challenge the infringement of Jay Treaty rights) as well as farmers and other employers on the US side who depended on unrestricted access to mobile labor, Congress reaffirmed the Jay Treaty in 1928, again granting Native Canadians free movement. Smith, "The INS and the Singular Status of North American Indians," 131–54. For a critique of how the field of US immigration history has dealt with the issue of Indigenous peoples, see also Volp, "The Indigenous as Alien," 289–325.

73 Yoshimitsu Suyematsu, interview with Tom Ikeda, April 22, 2014, Ontario, Oregon, Japanese American Museum of Oregon, Densho Digital Repository.

74 Lee, *A New History of Asian America*, 242.

75 Parnaby, "'The Best Men That Ever Worked the Lumber,'" 53–78.

76 Almojuela, interview.

77 Almojuela, interview.

78 See Ngai, *Impossible Subjects*, 109–16; and Tsu, *Garden of the World*, 178–84.

79 Rapada, interview.

80 Madayag, interview.

81 Magno Rudio, interview with Apolonio Buyagawan, 1974, Seattle, Washington, Apolonio K. Buyagawan Papers, University of Washington, Special Collections, Seattle, WA.

82 Baldoz, *The Third Asiatic Invasion*, 109–110.

83 Montgomery and McNett, "Historic Property Survey," 11.

84 Madayag, interview.

6. DEMOLITION ON THE EVE OF WAR

1 Berner, *Seattle 1920–1940*, 435. For more on Boeing's rapid expansion and labor struggles during World War II, see Myers, "Boeing Aircraft Company's Manpower," 183–95.

2 Schwantes, *The Pacific Northwest*, 408–11.

3 The lumber industry actually rebounded during World War II from its Depression-era slump, but was overtaken by the war economy and defense-related manufacturing. See Robbins, "The Social Context of Forestry," 413–27.

4 For more on the historical memory of Yesler Terrace, see Megan Asaka, "'40-Acre Smudge,'" 231–63.

5 Radford, *Modern Housing for America*, 59–110; Rogers, *Atlantic Crossings*, 461–84; and Lawrence J. Vale, *From the Puritans to the Projects*, 159–229.

6   Radford, *Modern Housing for America*, 190.

7   Bauer, "Slum Clearance or Housing?" 731.

8   Radford, *Modern Housing for America*, 190.

9   Schwantes, *The Pacific Northwest*, 414.

10   As quoted in *Seattle Housing Authority Annual Report*, 1940, Seattle Housing Authority Annual Reports (1940–2004), Office of the City Clerk, Seattle Municipal Archives.

11   The cooperation agreement, which formalized the relationship between the SHA and the city, focused almost entirely on slum clearance. Resolution No. 12732, November 6, 1939, Ordinances, Office of the City Clerk, Seattle Municipal Archives.

12   Housing Act of 1937, Pub. L. No. 75–412, 50 Stat. 888 (1937). The cooperation agreement repeated verbatim the language on slums and slum clearance from the Wagner-Steagall Act.

13   Seattle Housing Authority, Application for Financial Assistance for a Public Low Rent Housing Project, September 23, 1939, Subject Files, box 10, Seattle Housing Authority, Washington State Archives, Puget Sound Regional Branch.

14   The area is called First Hill today.

15   The King County Courthouse was located on the top of Profanity Hill until 1930. According to local lore, lawyers and others visiting the courthouse cursed as they walked up and down the hill, thus generating the nickname. Though not mentioned in the local stories, "Profanity Hill" also carried an obvious double meaning as the neighborhood grew into a center of prostitution and moral "profanity." See, for example, Paul Dorpat, "Seattle Neighborhoods: First Hill," HistoryLink, accessed September 25, 2021, https://www.historylink.org /file/3095.

16   Taylor, *The Forging of a Black Community*, 86–87.

17   US Federal Census, Districts K-4, M-5, O-2, Seattle, King County, 1940. All population statistics presented in this section come from the same census manuscript.

18   Seattle Housing Authority, *Real Property Survey*, 35–40 and 54–56.

19   The census recorded eighty-five fewer Profanity Hill residents than SHA's real property survey did. It also counted Japanese residents as 45 percent of Profanity Hill's total population, compared with the 33 percent noted in the SHA's statistics.

20   Among those of Japanese ancestry, US citizens far outnumbered non-US citizens within the demolition zone, 258 to 171.

21   For the legal and political context of the 1924 immigration act, see Ngai, *Impossible Subjects*, 17–55.

22 Miyamoto, *Social Solidarity among the Japanese in Seattle*, 18.

23 Note that these are just the businesses located within the demolition zone. R. L. Polk & Co., *Polk's Seattle City Directory* (1939).

24 The Seattle Buddhist Church is the original name. Today, it's called the Seattle Betsuin Buddhist Temple.

25 For more on the early history of the church, see Magden, *Mukashi, Mukashi*, 1–95. For photographs of the prewar Buddhist Church community and its rich social and cultural life, see also the Seattle Buddhist Temple Archives Collection, Densho Digital Repository, accessed December 19, 2021, http://ddr.densho .org/ddr/densho/38/.

26 R. L. Polk & Co., *Polk's Seattle City Directory* (1939).

27 Profanity Hill's adult population, which excludes adult children living with their parents, numbered at 650. Out of 650 residents, men outnumbered women, 411 to 239. Single men (including those who were divorced, widowed, or married but living separately from their wives) numbered 232; 141 of them were white (including European immigrants) and thirty-eight were Black. The remainder included thirty-two Japanese men, thirteen Filipino men, seven Chinese men, and one Indigenous man. Of these 232 single men, ninety-seven were born in the United States and 135 outside the United States, with men from Japan and Finland constituting the two largest immigrant groups (twenty each). US Federal Census, Seattle, King County, 1940.

28 Taylor, *The Forging of a Black Community*, 35.

29 In total, the 1940 census recorded twelve total interracial families within the demolition site.

30 US Federal Census, Seattle, 1940.

31 Svinth, "Nisei Boxer"; US Federal Census, Seattle, King County, 1940; May Sasaki and Chenoa Egawa, "The Egawa Family," *Nisei Veterans Committee Newsletter*, April 2012, accessed August 1, 2021, https://www.nvcfoundation .org/newsletter/2012/4/speakers-series--the-egawa-family/; and "Testimony of James P. Egawa," September 10, 1981, Commission on Wartime Relocation and Internment of Civilians Collection, Densho Digital Repository.

32 "Indefinite Leaves," *Minidoka Irrigator*, July 3, 1943.

33 "Testimony of James P. Egawa."

34 R. L. Polk & Co., *Polk's Seattle City Directory* (1939).

35 US Federal Census, Seattle, 1940.

36 Gene Akutsu, interview with Larry Hashima and Stephen Fugita, July 25, 1997, Seattle, Washington, Densho Digital Repository.

37 All the maps discussed are included in the SHA's application for financial assistance. For more about mapping as a tool of state power, see the work of James C. Scott, who argues that maps reflect the view of their makers,

summarizing complex worlds by highlighting certain aspects and omitting others. SHA, Application for Financial Assistance; and Scott, *Seeing Like a State*, esp. 87.

38   SHA, Application for Financial Assistance.

39   SHA, Application for Financial Assistance.

40   Photo collage included in *Seattle Housing Authority Annual Report*, 1940, Seattle Housing Authority Annual Reports (1940–2004), Office of the City Clerk, Seattle Municipal Archives.

41   Jesse Epstein, "Yesler Hill for Seattle's Low-Cost Housing Project," October 25, 1939, Speeches, Seattle Housing Authority, Washington State Archives, Puget Sound Regional Branch.

42   Klingle, *Emerald City*, 180–202.

43   Irene Burns Miller recalled in her memoir that "the press too would play a vital role in relocation . . . Fortunately, Hearst's *Post-Intelligencer* was managed by John Boettiger, President Roosevelt's son-in-law." Miller, *Profanity Hill*, 19.

44   Miller, *Profanity Hill*, 34.

45   "Yesler Hill Proposed for Housing Plan," *Seattle Post-Intelligencer*, October 1, 1939.

46   "Yesler Hill Residents Fond of Their Homes," *Seattle Post-Intelligencer*, February 26, 1940.

47   Quoted in Magden, *Mukashi, Mukashi*, 104.

48   For a recounting of the church's demolition and eventual relocation, see Magden, *Mukashi, Mukashi*, 104–14.

49   Irene Burns Miller, "The Relocation of Tenants on the Site of Yesler Terrace," January 13, 1941, Research Report Series, Seattle Housing Authority, Washington State Archives, Puget Sound Regional Branch.

50   Miller recounts the reaction by SHA officials to the charges of racial segregation in *Profanity Hill*, 74–76.

51   "Attorney Asks," *Northwest Enterprise*, November 29, 1940.

52   "Housing Authority Replies," *Northwest Enterprise*, November 29, 1940. Epstein also recalls the meeting in an interview with Howard Droker, claiming, "It was one of the largest audiences I've spoken to." Jesse Epstein, interview by Howard Droker, March 13, 1973, Howard Droker Collection, University of Washington Library, Special Collections.

53   SHA, Application for Financial Assistance.

54   Miller, *Profanity Hill*, 19.

55   *Seattle Housing Authority Annual Report*, 1941, Seattle Housing Authority Annual Reports (1940–2004), Office of the City Clerk, Seattle Municipal Archives.

56 For more on Asian American citizenship and New Deal policy, see Brooks, *Alien Neighbors*, 70–113.

57 On the limitations of the Housing Act of 1937, see Vale, *From the Puritans to the Projects*.

58 According to the 1940 census, the racial breakdown of the single male population within the demolition zone included thirty-eight Black men, thirty-two Japanese men, thirteen Filipino men, seven Chinese men, one Indigenous man, and 141 white men.

59 Epstein, interview by Droker.

60 The 1940 census recorded seventy-eight single, divorced, or widowed women living within the demolition site: forty-five white women, nineteen Black women, ten Japanese women, two Chinese women, and two Indigenous women.

61 *Seattle Housing Authority Annual Report*, 1940.

62 Miller, *Profanity Hill*, 111–17.

63 Miller, "The Relocation of Tenants."

64 Kashima, *Judgment without Trial*, 43–66 and 104–126.

65 "Buddhists Dedicate Their Local Temple," *Japanese American Courier*, October 10, 1941.

66 Ronald Magden describes how the events following Pearl Harbor related to the Buddhist Church. Magden, *Mukashi, Mukashi*, 94–110.

67 Taylor, *The Forging of a Black Community*, 159–84.

68 Taylor, *The Forging of a Black Community*, 159–69. For a discussion of discrimination in hiring at Boeing, see Myers, "Boeing Aircraft Company's Manpower Campaign," 183.

CONCLUSION

1 "Open for All?"

2 Levy, "Seattle Median Home Price Hits Record $820k."

3 "University Village through the Years," *Seattle P-I*, January 5, 2011; Rebecca Nelson, "Old University Village Appreciation Post," *Ravenna Blog*, January 5, 2011, http://www.ravennablog.com/old-university-village-appreciation-post/.

4 Waterman, "The Geographical Names," 188; and Waterman, *Puget Sound Geography*, 76.

5 Coll Thrush, "City of the Changers," 89–117.

6 "Garbage Dump Closure Asked," *Seattle Daily Times*, December 19, 1940. According to the article, residents in the surrounding areas filed a petition with the city to close the dump, describing it as "injurious to homes and families . . .

because of smoke, dust, vile and noxious odors" and stating that it "attracts rats, vermin, flies, and seagulls."

7   At the time, marshland was not considered desirable or lucrative from a real estate perspective, which helps to explain why this particular site was available to Japanese farmers. See Chrzastowski, *Historical Changes to Lake Washington*, 7.

8   Three Japanese American families occupied this land. Beginning in the mid-1920s, the Yoshinaka and Tamura families leased the land at 4657 and 4663 Union Bay Place. In the early 1930s, the Yoshinakas moved out (presumably back to Japan, as they are not listed in any US records after 1930) and the Tanagi family moved in to 4657 Union Bay Place, taking over the lease for a vegetable farm and house. For more information, see US Federal Census, District 22, Seattle, King County, Washington State, 1930; US Federal Census, District 13–14, Seattle, King County, Washington State, 1940; Kumasaka, *The Green Lake Japanese American Community*; and the Tanagi Collection, Densho Digital Repository, accessed November 29, 2021, https://ddr.densho.org/ddr -densho-136/.

9   Advertisement, *Seattle Daily Times*, April 15, 1943, 34; advertisement, *Seattle Daily Times*, April 16, 1943, 36; and advertisement, *Seattle Daily Times*, April 18, 1943, 38. The owners of the property took out a series of classified ads selling the farm equipment and materials.

10 "3 Years of Intensive Work in New Store," *Seattle P-I*, August 30, 1956, A3; "Big Ceremony Opens Rhodes 'U-Village,'" *Seattle P-I*, August 31, 1956, 6.

11 For more on Black migration to the West Coast during and after World War II, see Trotter, *Workers on Arrival*; Sides, *L.A. City Limits*; and Himes, *If He Hollers Let Him Go*.

BIBLIOGRAPHY

This bibliography is divided into sections, which represent the different type of sources used in the book. These sections include: manuscripts, newspapers, online databases, and published sources. It's my hope that organizing the bibliography this way will help guide future reading and research on the topic of race, labor migration, and urban history in Seattle and beyond.

MANUSCRIPT COLLECTIONS

Beinecke Rare Book & Manuscript Library, New Haven, Connecticut
 A.W. Smith Papers
 DeWitt Ayres Letters to His Family
 Frank R. and Kathryn M. Stenzel Collection of Western American Art
 Frank S. Bell Collection
King County Archives, Seattle, Washington
 Leases (1889–1969)
Minnesota Historical Society, St. Paul, Minnesota
 Great Northern Railroad Company Files
Museum of History and Industry, Seattle, Washington
 Brand Family Collection
 Pacific Coast Company Photograph Album
 Rainier Heat & Power Company International District Photograph Album
 Ziegler and Rankin Family Papers
Seattle Municipal Archives, Seattle, Washington
 Annual Reports
 Building Department
 Civil Service Commission
 Fire Department
 Police Department
 Seattle Housing Authority
  Clerk Files
  Comptroller Files
  Department of Design, Construction, and Land Use

        Fire Department (Building Inspection Log Book; Central Files;
           Fire Code Violation Cards)
        Health Department
        Office of Urban Conservation
        Ordinance Database
        Water Department (Central Files; Historical Files; Reports
           and Writings)

University of Oregon Library, Special Collections, Eugene, Oregon
        William C. Smith Papers

University of Washington Library, Special Collections, Seattle, Washington
        Building Service Employees International Union Local 6 Records
        Clark Kinsey Photograph Collection
        Daisho Miyagawa Papers
        George D. Hill Papers
        Hop Growers' Association of Snoqualmie, Washington Ledger
        Japanese Association of North America Records
        Kihachi Hirakawa Papers
        Margharete Ross Shotwell Papers
        Oliver S. Van Olinda Photographs and Ephemera
        Port Blakely Mill Company Records
        Ronald Magden Papers
        Seattle Hotel Operators Domeikai Records
        St. Paul & Tacoma Lumber Company Records
        Suda Takematsu Papers
        Theodore E. Peiser Photographs
        Washington State Oral/Aural History Program
        Watson C. Squire Papers
        Willard G. Jue Papers
        William F. Boyd Photograph Album

Washington State Archives, Puget Sound Regional Branch, Bellevue, Washington
        Seattle Housing Authority Collection

Washington State Historical Society, Tacoma, Washington
        A. S. Farquharson reminiscence
        Charles H. Ayer Manuscript Collection
        Ezra Meeker Manuscript Collection
        Oliver Matteson Collection
        Urban Pope Hadley Photograph Collection

Weyerhaeuser Archives, Federal Way, Washington
        Snoqualmie Falls Lumber Company
        Weyerhaeuser Timber Company Incoming Correspondence

White River Valley Museum, Auburn, Washington
       Ed Hart Memoirs
       Olson Family Collection
Wing Luke Asian Museum, Seattle, Washington
       Miscellaneous files

NEWSPAPERS

4L Bulletin
Bainbridge Island Gazette
Daily Pacific Tribune
Industrial Worker
Japanese American Courier
Minidoka Irrigator
Northwest Enterprise
Puget Sound Dispatch
Puget Sound Semi-Weekly

Puget Sound Weekly
Seattle Daily Times
Seattle Gazette
Seattle Post-Intelligencer
Seattle Weekly Gazette
Tacoma Daily Ledger
Union Guardian
Washington Statesman

ONLINE DATABASES

Ancestry (http://www.ancestrylibrary.com/)
Bureau of Land Management, General Land Office Records (http://www.glorecords
    .blm.gov)
Densho Digital Repository (https://ddr.densho.org/)
Forest History Society Oral History Collection (https://foresthistory.org/research
    -explore/oral-history-interview-collection/)
NewsBank, Historic Seattle Times (infoweb.newsbank.com)
Sanborn Fire Insurance Maps (https://www.loc.gov/collections/sanborn-maps/)
Seattle Civil Rights and Labor History Project (http://depts.washington.edu/civilr
    /index.htm)
Social Explorer (http://www.socialexplorer.com/)
UW Digital Collections (http://digitalcollections.lib.washington.edu/)
Washington Secretary of State, Washington Digital Newspapers (https://washington
    digitalnewspapers.org/)
WSU Early Washington Maps (http://content.libraries.wsu.edu/index.php/)

PUBLISHED SOURCES

Abbott, Carl. "Regional City and Network City: Portland and Seattle in the Twentieth
    Century." *Western Historical Quarterly* 23, no. 3 (1992): 293–322.

Adams, Emma Hildreth. *To and Fro, Up and Down in Southern California, Oregon, and Washington Territory.* Cranston & Stowe, 1888.

Anbinder, Tyler. *City of Dreams: The 400-Year Epic History of Immigrant New York.* New York: Houghton Mifflin Harcourt, 2016.

"A New Hop Country." *Littell's Living Age* 50, no. 2133 (1885): 384.

Armbruster, Kurt. "Orphan Road: The Railroad Comes to Seattle." *Columbia Magazine* 11, no. 4 (1997–98): 7–18.

Armitage, Susan. "Tied to Other Lives: Women in Pacific Northwest History." In *Women in Pacific Northwest History,* edited by Karen J. Blair, 5–24. Seattle: University of Washington Press, 1988.

Asaka, Megan. "'40-Acre Smudge': Race and Erasure in Prewar Seattle." *Pacific Historical Review* 87, no. 2 (2018): 231–63.

Asher, Brad. *Beyond the Reservation: Indians, Settlers, and the Law in Washington Territory, 1853–1889.* Norman: University of Oklahoma Press, 1999.

Atkinson, David C. *The Burden of White Supremacy: Containing Asian Migration in the British Empire and the United States.* Chapel Hill: University of North Carolina Press, 2016.

Atwood, A. *Glimpses in Pioneer Life on Puget Sound.* Seattle: Denny-Coryell, 1903.

Avrich, Paul. *Sacco and Vanzetti: The Anarchist Background.* Princeton: Princeton University Press, 1996.

Azuma, Eiichiro. *Between Two Empires: Race, History, and Transnationalism in Japanese America.* New York: Oxford University Press, 2005.

———. "Racial Struggle, Immigrant Nationalism, and Ethnic Identity: Japanese and Filipinos in the California Delta." *Pacific Historical Review* 67, no. 2 (1998): 163–99.

Bagley, Clarence. *History of Seattle from the Earliest Settlement to the Present Time.* Seattle: S. J. Clarke, 1916.

Baldoz, Rick. *The Third Asiatic Invasion: Empire and Migration in Filipino America, 1898–1946.* New York: New York University Press, 2011.

Bancroft, Hubert Howe, and Frances Fuller Victor. *History of Washington, Idaho, and Montana: 1845–1889.* San Francisco: History, 1890.

Barman, Jean, and Bruce McIntyre Watson. *Leaving Paradise: Indigenous Hawaiians in the Pacific Northwest, 1787–1898.* Honolulu: University of Hawai'i Press, 2006.

Bass, Sophie Frye. *Pig-Tail Days in Old Seattle.* Portland: Metropolitan Press, 1937.

Bauer, Catherine. "Slum Clearance or Housing?" *Nation* 137 (December 27, 1933): 730–31.

Berner, Richard. *Seattle 1900–1920: from Boomtown, Urban Turbulence, to Restoration.* Seattle: Charles Press, 1991.

———. *Seattle 1921–1940: From Boom to Bust.* Seattle: Charles Press, 1992.

————. "The Port Blakely Mill Company, 1876–89." *The Pacific Northwest Quarterly* 57, no. 4 (1966): 158–71.

Bird, Stewart, Dan Georgakas, and Deborah Shaffer, eds. *Solidarity Forever: An Oral History of the IWW*. Chicago: Lake View Press, 1985.

Blair, Karen J., ed. *Women in Pacific Northwest History*. Seattle: University of Washington Press, 1988.

Blomley, Nicholas. *Unsettling the City: Urban Land and the Politics of Property*. New York: Routledge, 2003.

Boag, Peter. *Same-Sex Affairs: Constructing and Controlling Homosexuality in the Pacific Northwest*. Berkeley: University of California Press, 2003.

Brewer, Susan A. "Selling Empire: American Propaganda and War in the Philippines." *Asia-Pacific Journal* 11, no. 40 (2013): 1–26.

Brody, David. *Workers in Industrial America: Essays on the Twentieth Century Struggle*. 2nd ed. New York: Oxford University Press, 1993.

Brooks, Charlotte. *Alien Neighbors, Foreign Friends: Asian Americans, Housing, and the Transformation of Urban California*. Chicago: University of Chicago Press, 2009.

Brown, Jovanna J. "Treaty Rights: Twenty Years after the Boldt Decision." *Wicazo Sa Review* 10, no. 2 (1994): 1–16.

Buchanan, Iva L. "Lumbering and Logging in the Puget Sound Region in Territorial Days." *Pacific Northwest Quarterly* 27, no. 1 (1936): 34–53.

Bull, W. H. "Indian Hop Pickers on Puget Sound." *Harper's Weekly* 36 (June 4, 1892): 546.

Bulosan, Carlos. *America Is in the Heart*. Seattle: University of Washington Press, 1973.

Burke, Padraic. *A History of the Port of Seattle*. Seattle: Port of Seattle, 1976.

Canada Department of Indian Affairs. *Dominion of Canada: Annual Report of the Department of Indian Affairs for the Year Ending 31st December 1885*. Ottawa: Maclean, Roger & Co., 1886.

Carlson, Keith Thor, ed. *A Stó:lō Coast Salish Historical Atlas*. Seattle: University of Washington Press, 2001.

Chang, Kornel. "Enforcing Transnational White Solidarity: Asian Migration and the Formation of the U.S.-Canadian Boundary." *American Quarterly* 60, no. 3 (2008): 671–96.

————. *Pacific Connections: The Making of the U.S.-Canada Borderlands*. Berkeley: California University Press, 2012.

Cheng, Lucie, and Edna Bonacich, eds. *Labor Immigration under Capitalism: Asian Workers in the United States before World War II*. Berkeley: University of California Press, 1984.

Chew, Ron, ed. *Reflections of Seattle's Chinese Americans: The First 100 Years*. Seattle: Wing Luke Museum, 1994.

Child, Brenda. "The Boarding School as Metaphor." *Journal of American Indian Education* 57, no. 1 (2018): 37–57.

Chin, Doug. *Seattle's International District: The Making of a Pan-Asian Community*. Seattle: International Examiner Press, 2001.

Choy, Catherine Ceniza. *Empire of Care: Nursing and Migration in Filipino American History*. Durham: Duke University Press, 2003.

Chrzastowski, Martin. *Historical Changes to Lake Washington and the Route of the Lake Washington Ship Canal, King County, Washington*. US Geological Survey, 1983.

Clifford, James. *Routes: Travel and Translation in the Late Twentieth Century*. Cambridge, MA: Harvard University Press, 1997.

Cole, Douglas, and David Darling. "History of the Early Period." In *Handbook of North American Indians*. Vol. 7, *Northwest Coast*, edited by Wayne Suttles and William Sturtevant, 119–34. Washington, DC: Government Printing Office, 1990.

Coman, Edwin T., Jr., and Helen M. Gibbs. *Time, Tide, and Timber: A Century of Pope & Talbot*. Palo Alto: Stanford University Press, 1949.

Commission on Industrial Relations. *Industrial Relations: Final Report and Testimony Submitted to Congress by the Commission on Industrial Relations*. Washington, DC: Government Printing Office, 1916.

Cordova, Fred. *Filipinos: Forgotten Asian Americans*. Demonstration Project for Asian Americans, 1983.

Cox, Thomas. *Mills and Markets: A History of the Pacific Coast Lumber Industry to 1900*. Seattle: University of Washington Press, 1974.

Crawford, Margaret. *Building the Workingman's Paradise: The Design of American Company Towns*. New York: Verso, 1995.

Cronon, William. *Nature's Metropolis: Chicago and the Great West*. New York: W. W. Norton, 1992.

Cuison, Rose Villazor. "Rediscovering *Oyama v. California*: At the Intersection of Property, Race, and Citizenship." *Washington University Law Review* 87, no. 5 (2010): 979–1042.

Cummings, BJ. *The River that Made Seattle: A Human and Natural History of the Duwamish*. Seattle: University of Washington Press, 2020.

Dahlie, Jorgen. *A Social History of Scandinavian Immigration, Washington State, 1895–1910*. New York: Arno Press, 1980.

Daniels, Roger. *Asian America: Chinese and Japanese in the United States Since 1850*. Seattle: University of Washington Press, 1988.

Day, Iyko. *Alien Capital: Asian Racialization and the Logic of Settler Colonial Capitalism*. Durham: Duke University Press, 2016.

Denny, Arthur Armstrong. *Pioneer Days on Puget Sound.* Seattle: C. B. Bagley, 1888.

Dillingham, William P., Henry A. Millis, and United States Immigration Commission. *Immigrants in Industries: Pt. 25; Japanese and Other Immigrant Races in the Pacific Coast and Rocky Mountain States.* Vols. 23–25. Washington, DC: Government Printing Office, 1911.

Dover, Harriet Shelton. *Tulalip, From My Heart: An Autobiographical Account of a Reservation Community.* Seattle: University of Washington Press, 2013.

Dubofsky, Melvyn. *We Shall Be All: A History of the Industrial Workers of the World.* Urbana-Champaign: University of Illinois Press, 2000.

Dubrow, Gail. *Sento at Sixth and Main: Preserving Landmarks of Japanese American Heritage.* Seattle: University of Washington Press, 2002.

Duwamish Indians et al., claimants. *The Duwamish, Lummi, Whidbey Island, Skagit, Upper Skagit, Swinomish, Kikiallus, Snohomish, Snoqualmie, Stillaguamish, Suquamish, Samish, Puyallup, Squaxin, Skokomish, Upper Chehalis, Muckleshoot, Nooksack, Chinook and San Juan Islands Tribes of Indians, Claimants, vs. United States of America, Defendant, Consolidated Petition No. F-275.* Seattle: Argus Press, 1933.

Edmonds, Penelope. *Urbanizing Frontiers: Indigenous Peoples and Settlers in 19th-Century Pacific Rim Cities.* Vancouver: University of British Columbia Press, 2010.

Eells, Myron. *Ten Years of Missionary Work Among the Indians at Skokomish, Washington Territory, 1874–1884.* Boston: Congregational Sunday School and Publishing Society, 1886.

1876 Seattle Business Directory. Seattle: B. L. Northup, 1876.

España-Maram, Linda. *Creating Masculinity in Los Angeles's Little Manila: Working-Class Filipinos and Popular Culture, 1920s–1950s.* New York: Columbia University Press, 2006.

Ficken, Robert. *The Forested Land: A History of Lumbering in Western Washington.* Seattle: University of Washington Press, 1987.

———. "The Wobbly Horrors: The Pacific Northwest Lumbermen and the Industrial Workers of the World, 1917–1918." *Labor History* 24 (1983): 325–41.

Finger, John. "Seattle's First Sawmill, 1853–1869: A Study of Frontier Enterprise." *Forest History* 15, no. 4 (1972): 24–31.

Fisher, Colin. *Urban Green: Nature, Recreation, and the Working Class in Industrial Chicago.* Chapel Hill: University of North Carolina Press, 2015.

Fletcher, Bill, Jr. "Race Is About More Than Discrimination: Racial Capitalism, the Settler State, and the Challenges Facing Organized Labor in the United States." *Monthly Review* 72, no. 3 (2020): 21–31.

Foner, Philip S. *History of the Labor Movement in the United States.* Vol. 4, *The Industrial Workers of the World, 1905–1917.* New York: International, 1965.

Frank, Dana. *Purchasing Power: Consumer Organizing, Gender, and the Seattle Labor Movement, 1919–1929*. New York: Cambridge University Press, 1994.

———. "Race Relations and the Seattle Labor Movement, 1915–1929." *Pacific Northwest Quarterly* 36, no. 1 (1994/1995): 35–44.

Friday, Chris. *Organizing Asian American Labor: The Pacific Coast Canned-Salmon Industry, 1870–1942*. Philadelphia: Temple University Press, 1994.

Friedheim, Robert L. *The Seattle General Strike*. Centennial ed. Seattle: University of Washington Press, 2018.

Fuentes, Marissa. *Dispossessed Lives: Enslaved Women, Violence, and the Archive*. Philadelphia: University of Pennsylvania Press, 2016.

Fujita-Rony, Dorothy. *American Workers, Colonial Power: Philippine Seattle and the Transpacific West, 1919–1941*. Berkeley: University of California Press, 2003.

———. "Water and Land: Asian Americans and the U.S. West." *Pacific Historical Review* 76, no. 4 (November 1, 2007): 563–74.

Genetin-Pilawa, C. Joseph. *Crooked Paths to Allotment: The Fight over Federal Indian Policy after the Civil War*. Chapel Hill: University of North Carolina Press, 2012.

Geoghegan, John. "The Migratory Worker in Seattle: A Study in Social Disorganization and Exploitation." PhD diss., University of Washington, 1923.

Giraldez, Arturo. *The Age of Trade: The Manila Galleons and the Dawn of the Global Economy*. Lanham, MD: Rowman & Littlefield, 2015.

Gompers, Samuel, and Herman Gutstadt. *Meat vs. Rice: American Manhood against Asiatic Coolieism; Which Shall Survive?* Reprinted by Asiatic Exclusion League of San Francisco. San Francisco: Allied Printing, 1908.

Grant, Francis F. *Ordinances Relating to Buildings, City of Seattle*. Seattle: Lowman & Hanford, 1910.

Groth, Paul. *Living Downtown: The History of Residential Hotels in the United States*. Berkeley: University of California Press, 1994.

Guilmet, George M., Robert T. Boyd, David L. Whited, and Nile Thompson. "The Legacy of Introduced Disease: The Southern Coast Salish." *American Indian Culture and Research Journal* 15, no. 4 (1991): 1–32.

Hansen, Arthur, ed. *Japanese American World War II Evacuation Oral History Project, Part IV: Resisters*. 1995.

Harmon, Alexandra. "Coast Salish History." In *Be of Good Mind: Essays on the Coast Salish*, edited by Bruce Granville Miller, 30–54. University of British Columbia Press, 2007.

———. *Indians in the Making: Ethnic Relations and Indian Identities around Puget Sound*. Berkeley: University of California Press, 1998.

Harrington, Sheila, and Judi Stevenson, eds. *Islands in the Salish Sea: A Community Atlas*. Surrey: The Land Trust Alliance of British Columbia, 2005.

Harris, Cole. *Making Native Space: Colonialism, Resistance, and Reserves in British Columbia*. Vancouver: University of British Columbia Press, 2003.

———. *The Resettlement of British Columbia: Essays on Colonialism and Geographical Change*. Vancouver: University of British Columbia Press, 1997.

Hayden, Dolores. *The Power of Place: Urban Landscapes as Public History*. Cambridge, MA: MIT Press, 1995.

Hayner, Norman S. *Hotel Life*. Chapel Hill: University of North Carolina Press, 1936.

———. "Hotel Life and Personality," *American Journal of Sociology* 33, no. 5 (1928): 784–95.

Hebner, Edna. *Memories of a Mill Town: Snoqualmie Falls, Washington 1917 to 1932*. North Bend: Snoqualmie Valley Historical Museum, 1984.

Hendrick, Burton J. "The 'Recall' in Seattle: How the People Dislodged a Mayor under Whose Administration the 'Vice Syndicate'—Gamblers, Saloonkeepers, and Exploiters of Women—Ruled a City." *McClure's Magazine* 37, no. 6 (October 1911): 647–63.

"Henry Yesler and the Founding of Seattle." *Pacific Northwest Quarterly* 42, no. 4 (1951): 271–76.

Hernandez, Kelly Lytle. "Hobos in Heaven: Race, Incarceration, and the Rise of Los Angeles, 1880–1910." *Pacific Historical Review* 83, no. 3 (2014): 410–47.

Herod, Andrew. *Labor Geographies: Workers and the Landscapes of Capitalism*. New York: Guilford Press, 2001.

Hill-Tout, Charles. *The Salish People: The Squamish and the Lilloet*. Vancouver: Talonbooks, 1978.

Himes, Chester. *If He Hollers Let Him Go*. New York: Doubleday Doran, 1945.

Hing, Bill Ong. *Making and Remaking Asian America through Immigration Policy, 1850–1990*. Palo Alto: Stanford University Press, 1993.

Hotchkiss, William E. "Labor in the Inland Empire Lumber Territory." December 1917. President's Mediation Commission Records, 1917–1918. Frederick, MD: University Publications of America, 1985.

"Hotel Rates." *Carpenter* 2, no. 10 (October 1913): 24.

Howd, Cloice. *Industrial Relations in the West Coast Lumbering Industry*. Washington, DC: Government Printing Office, 1924.

Howe, R. S. *The Great Northern Country, Illustrating and Describing the Country, Industry and Scenery along the Lines of the Great Northern Railway and Northern Steamship Company*. St. Paul: Great Northern Railway, 1903.

Hu Pegues, Juliana. *Space-Time Colonialism: Alaska's Indigenous and Asian Entanglements*. Chapel Hill: University of North Carolina Press, 2021.

Hume, Harry, ed. *Prosperous Washington: A Series of Articles Descriptive of the Evergreen State, Its Magnificent Resources, and Its Present and Probable Development*. Seattle: Seattle Post-Intelligencer Press, 1906.

Hunter, Tera. *To 'Joy My Freedom: Southern Black Women's Lives and Labors after the Civil War*. Cambridge, MA: Harvard University Press, 1997.

Ichioka, Yuji. *The Issei: The World of the First Generation Japanese Immigrants, 1885–1924*. New York: Free Press, 1988.

Immerwahr, Daniel. *How to Hide an Empire*. New York: Picador, 2020.

Itō, Kazuo. *Issei: A History of Japanese Immigrants in North America*. Seattle: Japanese Community Service, 1973.

IWW Deportation Cases: Hearings before a Subcommittee of the Committee on Immigration and Naturalization. Washington, DC: Government Printing Office, 1920.

Jacobson, Matthew. *Barbarian Virtues: The United States Encounters Foreign People at Home and Abroad, 1876–1917*. New York: Hill and Wang, 2000.

———. *Whiteness of a Different Color: European Immigrants and the Alchemy of Race*. Cambridge, MA: Harvard University Press, 1999.

Jackson, Kenneth. *Crabgrass Frontier: The Suburbanization of the United States*. New York: Oxford University Press, 1985.

Japanese American National Museum, *Japanese American History: An A to Z Reference from 1868 to the Present*. New York: Facts on File, 1993.

Jones, Kendall. "The Hops Capital of the World Is in Eastern Washington." *Seattle Magazine* (September 2017). Accessed December 8, 2021. https://seattlemag.com /news-and-features/hops-capital-world-eastern-washington.

Jung, Moon-Ho. *Coolies and Cane: Race, Labor, and Sugar in the Age of Emancipation*. Baltimore: Johns Hopkins University Press, 2006.

Kaiser, James G. *Crown Lumber Company and the Early Growth of Mukilteo*. Oak Harbor: Pack Rat Press, 1990.

Kanazawa, Mark. "Immigration, Exclusion, and Taxation: Anti-Chinese Legislation in Gold Rush California." *Journal of Economic History* 65, no. 3 (2005): 779–805.

Kaplan, Amy. *The Anarchy of Empire in the Making of U.S. Culture*. Cambridge, MA: Harvard University Press, 2002.

Karuka, Manu. *Empire's Tracks: Indigenous Nations, Chinese Workers, and the Transcontinental Railroad*. Berkeley: University of California Press, 2019.

Kashima, Tetsuden. *Judgment without Trial: Japanese American Imprisonment during World War II*. Seattle: University of Washington Press, 2004.

Keliiaa, Caitlin. "Unsettling Domesticity: Native Women and 20th-Century U.S. Indian Policy in the San Francisco Bay Area." PhD diss., UC Berkeley, 2019.

Klingle, Matthew. *Emerald City: An Environmental History of Seattle*. New Haven: Yale University Press, 2007.

Kornbluh, Joyce L., ed. *Rebel Voices: An I.W.W. Anthology*. Chicago: Charles H. Kerr, 1988.

Kramer, Paul. *The Blood of Government: Race, Empire, the United States & the Philippines*. Chapel Hill: University of North Carolina Press, 2006.

Kumasaka, Roland. *The Green Lake Japanese American Community, 1900–1942.* Seattle: Green Lake Japanese American Community Booklet Committee, 2005.

Kurokawa, Katsutoshi. "The Condition of Japanese Immigrants in Seattle and its Vicinity, 1925–1929." *Economic Association of Okayama University* 36, no. 4 (2005): 155–66.

Kurashige, Scott. *The Shifting Grounds of Race: Black and Japanese Americans in the Making of Multiethnic Los Angeles.* Princeton: Princeton University Press, 2008.

Lake, Marilyn, and Henry Reynolds. *Drawing the Global Colour Line: White Men's Countries and the International Challenge of Racial Equality.* Cambridge: Cambridge University Press, 2008.

Lawrence, Bonita. "Gender, Race, and the Regulation of Native Identity in Canada and the United States: An Overview." *Hypatia* 18, no. 2 (2003): 3–31.

Lee, Erika. *At America's Gates: Chinese Immigration during the Exclusion Era.* Chapel Hill: University of North Carolina Press, 2003.

———. *The Making of Asian America: A History.* New York: Simon & Schuster, 2015.

Lee, Shelley Sang-Hee. *A New History of Asian America.* New York: Routledge, 2014.

———. *Claiming the Oriental Gateway: Prewar Seattle and Japanese America.* Philadelphia: Temple University Press, 2010.

———. "The Contradictions of Cosmopolitanism: Consuming the Orient at the Alaska-Yukon-Pacific Exposition and the International Potlatch Festival, 1909–1934." *Western Historical Quarterly.* 38, no. 3 (2007): 277–302.

Leighton, Caroline. *Life at Puget Sound: With Sketches of Travel in Washington Territory, British Columbia, Oregon, and California, 1865–1881.* Boston: Lee & Shepard, 1883.

Lentz, Katherine Jane. "Japanese-American Relations in Seattle." MA thesis, University of Washington, 1924.

Levy, Nat. "Seattle Median Home Price Hits Record $820k." *GeekWire,* April 6, 2018.

Lew-Williams, Beth. "Before Restriction Became Exclusion: America's Experiment in Diplomatic Immigration Control." *Pacific Historical Review* 83, no. 1 (2014): 24–56.

———. *The Chinese Must Go: Violence, Exclusion, and the Making of the Alien in America.* Cambridge, MA: Harvard University Press, 2018.

Loomis, Erik. *Empire of Timber: Labor Unions and the Pacific Northwest Forests.* New York: Oxford University Press, 2017.

Lui, Mary Ting Yi. *The Chinatown Trunk Mystery: Murder, Miscegenation, and Other Dangerous Encounters in Turn-of-the-Century New York City.* Princeton: Princeton University Press, 2005.

Lundstrom, Catrin, and Benjamin Teitelbaum. "Nordic Whiteness: An Introduction." *Scandinavian Studies* 89, no. 2 (Summer 2017): 151–58.

Mabalon, Dawn Bohulano. *Little Manila Is in the Heart: The Making of the Filipino/a American Community in Stockton, California.* Duke University Press, 2013.

Magden, Ronald E. *History of Seattle Waterfront Workers, 1884–1934.* Tacoma: Tacoma Longshore Books, 1991.

———. *Mukashi, Mukashi: Long, Long Ago: The First Century of the Seattle Buddhist Church.* Seattle: Seattle Betsuin Buddhist Temple, 2008.

Matsumoto, Valerie J. *Farming the Home Place: A Japanese American Community in California, 1919–1982.* Ithaca: Cornell University Press, 1994.

Matsumoto, Valerie J., and Blake Allmendinger, eds. *Over the Edge: Remapping the American West.* Berkeley: University of California Press, 1999.

Mawani, Renisa. *Colonial Proximities: Crossracial Encounters and Juridical Truths in British Columbia, 1871–1921.* Vancouver: University of British Columbia Press, 2010.

———. "'The Iniquitous Practice of Women': Prostitution and the Making of White Spaces in British Columbia, 1898–1905." In *Working through Whiteness: International Perspectives,* edited by Cynthia Levine-Rasky, 43–68. Albany: State University of New York Press, 2002.

McConnell, Opal. *Mukilteo: Pictures and Memories.* Seattle: Ballard, 1977.

Meany, Edmond S., Jr. "The History of the Lumber Industry in the Pacific Northwest to 1917." PhD diss., Harvard University, 1935.

Meares, John. *Voyages Made in the Years 1788 and 1789 from China to the North West Coast of America.* London: Logographic Press, 1790.

Meeker, Ezra. *The Busy Life of Eighty-Five Years of Ezra Meeker.* Seattle: Ezra Meeker, 1916.

———. *Hop Culture in the United States: Being a Practical Treatise on Hop Growing in Washington Territory, from the Cutting to the Bale.* Puyallup: E. Meeker & Co., 1888.

———. *Ox-Team Days on the Oregon Trail.* Yonkers-on-Hudson: World Book Company, 1922.

———. *Pioneer Reminiscences of Puget Sound: The Tragedy of Leschi.* Seattle: Lowman & Hanford, 1905.

Mercene, Floro L. *Manila Men in the New World: Filipino Migration to Mexico and the Americas from the Sixteenth Century.* Quezon City: The University of the Philippines Press, 2007.

Miller, Irene Burns. *Profanity Hill.* Everett: Working Press, 1979.

———. *The Relocation of Tenants on the Site of Yesler Terrace.* Seattle: Housing Authority of Seattle, 1941.

Miller, Jay. *Lushootseed Culture and the Shamanic Odyssey: An Anchored Radiance.* Lincoln: University of Nebraska Press, 1999.

Mitchell, Don. *The Lie of the Land: Migrant Workers and the California Landscape.* Minneapolis: University of Minnesota Press, 1996.

Miyamoto, Frank S. *Social Solidarity among the Japanese in Seattle.* Seattle: University of Washington Press, 1939.

Molina, Natalia. *Fit to Be Citizens? Public Health and Race in Los Angeles, 1879–1940.* Berkeley: University of California Press, 2006.

Montgomery, Marcia, and James McNett. "Historic Property Inventory of Japanese, Filipino and Indipino Agricultural Properties on Bainbridge Island, Washington." January 7, 2015. Available via the National Park Service Integrated Resource Management Application Database. Accessed July 31, 2021. https://irma.nps.gov /DataStore/DownloadFile/581233.

Moreton-Robinson, Aileen. *The White Possessive: Property, Power, and Indigenous Sovereignty.* Minneapolis: University of Minnesota Press, 2015.

Morgan, Murray. *Skid Road: An Informal Portrait of Seattle.* Seattle: University of Washington Press, 2018.

Morse, Kathryn. *The Nature of Gold: An Environmental History of the Gold Rush.* Seattle: University of Washington Press, 2003.

Mumford, Kevin. *Interzones: Black/White Sex Districts in Chicago and New York in the Early Twentieth Century.* New York: Columbia University Press, 1997.

Muszynski, Alicja. *Cheap Wage Labour: Race and Gender in the Fisheries of British Columbia.* Montreal: McGill-Queen's University Press, 1996.

Myers, Polly Reed. "Boeing Aircraft Company's Manpower Campaign during World War II." *Pacific Northwest Quarterly* 98, no. 4 (2007): 183–95.

Nagai, Kafū. "An Early Account of Japanese Life in the Pacific Northwest." Edited and translated by Stephen W. Kohl. *Pacific Northwest Quarterly* (April 1979): 58–68.

Nelson, Bruce. *Workers on the Waterfront: Seamen, Longshoremen, and Unionism in the 1930s.* Urbana: University of Illinois Press, 1990.

Nelson, Robert K., LaDale Winling, Richard Marciano, Nathan Connolly, et al. "Mapping Inequality: Redlining in New Deal America." In *American Panorama,* edited by Robert K. Nelson and Edward L. Ayers. Accessed July 30, 2021. https:// dsl.richmond.edu/panorama/redlining/#loc=5/39.1/-94.58.

Newbill, James G. "Farmers and Wobblies in the Yakima Valley, 1933." *Pacific Northwest Quarterly* 68, no. 2 (1977): 80–87.

Newell, Dianne. *Tangled Webs of History: Indians and the Law in Canada's Pacific Coast Fisheries.* Toronto: University of Toronto Press, 1993.

"News Items." *Youth's Companion* 1, no. 5 (1881): 110–20.

"News Narrative." *Public* 14, no. 667 (1911): 34.

Ngai, Mae. *Impossible Subjects: Illegal Aliens and the Making of Modern America.* Princeton: Princeton University Press, 2004.

———. *The Chinese Question: Gold Rushes and Global Politics.* New York: W. W. Norton, 2021.

Nicolaides, Becky. *My Blue Heaven: Life and Politics in the Working-Class Suburbs of Los Angeles, 1920–1965.* Chicago: University of Chicago Press, 2002.

Nishinoiri, John Isao. "Japanese Farms in Washington." MA thesis, University of
Washington, 1926.

Odo, Franklin, ed. *The Columbia Documentary History of the Asian American Experience*. New York: Columbia University Press, 2002.

Office of the Commissioner of Indian Affairs. *Report of the Commissioner of Indian Affairs for the Year 1865*. Washington, DC: Government Printing Office, 1865.

———. *Report of the Commissioner of Indian Affairs for the Year 1866*. Washington,
DC: Government Printing Office, 1866.

———. *Report of the Commissioner of Indian Affairs for the Year 1867*. Washington,
DC: Government Printing Office, 1867.

Ogburn, William F. "Causes and Remedies of Labor Unrest in the Lumber Industry."
University of Washington Forest Club Annual 6 (1918): 11–14.

Okihiro, Gary. *Margins and Mainstreams: Asians in American History and Culture*.
Seattle: University of Washington Press, 1994.

Oliver, E. S. "Sawmilling on Grays Harbor in the Twenties: A Personal Reminiscence."
Pacific Northwest Quarterly 69, no. 1 (January 1978): 1–18.

"Open for All? Booming Seattle Struggles to Stay Affordable." *Economist*, August 9,
2018.

Ordinances of the City of Seattle Published by Order of the Common Council. Seattle:
A. E. Hanford, 1880.

Pacyga, Dominic. *Polish Immigrants and Industrial Chicago: Workers on the South
Side, 1880–1922*. Chicago: University of Chicago Press, 1991.

———. *Slaughterhouse: Chicago's Union Stock Yard and the World It Made*. Chicago:
University of Chicago Press, 2015.

Painter, Nell Irvin. *The History of White People*. New York: W. W. Norton, 2010.

Parham, Vera. "'All Go to the Hop Fields': The Role of Migratory and Wage Labor
in the Preservation of Indigenous Pacific Northwest Culture." In *Native Diasporas: Indigenous Identities and Settler Colonialism in the Americas*, edited by
Gregory D. Smithers and Brooke N. Newman, 317–46. Lincoln: University of
Nebraska Press, 2014.

Parnaby, Andrew. "'The Best Men That Ever Worked the Lumber': Aboriginal Longshoremen on Burrard Inlet, BC, 1863–1939." *Canadian Historical Review* 87, no. 1
(2006): 53–78.

Peffer, George. *If They Don't Bring Their Women Here: Chinese Female Immigration
before Exclusion*. Urbana-Champaign: University of Illinois Press, 1999.

Peiss, Kathy. *Cheap Amusements: Working Women and Leisure in Turn-of-the-
Century New York*. Philadelphia: Temple University Press, 1986.

Perry, Adele. *On the Edge of Empire: Gender, Race, and the Making of British Columbia, 1849–1871*. Toronto: University of Toronto Press, 2001.

Phelps, Thomas. *Reminiscences of Seattle, Washington Territory and of the U.S. Sloop-of-War Decatur during the Indian War of 1855–56*. Fairfield: Ye Galleon Press, 1970.

Pierce, Jason. *Making the White Man's West: Whiteness and the Creation of the American West*. Boulder: University of Colorado Press, 2016.

President's Median Commission. *Report of President's Mediation Commission to the President of the United States*. Washington, DC: Government Printing Office, 1918.

Price, Andrew, Jr. *Port Blakely: The Community Captain Renton Built*. Seattle: Magna Press, 1989.

Proceedings, Tenth Session of the Pacific Logging Congress. Portland: Timberman, 1919.

Prosch, Thomas. *David S. Maynard and Catherine T. Maynard: Biographies of Two of the Oregon Immigrants of 1850*. Lowman & Hanford Printing: Seattle, 1906.

Putman, John. *Class and Gender Politics in Progressive-Era Seattle*. Las Vegas: University of Nevada Press, 2008.

Rabban, David M. "The IWW Free Speech Fights and Popular Conceptions of Free Expression before World War I." *Virginia Law Review* 80, no. 5 (1994): 1055–1158.

Radford, Gail. *Modern Housing for America: Policy Struggles in the New Deal Era*. Chicago: University of Chicago Press, 1996.

Raibmon, Paige. *Authentic Indians: Episodes of Encounter from the Late-Nineteenth-Century Northwest Coast*. Durham: Duke University Press, 2005.

Rajala, Richard. "A Dandy Bunch of Wobblies: Pacific Northwest Loggers and the Industrial Workers of the World." *Labor History* 37, no. 2 (1996): 205–34.

Reddick, SuAnn, and Cary Collins. "Medicine Creek to Fox Island: Cadastral Scams and Contested Domains." *Oregon Historical Quarterly* 106, no. 3 (Fall 2005): 374–97.

Redfield, Edith Sanderson. *Seattle Memories*. Boston: Lothrop Lee & Shepard, 1930.

Reid, Josh. *The Sea Is My Country: The Maritime World of the Makah, an Indigenous Borderlands People*. New Haven: Yale University Press, 2015.

Resner, Herbert. *Trees and Men*. Seattle: Works Progress Administration, 1938.

R. L., Polk & Co. *Polk's Seattle City Directory*. Seattle: Acme, 1896.

———. *Polk's Seattle City Directory*. Seattle: Acme, 1901.

———. *Polk's Seattle City Directory*. Seattle: Acme, 1905.

———. *Polk's Seattle City Directory*. Seattle: Acme, 1939.

Robbins, William G. "Extinguishing Indian Land Title in Western Oregon." *Indian Historian* 7, no. 2 (1974): 10–14.

———. "The Social Context of Forestry: The Pacific Northwest in the Twentieth Century." *Western Historical Quarterly* 16, no. 4 (1985): 413–27.

Rogers, Daniel T. *Atlantic Crossings: Social Politics in a Progressive Age*. Cambridge, MA: Harvard University Press, 1998.

Rothstein, Richard. *The Color of Law: A Forgotten History of How Our Government Segregated America*. Reprint edition. New York: Liverlight, 2018.

Runblom, Harald, and Hans Norman, eds. *From Sweden to America: A History of the Migration*. Minneapolis: University of Minnesota Press, 1976.

Sale, Roger. *Seattle: Past to Present*. Seattle: University of Washington Press, 1976.

Saxton, Alexander. *The Indispensable Enemy: Labor and the Anti-Chinese Movement in California*. Berkeley: University of California Press, 1971.

Schmid, Calvin. *Growth and Distribution of Minority Races in Seattle, Washington*. Seattle: Seattle Public Schools, 1964.

———. *Social Trends in Seattle*. Seattle: University of Washington Press, 1944.

Schmid, Calvin, and Charles E. Nobbe. "Socio-Economic Differentials Among Non-white Races in the State of Washington." *Demography* 2 (1965): 549–66.

Schwantes, Carlos. *The Pacific Northwest: An Interpretive History*. Lincoln: University of Nebraska Press, 1989.

———. *Railroad Signatures Across the Pacific Northwest*. Seattle: University of Washington Press, 1993.

Scott, James C. *Seeing Like a State: How Certain Schemes to Improve the Human Condition have Failed*. New Haven: Yale University Press, 1998.

Seattle Civil Rights & Labor History Project. "Segregated Seattle." Accessed July 30, 2021. https://depts.washington.edu/civilr/segregated.htm.

Seattle Housing Authority. *Real Property Survey, 1939–1940*. Seattle: Works Projects Administration, 1941.

Seiber, Richard A., ed. *Memoirs of Puget Sound: Early Seattle, 1853–1856; The Letters of David and Catherine Blaine*. Seattle: Ye Galleon Press, 1978.

Seltz, Jennifer. "Epidemics, Indians, and Border-Making in the Nineteenth-Century Pacific Northwest." In *Bridging National Borders in North America: Transnational and Comparative Histories*, edited by Benjamin Johnson, Andrew Graybill, Gilbert Joseph, and Emily Rosenberg, 91–114. Durham: Duke University Press, 2010.

Semple, Eugene. *Report of the Governor of Washington Territory to the Secretary of the Interior, 1888*. Washington, DC: Government Printing Office, 1888.

Shah, Nayan. "Between 'Oriental Depravity' and 'Natural Degenerates': Spatial Borderlands and the Making of Ordinary Americans." *American Quarterly* 57, no. 3 (October 3, 2005): 703–25.

———. *Contagious Divides: Epidemics and Race in San Francisco's Chinatown*. Berkeley: University of California Press, 2001.

———. *Stranger Intimacy: Contesting Race, Sexuality, and the Law in the North American West*. Berkeley: University of California Press, 2011.

Sides, Josh. *L.A. City Limits: African American Los Angeles from the Great Depression to the Present*. Berkeley: University of California Press, 2006.

Smith, Marian. "The INS and the Singular Status of North American Indians." *American Indian Culture and Research Journal* 21, no. 1 (1997): 131–54.

Smith, Walker C. *The Everett Massacre: A History of the Class Struggle in the Lumber Industry.* Chicago: IWW Publishing Bureau, 1916.

Squire, Watson C. *Report of the Governor of Washington Territory for the Year 1884.* Washington, DC: Government Printing Office, 1885.

———. *Report of the Governor of Washington Territory to the Secretary of the Interior, 1886.* Washington, DC: Government Printing Office, 1886.

Stanger-Ross, Jordan. "Municipal Colonialism in Vancouver: City Planning and the Conflict over Indian Reserves, 1928–1950s." *Canadian Historical Review* 89, no. 4 (2008): 541–80.

Stevens, Todd. "Brokers between Worlds: Chinese Merchants and Legal Culture in the Pacific Northwest, 1852–1925." PhD diss., Princeton University, 2003.

Suzuki, Masao. "Important or Impotent? Taking Another Look at the 1920 California Alien Land Law." *The Journal of Economic History* 64, no. 1 (2004): 125–43.

Svinth, Joseph R. "Nisei Boxer: Fred Egawa." *Journal of Combative Sport,* November 2000.

Tanaka, Stefan Akio. "The Nikkei on Bainbridge Island, 1883–1942: A Study of Migration and Community Development." MA thesis, University of Washington, 1977.

Taylor, Quintard. "Blacks and Asians in a White City: Japanese Americans and African Americans in Seattle, 1890–1941." *Western Historical Quarterly* 22, no. 4 (1991): 401–29.

———. *The Forging of a Black Community: Seattle's Central District from 1870 through the Civil Rights Era.* Seattle: University of Washington Press, 1994.

"The New Immigration Movement." *Northwest Illustrated Monthly Magazine* 14 (1896): 7–9.

The Statutes at Large and Treaties of the United States of America from December 1, 1851 to March 3, 1855. Vol. 10. Boston: Little, Brown, 1855.

Thrush, Coll. "City of the Changers: Indigenous People and the Transformation of Seattle's Watersheds." *Pacific Historical Review* 75, no. 1 (2006): 89–117.

———. *Native Seattle: Histories from the Crossing-Over Place.* Seattle: University of Washington Press, 2008.

Todes, Charlotte. *Labor and Lumber.* New York: International, 1931.

Tollefson, Kenneth D. "Political Organization of the Duwamish." *Ethnology* 28, no. 2 (1989): 135–49.

Tomlan, Michael. *Tinged with Gold: Hop Culture in the United States.* Athens: University of Georgia Press, 1992.

Trotter, Joe. *Workers on Arrival: Black Labor in the Making of America.* Berkeley: University of California Press, 2019.

Tsu, Cecilia M. *Garden of the World: Asian Immigrants and the Making of Agriculture in California's Santa Clara Valley*. New York: Oxford University Press, 2013.

Tyler, Robert. *Rebels of the Woods: The I.W.W. in the Pacific Northwest*. Corvallis: Oregon State University Press, 1967.

United States Army Corps of Engineers. *Annual Report of the Chief of Engineers, United States Army to the Secretary of War for the Year 1885*. Washington, DC: Government Printing Office, 1885.

United States Department of Commerce. *Thirteenth Census of the United States Taken in the Year 1910*. Vol. 8, *Manufactures*. Washington, DC: Government Printing Office, 1913.

United States House of Representatives. *Japanese Immigration: Hearings before the Committee on Immigration and Naturalization*. Washington, DC: Government Printing Office, 1921.

United States Senate. *Relations with Canada: Testimony Taken by the Select Committee on Relations with Canada, United States Senate*. Washington, DC: Government Printing Office, 1890.

Urban, Andrew. *Brokering Servitude: Migration and the Politics of Domestic Labor during the Long 19th Century*. New York: New York University Press, 2018.

Vale, Lawrence. *From the Puritans to the Projects: Public Housing and Public Neighbors*. Cambridge, MA: Harvard University Press, 2000.

Vargas, Zaragosa. *Proletarians of the North: A History of Mexican Industrial Workers in Detroit and the Midwest, 1917–1933*. Berkeley: University of California Press, 1999.

Volp, Leti. "The Indigenous as Alien." *UC Irvine Law Review* 5, no. 2 (2015): 289–325.

Wadewitz, Lissa. *The Nature of Borders: Salmon, Boundaries, and Bandits on the Salish Sea*. Seattle: University of Washington Press, 2012.

———. "Pirates of the Salish Sea: Labor, Mobility, and Environment in the Transnational West." *Pacific Historical Review* 75, no. 4 (2006): 587–627.

Wagner, Eric. *Once and Future River: Reclaiming the Duwamish*. Seattle: University of Washington Press, 2016.

Washington Territorial Legislature, *Statutes of the Territory of Washington, Made and Passed*. Olympia: T. F. McElroy Printer, 1865.

Washington Territorial Legislature. *Statutes of the Territory of Washington, Made and Passed by the Legislative Assembly*. Olympia: Chas. Prosch Printer, 1868.

———. *Statutes of the Territory of Washington, Made and Passed by the Legislative Assembly*. Olympia: James Rodgers Printer, 1869.

Waterman, T. T. *Puget Sound Geography*. Edited by Vi Hilbert, Jay Miller, and Zalmai Zahir. Seattle: Lushootseed Press, 2001.

———. "The Geographical Names Used by the Indians of the Pacific Coast." *American Geographical Society* 12, no. 2 (1922): 175–94.

Watt, Roberta Frye. *The Story of Seattle.* Seattle: Lowman and Hanford, 1931.

Whaley, Gray H. *Oregon and the Collapse of Illahee: U.S. Empire and the Transformation of an Indigenous World, 1792–1859.* Chapel Hill: University of North Carolina Press, 2010.

Wharf, Barney. "Regional Transformation, Everyday Life, and Pacific Northwest Lumber Production." *Annals of the Association of American Geographers* 78, no. 2 (1988): 326–46.

Wilkinson, Charles. *Blood Struggle: The Rise of Modern Indian Nations.* New York: W. W. Norton, 2005.

Williams, Carol, ed. *Indigenous Women and Work: From Labor to Activism.* Urbana: University of Illinois Press, 2012.

Williams, David B. *Homewaters: A Human and Natural History of Puget Sound.* Seattle: University of Washington Press, 2021.

Winling, LaDale C., and Todd M. Michney. "The Roots of Redlining: Academic, Governmental, and Professional Networks in the Making of the New Deal Lending Regime." *Journal of American History* 108, no. 1 (2021): 42–69.

Wong, Marie Rose. *Building Tradition: Pan-Asian Seattle and Life in the Residential Hotels.* Seattle: Chin Music Press, 2018.

Woods, Louis Lee. "The Federal Home Loan Bank Board, Redlining, and the National Proliferation of Racial Lending Discrimination, 1921–1950." *Journal of Urban History* 38 (2012): 1036–59.

Wray, Jacilee, ed. *Native Peoples of the Olympic Peninsula: Who We Are.* Norman: University of Oklahoma Press, 2015.

Wray, William D. *Mitsubishi and the NYK, 1870–1914: Business Strategy in the Japanese Shipping Industry.* Cambridge, MA: Harvard University Press, 1984.

Wright, E. W., ed. *Lewis & Dryden's Marine History of the Pacific Northwest.* Portland: Lewis & Dryden, 1895.

Yamamoto, Hisaye. *Seventeen Syllables and Other Stories.* New Brunswick: Rutgers University Press, 1989.

INDEX

Abbott, Carl, 192n8

Acena, Jose, 147

Acor family, 181–82, 182–83*fig.*

African Americans: migration into Seattle, 10, 194n33; pathways to the middle class for, 179; and police tax, 33, 198n53; on Profanity Hill, 167–68; and racial discrimination in Seattle, 10–11, 16, 186, 189, 190; and Yesler Terrace, 177–78

agriculture: Chinese workers in, 14; dispossession of the Japanese in, 143; Filipino workers in, 138, 140; Great Depression and, 137; Indigenous workers in, 35; relationships among workers, 15; seasonality and Indigenous autonomy, 6; shift from Puget Sound to Eastern Washington, 74; and transient populations, 3. *See also* Bainbridge Island; Filipino workers; hop farms; Japanese farmers

Ah Ty, 41

Akutsu, Gene, 169

Akutsu, Jim, 168

Alaska-Yukon-Pacific (AYP) Exposition (1909), 111

alien land laws, 143, 157, 164, 218n28

Alin, Romero, 142

Almojuela, Dorothy (Nahanee), 153–54, 155–56

Almojuela, Tom, 153, 156

American Federation of Labor (AFL), 96, 97, 99, 211n91

Anderson, Signe, 90

Angeles, Mariano, 142

anti-Chinese hostility: attack on a hop farm's "China Camp," 65–66; expulsion of Chinese from Seattle region, 15, 68–69, 73; hop farmers' exploitation of, 66–67; and immigration restrictions, 63–64, 75; increased Chinese migration and, 204n83; mixed with fascination, 35, 198n58; view of Chinese as threats, 37, 73

anti-Japanese hostility, 134–35, 183–85, 184*fig.*, 188–89. *See also* Japanese American incarceration

Anti-Japanese League, 135

Aquino, Elaulio, 152*fig.*

Arai, Allen K., 185

Ash, Ellis, 176

Asher, Brad, 197n37

Asian migratory workers, exclusion of, 10, 193n20. *See also under* Chinese; Filipino; Japanese

assimilation: domestic employment as project of, 42, 108; forced programs of, 50, 60, 68; Japanese and, 107–8; marriage and, 107; pathways for European laborers, 108

authorities, Seattle. *See* city authorities

Ayer, Charles, 61

Azuma, Eiichiro, 120, 146

Bagley, Clarence, 22, 47

Bagley, Herman, 41

Bainbridge Gardens, 148, 150

Bainbridge Island: appeal to Filipino workers, 148–49; Coast Salish workers on, 153, 155–56; effect of World War II on, 157–58;

Columbia & Puget Sound Railroad (formerly Seattle & Walla Walla), 63

Columbia Hotel, 132

commercial district in Seattle, 52–53; Chinese commerce in, 54–55

Congress Hotel, 129

Conklin, Mary Ann (Madame Damnable), 24–25

Corpuz, Anacleto, 137, 138

Cox, Thomas, 192n13

Crawford, Margaret, 212n108

crime, 116–19, 180

Cronon, William, 2

Crown Lumber, 90*fig.*, 94, 107–8

Dahlie, Jorgen, 88

Dawes Act of 1887, 68

DeCano, Pio, 157

defense industries, 127

Denny, Arthur, 18–20, 21–23, 24

Department of Labor, 103

De Vera, Arlene, 146

Diller, Leonard, 113

Diller Hotel, 113, 114*fig.*, 127

Dilling, George, 117, 121, 132

displacement, 3, 16, 38, 189. *See also* Chinese workers; Duwamish people; Indigenous peoples; Japanese American incarceration; Profanity Hill

dock and shipyard workers, 155, 157, 159, 191n7

domestic service, 41–42, 51

Donation Land Claim Act of 1850, 19, 29, 46, 47, 195n5

Dover, Harriette Shelton, 48; *Tulalip, from My Heart*, 46

Duwamish people: dispossession of, 3, 10, 14, 27, 42, 75, 194n25; maritime mobility of, 6; reservation for, 28; Seattle as homeland of, 188; settler's reliance on, 17, 20, 21; as source of labor, 8–9; traditional life and networks for, 20

dᶻidᶻəlalič, 5, 22, 44, 192n12

Eatonville Lumber Company, 94–95*map*

economy, regional. *See* regional economy

Eells, Myron, 60, 207n16

Egawa, Fred, family of, 168

Egawa, James, 168

employment agencies: and the IWW, 98, 101, 211n95; Japanese agencies, 118; lumber industry's use of, 81–83, 85–86, 207n20, 207n24; in the southern district, 91. *See also* labor-contracting businesses

Epstein, Jesse, 162, 172, 173–74, 177–78, 180, 224n52

European and white laborers: in the lumber industry, 100*fig.*; migration to Seattle, 87–88; and new immigration policies, 101–3; and racial exclusion, 89; in Seattle's seasonal economy, 7, 78; as skilled labor in the lumber industry, 86*fig.*; transiency of, 104. *See also* Scandinavians

Executive Order 9066, 157, 168

extractive industries: decline of, 15, 137; importance in Seattle's economy, 3; scholarship on laborers in, 2–3, 14; seasonality and Indigenous autonomy, 6. *See also* agriculture; coal mining; hop farms; lumber industry; salmon canneries

farmers. *See* agriculture

Felker, Leonard, 25

Ficken, Robert, 211n97

Filipino migration, history of, 7, 139–40, 191n6

Filipino workers: appeal of strawberry harvesting to, 149; campaigns to improve conditions for, 151; hostility and racism toward, 138, 141; housing for, 136, 144–45, 183; population in the Northwest, 138; reliance on Japanese businesses, 142; social relationships of, 138, 146–51, 219n50; temporary work for, 15, 136–37, 138, 140–41, 218n23

fire department: harassment campaign of, 15, 132–33, 134, 135; inspections of the fire department (*continued*)

Tenderloin, 134; power of, 132; and zoning of laundries, 40–41

Floresca, Fred, 141

Foner, Philip, 97

Foreign Miners' Tax of 1850, 133

Frank, Dana, 99, 211n91

Friday, Chris, 68

Fujii, Chojiro, 118, 124

Fujii, Yukiko, 123, 124

Fujii Hotel, 118

Fujita-Rony, Dorothy, 10

Furuya, Masajiro, 84–85, 87, 208n35

Gatzert, Bailey, 41

Gentlemen's Agreement of 1907–8, 107, 121, 122, 140, 165

Gill, Hiram, 117

Gompers, Samuel, 98

Great Depression, 15, 137, 141, 162, 175

Great Northern Hotel, 118, 144–45

Great Northern Railway, 80, 84, 87, 88–89

Great Northern Steamship Company, 84

Great Seattle Fire (1889), 113

Guiberson, Harumi, 133

Hanihara, Masanao, 120

Harmon, Alexandra, 20, 23, 196n9

Harui, Zenhichi, 148, 149

Hayes, C. P., 69

Hayner, Norman, 15, 192n8

Haywood, William "Big Bill," 99

Hearst, William Randolph, 175

Hebner, Edna, 104–5

Higa, May Ota, 144, 146

Hilderbidle, Lois, 41

Hill, George, 66

Hill, James, 83–84, 87, 88, 208n30

Hirakawa, Kihachi, 84

Hooverville, 15, 160, 175

hop farms: Chinese and Indigenous pickers on, 44–45, 49–51, 53–55, 72*fig.*, 75*fig.*; coal mining as source of labor for, 56, 64–65;

colonial control undermined through, 60; decline of, 73–74, 76; establishment and growth of, 46–47, 48, 61; expansion beyond river valleys, 62–63; historical importance of, 15; hop harvest of 1877, 56–62; preference for Indigenous workers, 67–68; Puget Sound geography and, 44; rival growers and racial tensions, 66; Seattle as center of labor contracting for, 14, 51–56; as Seattle's first major agricultural industry, 45; short season of picking on, 48–49, 53–54; as tourist attraction, 74, 200n6; white women and children as pickers on, 69–71; workers' growing dissatisfaction with, 61–62

Hop Sing Wash House, 39*fig.*, 41

Hotchkiss, Willard E., 101

hotels: and building codes, 124, 125, 127, 129; and control of occupants' relationships, 12–13; definition of, 213n18; as dominant form of housing, 15; first-class, 113, 122; as housing for laborers, 15; increases in numbers of, 111, 118; role in Filipinos' lives, 142; south of Yesler Way, 114–15. *See also* Japanese hoteliers

House Committee on Immigration and Naturalization, 134

housing: differential housing for Filipinos, 145–46; federal government's role in provision of, 160–61; increases in short-term accommodations, 112; lodging houses, 115–16, 117–18, 213n18; in lumber towns, 104, 105–6, 106*fig.*; and Profanity Hill's concentration of nonwhite population, 164–65; racially segregated, 92–93, 94–95, 94–95*map. See also* hotels; Wagner-Steagall Act (1937)

Hughes, William, 185

Hunter, Tera, 39

Hu Pegues, Juliana, 205n124

Ichioka, Yuji, 118, 143

Ikeda, Victor, 130

Illahee brothel, 30

immigration: and Europeans, 101–2; First Nations people and, 154, 220n72; increases with opening of shipping route to Seattle, 84; lax enforcement of laws, 63–64; problem of Japanese immigration, 134–35; restrictions on, 14, 15, 193n20. *See also* Chinese Exclusion Act of 1882; Gentlemen's Agreement of 1907–8

Immigration Act of 1917, 102

Immigration Act of 1924, 138, 143, 166, 221n72

imperial economy: Filipino migration and, 139–40; in Seattle, 6; of the US, 193n15

Indian agents, 60, 70, 197n43, 204n93

Indigenous Hawaiians, 33, 195n5

Indigenous lands: dᶻidᶻəlalič in, 5, 22, 192n12; and Ordinance 5, 28–29; settlers' occupation of, 19–20, 38, 47, 201n11; slu?wił in, 188; treaties with US government and, 27–28; and Yesler's sawmill, 24

Indigenous peoples: assistance to early settlers, 22; autonomy of, 6; in canneries and hop farming, 50; dispossession of, 10, 52, 57, 80, 195n2; epidemics' impact on, 21; intersection with Chinese workforce, 14–15; in labor negotiations with hop farmers, 54, 62, 64; in the lumber industry, 206n11; maintenance of traditions in work contexts, 58, 59*fig.*, 153, 200n6; maritime mobility of, 4, 5, 20, 45, 153; missionaries' views of, 60; popularity of hop picking for, 53–54, 56, 57, 72*fig.*, 200n6; as public health and safety threat, 31, 197n43; purchasing power of, 52; and violence against Chinese workers, 67; at Yesler's mill, 18*fig.*, 25. *See also* Coast Salish peoples; Duwamish people; hop farms; reservations

Indigenous women: in canning industry, 50; in the northern district, 41–42; as strawberry harvesters, 155–56; as target of ordinances, 29–31; as washerwomen, 38–39

Industrial Worker, 77, 82*fig.*, 98

Industrial Workers of the World (IWW): arrests and deportation of members of, 102; arrival of, 78; and discontent among white workers, 103; exposure of worker discontent, 15; free speech movement of, 98–99; and interracial solidarities, 96; and Japanese workers, 99; legacy in the Pacific Northwest of, 108, 211n97; mission of, 96; organizing in the lumber industry, 96–97; popularity of, 103–4; and Scandinavians, 99–100, 105; as threat to Pacific Northwest society, 100–101; welcoming of Asian workers, 97–98

International Union of Timber Workers, 81

interracial alliances, 12

interracial marriages and relationships, 29, 146–48, 153–54, 156, 219n50, 223n29

interracial sociability, 71–72

Ito, Chusaburo, 185

IWW. *See* Industrial Workers of the World (IWW)

Japan: monitoring of overseas citizens by, 120, 121; Seattle's relationship with, 125; trade with Seattle, 83

Japanese American incarceration, 157–58, 168, 184

Japanese Americans, 16, 179, 184*fig.*, 222n20

Japanese Association of North America, 122, 124

Japanese farmers: accommodations for Filipinos provided by, 150; circumvention of alien land law by, 149–50, 218n28; decline in Washington farming by, 218n29; and decline of agriculture, 16; loss of farms, 157; in Puget Sound, 217n5; recruitment of Coast Salish pickers, 153–54, 154*fig.*; recruitment of Filipino workers, 15, 148–49, 155; and use of marshland, 189, 226nn7–8

Japanese hoteliers: entrance into hotel management, 117–18; expansion beyond Japantown, 127–29, 128*map*, 215n63, 216n70; as family business, 130, 131*fig.*; and Filipino

Ota, Tokio, 144, 219n34
Ozawa v. United States, 165

Pacific National Lumber Company, 86
Pacific Northwest: Asian and Indigenous
  laborers in, 193n18; labor struggles in, 96;
  marine geography of, 4, 5*map*, 192n11;
  promotion of, 61; salmon canning indus-
  try in, 50. *See also* regional economy;
  transpacific labor migration
Page Act of 1875, 102
Paige, George, 28
Parham, Vera, 58
Paris Hotel, 145–46
Parnaby, Andrew, 155
Pensionado Act of 1903, 140
Philippines, 138, 139
P-I. See *Seattle Post-Intelligencer* (the P-I)
Pierce, Jason, 88
Pinnell, John, 30
Pioneer Square, 194n23
Point Elliott Treaty, 27, 28, 47
Point Julia (later Little Boston), 80
Point No Point Treaty, 27, 47, 80
police department, 117, 199n77
police tax, 33, 37
Pope, Andrew, 79, 80
Port Blakely Mill Company, 85, 208n35,
  208n39
Port Gamble, 13, 79–80, 80
Port Gamble S'Klallam reservation, 80,
  207n12
Prince Albert (ship), 29
Profanity Hill: Black population of, 167–68;
  as center of prostitution, 164; defined as
  a slum, 169; displacement of population
  of, 160, 169, 179; interracial families in,
  168, 223n29; Japanese population in, 165–
  66, 171, 173, 222nn19–20; maps of, 169–71;
  nonwhite housing in, 164; pain in evictions from, 176; photographs of, 172, 173,
  174*fig.*, 176; relocation of those evicted
  from, 182–83; single men and women in,

166–67, 223n27, 225n58, 225n60; as slum
  clearance site, 15, 163, 170–71; social interaction in, 169; source of name, 222n15;
  stigmatized as a slum, 163, 172–73, 174*fig.*,
  176; as Yesler Hill, 163–64. *See also*
  Epstein, Jesse; Seattle Housing Authority
  (SHA); Yesler Terrace
prostitution, 30, 31, 116, 118, 122
public health and safety: Chinese as health
  menace, 199n82; Chinese laundries as
  hazardous, 38, 40; crackdown on Tenderloin lodging houses, 121; Indigenous peoples as threat to, 31, 197n43; and Japanese
  hotels, 119; quarantines and, 29–30
public housing, 161–62, 169, 172, 180. *See also*
  Yesler Terrace
Public Works Administration (PWA), 161
Puget Sound basin, description of, 44, 46
Puget Sound Dispatch, "No Mongolians," 37
Putman, John, 117
Puyallup reservation, 57
Puyallup Valley: Chinese population of,
  202n49; demographics of, 56–57; hop
  farms in, 46–47; importance of river to,
  202n35; Indigenous roots of, 57; racial
  stratification of housing and work in,
  57–58; Sunday "boomtowns" in, 59–60,
  71–72

Quong Chong & Co., 55, 202n43

race relations, official views of, 178
racial exclusion: of Asians, 104; of Chinese,
  37–38, 102, 203n83; in enforcement of city
  ordinances, 30; function in regional economy, 9, 193n20; housing in, 57–58; in
  immigration acts and agreements, 121,
  166–67; intermarriage and, 29; of Japanese, 89, 93–95, 107, 142–43; of Jews,
  209n54; by labor unions, 97–98; in Seattle's history, 8, 10, 189; of single white
  men, 107; and slum clearance projects,
  160; Washington Territory legislation

and, 33; whiteness and, 79; and Yesler
Terrace, 177–79. *See also* city ordinances;
north-south division in Seattle; slum
clearance projects
racism: anti-Asian, 97–98, 133–34, 135; anti-
Filipino, 138, 141; in discriminatory penalties and taxation, 133; as seen on maps,
119*map*. *See also* African Americans; anti-
Chinese hostility; anti-Japanese hostility
Raibmon, Paige, 6, 74, 200n6
railroads: hop businesses' reliance on, 69;
hostility toward employment of Chinese
by, 37; and Japanese trade and workers,
83–85; Kalama line, 49; lumber industry
and, 49, 80; need for local markets, 87;
recruitment of white settlers to the West,
88; Seattle's first lines, 62; and tourism,
74. *See also* Great Northern Railway;
Seattle & Walla Walla Railroad
Rapada, Doreen, 149, 150
Redfield, Edith Sanderson, 26
redlining, 8
regional economy: importance of Indigenous
and Chinese interconnection to, 44–45;
and Indigenous-white relationships,
197n37; Seattle's role in, 78; shift to manufacturing, 16, 159. *See also* agriculture;
Bainbridge Island; Chinese laundries; hop
farms; Japanese hoteliers; lumber industry; salmon canneries; Seattle
reservations: Indigenous peoples living outside of, 27, 28, 50, 53, 60, 197n36; Indigenous relocation to, 50; and settlers' land
grabs, 47; treaties and settlers' objections
to, 8, 27–28
Rinonos, Ben, 136, 138
river transportation networks: and hop farm
pickers, 54; hop farm's dependence on, 47,
49–51, 202n35; and lumber industry, 78;
and railroads, 62
Robbins, William G., 19
Roosevelt, Franklin Delano, 161, 175, 189
Roosevelt, Theodore, 121

Rudio, Magno, 157
Russell House (Tokio), 118, 126–27, 134,
144–45

salmon canneries: division of labor in, 58;
Filipino workers at, 136, 140, 141, 145, 149;
during the Great Depression, 137–38;
growth of, 50; Indigenous workers in, 35,
155, 156; Japanese authority in, 141; Japanese workers in, 1; near collapse of industry, 61; rebound in work at, 69; seasonality
of work in, 2, 49; as source of labor for
hop farms, 49–51, 55; Wa Chong Company
and, 36
Sanborn map (1884), 36, 199n75
San Francisco, 37, 38, 116, 121, 133–34, 199n73,
199n82
Sato, Dorothy, 130
sawdust, double meaning of, 31, 43
the Sawdust: Chinese laundries in, 38–39; as
concentrated source of labor, 51, 77; containment of Indigenous peoples to, 29;
creation of, 17, 18; definition and character
of, 26, 193n23; fire zone established in,
40; growth of, 14; heterogeneity of, 7–8,
91–92, 95–96; Klondike gold rush and
growth of, 82; as stigmatized slum district, 9; tidal flooding in, 25
sawmills, 17, 21–22, 24, 79. *See also* lumber
industry; Yesler, Henry, sawmill of
Saxton, Alexander, 66–67
Scandinavians: as "good foreigners," 87,
88–91; and the IWW, 99; as loggers, 93;
lumber towns and, 105; and proximity to
Japanese laborers, 78; working conditions
and radicalism of, 103
Schwantes, Carlos, 137
Scott, James C., 223n37
Seattle: as challenging city for historical
study, 11; decline of Japanese population
in, 165–66; exclusionary roots of, 189–90;
expansion of commerce in, 112; as "Gateway to the Orient," 83–87, 111, 125; growth